THE
LOGODAEDALIAN'S DICTIONARY

of Interesting and Unusual Words

——THE——
LOGODAEDALIAN'S DICTIONARY

of Interesting and Unusual Words

George Stone Saussy III

University of South Carolina Press

Copyright © University of South Carolina 1989
Copyright © 1984 George Stone Saussy

Published in Columbia, South Carolina, by the
University of South Carolina Press

First published in the United States of America as *The Oxter English Dictionary*
by Facts on File Publications, 1984

Published in the United Kingdom as *The Penguin Dictionary of Curious and
Interesting Words* by the Penguin Group, 1986

Library of Congress Cataloging-in-Publication Data

Saussy, George Stone.
    The logodaedalion's dictionary of interesting and unusual words /
  George Stone Saussy III.
      p.   cm.
   Rev. ed. of: The oxter English dictionary. c 1984.
   Includes bibliographical references.
   ISBN 0-87249-683-X
    1. Vocabulary.   2. English language—Glossaries, vocabularies,
etc. I. Saussy, George Stone. Oxter English dictionary.
II. Title.
PE1449.S288   1989
428.1—dc20   89-22707
                                         CIP

CONTENTS

INTRODUCTION

*Many words that have died will be born again, and those now
respected shall be slain, if custom wills it in whose power is
judgment, law and rule of speech.*
        —Horace, *Epistula ad Pisones (traditional title: Ars Poetica)*

The Logodaedalist's Lexicon is a collection of unusual words defined
and used in context from the works of best-selling and less-selling
writers published from 1945 to the present. Over 1,300 words are
defined and over 90 authors and 200 books are represented. Originally
published as *The Oxter English Dictionary* in 1984 and in paperback
in 1986 as *The Penguin Dictionary of Curious and Interesting Words*,
this edition contains an appendix of words I discovered since then and
a list of sources that identifies the authors and titles included.

I am not a professional lexicographer nor an etymologist. I am
an amateur (from the Latin *amator*), not in the sense of a diletante, but
as a lover, one who pursues his muse with a passion.

It is not that amateurs can afford to dabble everywhere; they
ought to dabble everywhere, and damn the scientific prigs
who try to shut them up in some narrow *oubliette.*
        —Fowles, John, *The French Lieutenant's Woman,* p. 58.

Several years ago, I was re-reading John Gardner's *Jason and
Medeia.* I found his vocabulary fascinating in its diversity and
frustrating in that many of the words were not to be found in my trusty
Webster's Collegiate. A quest began for words I didn't know and
which were not easily accessible. As I read or reread the works of John
Barth, Anthony Burgess, William Gaddis, Mark Helprin, R. M.
Koster, Vladimir Nabokov, and Thomas Pynchon, I realized that
Gardner was not a lonely logodaedalist in a land of fourth-grade
vocabularies. Authors of old favorites I discovered to have used many
words which I had skipped over. Moreover, I found more than one
author using the same strange word or the same word with different
meanings. Intrigued and challenged, I acquired a taste—later an
obsession—for words I did not know the meaning of or which had
additional and uncommon definitions.

The compulsion to assemble these words, their definitions, and
contextual quotations grew from a craving into an addiction, as I
stalked the library stacks for ever another fix to assuage my appetite.
The fruit of that quest now lies in your hands.

INTRODUCTION

The purpose of this book is to entertain. Often the excerpts utilizing the words are enjoyable as examples of the writer's skill or pleasure in the use of language. Some of the usages are obviously intended humorously. Others are attempts to achieve precision of meaning. *The Logodaedalian's Dictionary* is not a pedagogical instrument, though it will no doubt have instructional value. Many of these words deserve resurrection; but I have not compiled a "Thirty Days to a More Esoteric Vocabulary." Be warned: obfuscation and obscurantism are frequently punished by ostracism and obscurity.

Walker Percy, in *The Message in the Bottle*, warns that: "A word, by the very fact of its having been lost to common usage or by its having undergone a change in meaning, is apt to acquire thereby an unmerited potency. One is aware of skirting the abyss as soon as one begins to repose virtue in the obscure." With that caveat in mind we can still take heart for the growth and diversity of the language, as proclaimed by Alexander Theroux in "Theroux Metaphrastes": "Those who fear embellishment are only wharfingers mismeasuring you and your freight. The man who disvalues words is always a vaticide." The need for precision of meaning has been stated by Anthony Burgess in *Enderby*: "It's only by the exact use of words that people can begin to understand themselves."

I do not equate the command of an unusual vocabulary with literary merit. Many of my favorite writers eschew obfuscation or simply do not use diverse vocabularies. Some cases may well represent errors in authorial taste or judgment—mere linguistic ostentation. One of my sources, Robert Nye, has decreed: "A useless word is a crime against the spirit of intelligence. It is an intellectual infanticide." Yet one man's pleonasm is another's paronomastic pet. There are many examples in which an uncommon word expresses the precise shade of meaning intended. When *By Love Possessed* was attacked for its difficult vocabulary, James Gould Cozzens noted: "The charge, stated or implied, that I look up hard words to impress the boobs I think can be answered by pointing out that normally no boob would so much as try to read beyond a first page of mine. Sometimes the long word will be the right word and I don't scruple to use it—if the reader doesn't know it it's time he learned. . . . "

There is an aptness to my book being republished by the U.S.C. Press. When I was in the seventh grade, my father returned to the University of South Carolina to complete his Bachelor's degree at the

INTRODUCTION

behest of the Marine Corps. He took a vocabulary course popularly called *I Want A Word* based on a book of the same name written by a Carolina professor, Dr. Havilah Babcock. My parents and I would discuss that collection of interesting words at home and I was given an incalculable boost in the direction of vocabularistic virtuosity.

I have been fortunate in securing the assistance of some of the authors cited herein; their comments on particular words are incorporated within the definitions. Excerpts from letters to me discussing their approaches to language are assembled under AUTHOR RESPONSES. I thank each of these writers for taking the time and trouble to reply to my queries. I gratefully acknowledge the extraordinary editorial labors of Judith Baughman on the original edition, David Fischer on the appendix, as well as the encouragement, suggestions, and criticism of a legion of forebearing friends.

HOW TO USE THIS DICTIONARY

The following sample entries illustrate the format and plan of *The Penguin Dictionary of Curious and Interesting Words*.

ABLUTE: *verb* to cleanse "but with a ceremonial ring to it, as having had performed reglementary pre-ritual ablutions" (Koster). ABLUTED, *adj.* Compare LUSTRATION

> ... the black girl, having seized his hands, now led them up, like lifeless flannels or sponges, over her smooth stomach to ablute the cones of dark-tipped flesh above. ...
>
> —Fowles, *Mantissa*, pp. 33–34.

> The girls led Genghis—abluted, tunicked, wanged— through the celebrants and stood him just inside the circle.
>
> —Koster, *Mandragon*, p. 218.

ARTEMID: *adj* having the characteristics of Artemis, Diana the Huntress, goddess of chastity. Compare DRYAD, MAELID, NAIAD

> There were days when her body was artemid, an ore-ad's, † the flat belly grooved and brown, butt, breasts, and hips strict and firm. ...
>
> —Davenport, "The Dawn in Erewhon," *Tatlin!*, p. 257.

BOLUS: *noun* lump, large pill. See also DIGLOT. Compare HOLUS-BOLUS

—Grandfather Hippagoras ... was physicking the ass, sticking a turpentine and onion bolus down it.
> —Davenport, "The Antiquities of Elis,"
> *Da Vinci's Bicycle,* p. 144.

BOREAL : *adj* northern. See TRAMONTANA. Compare SEPTENTRIONAL

The word to be defined appears in full capitals and is followed by its part of speech and its definition. In a few cases the word's meaning is so clearly defined by its literary quotation that the reader is instructed merely to *See quotation.* When a writer has supplied the compiler• with a gloss on a word, this commentary becomes part of the definition—as shown in the first example. Koster's discussion of ABLUTE is placed within quotation marks, and the writer is identified within parentheses.

Following each word's definition appear any variant forms of the word illustrated in the quotations. For example, although ABLUTE is defined as a verb and functions as a verb construction in the Fowles quotation, it becomes an adjective in the passage from Koster. This adjectival form is, therefore, specified following the definition.

Cross-references often follow definitions: *Compare, See, See also,* and †:

Compare directs the reader to other words—usually synonyms or antonyms—which appear in the dictionary. Thus the ABLUTE entry provides LUSTRATION for comparison; ARTEMID provides DRYAD, MAELID, and NAIAD; BOLUS provides HOLUS-BOLUS; and BOREAL provides SEPTENTRIONAL.

See has been used to avoid repetition of quotations. In the fourth entry above, both BOREAL and TRAMONTANA are found in a single quotation printed only under TRAMONTANA.

See also, illustrated by the BOLUS example, informs the reader that the word also appears in a quotation for DIGLOT.

A dagger (†) following a word within a quotation alerts the reader that the word is itself defined elsewhere in the book. Thus OREAD, which appears in the quotation for ARTEMID, has a separate entry.

A complete bibliography of sources appears at the end of this dictionary.

THE LOGODAEDALIAN'S DICTIONARY

of Interesting and Unusual Words

Use your definitionary.
It's one of the last few pleasures left in life.

—Alexander Theroux

A

ABAXIAL : *adj* off the centerline, eccentric. Compare OBLI-
QUITY

I mime and burlesque my own nature in an abaxial
attempt to get it clear. . . .
—Gardner, *The Wreckage of Agathon*, p. 53.

ABDITORY : *noun* a hidden or secret place

. . . what abditories of weakness, secret guile they
keep. . . .
—Gardner, *Jason and Medeia*, p. 12.

ABLUTE : *verb* to cleanse "but with a ceremonial ring to it,
as having had performed reglementary pre-ritual ablutions"
(Koster). ABLUTED, *adj*. Compare LUSTRATION

. . . the black girl, having seized his hands, now led them
up, like lifeless flannels or sponges, over her smooth
stomach to ablute the cones of dark-tipped flesh above. . . .
—Fowles, *Mantissa*, pp. 33-34.

The girls led Genghis—abluted, tunicked, wanged—
through the celebrants and stood him just inside the
circle.

—Koster, *Mandragon*, p. 218.

ABREACTION : *noun* a talking or acting out of suppressed desires or fears; a secular version of exorcism. Compare APOTROPAIC, DIABOLIFUGE

... the cave of an oracle: steam drifting, sibylline† cries arriving out of the darkness ... Abreactions of the Lord of the Night.
—Pynchon, *Gravity's Rainbow,* p. 48.

ACARPOUS : *adj* sterile, fruitless

... the first faint shadows of ... "my acarpous destiny". ...
—Nabokov, *Ada,* p. 219.

ACEDIA : *noun* an affliction involving loss of interest in things intellectual, spiritual, and physical

"But for sloth," said Sir Gawaine, "a tendency towards acedia is his only weakness."
—Berger, *Arthur Rex,* p. 181.

ACROAMATICAL : *adj* literally, "divulged only to the ear in private"; esoteric, arcane, abstruse

It was something so acroamatical, so exotically tortuous a refinement, so remote from his liberal enough conception of a decently and considerately embellished ... escalier to venereant† ecstasy, that he took immediate fright.
—Burgess, *Honey for the Bears,* p. 21.

ACROMEGALIC : *adj* having oversized arms and legs and/or excessive growth. Compare HYPERTROPHIA

At that moment a match flared on the far side of the room and illuminated the ruddy acromegalic features of Smirke. ...
—Boyle, *Water Music,* p. 133.

ADFENESTRATE : *verb* "to sneak through a window" (Koster). Compare antonym DEFENESTRATE

AGON

Two hours before dawn members of Acción Dinámica adfenestrated themselves into the palace.
—Koster, *The Prince*, p. 32.

ADSCITITIOUS : *adj* supplemental, extrinsic, superfluous

". . . Good old Biff."
"It won't last. It's a thoroughly adscititious soubriquet."
"I shan't give you the satisfaction of asking you what adscititious means."
"Irrelevant."
—DeVries, *Slouching Towards Kalamazoo*, pp. 30-31.

AFFRICATIVE : *adj* characterized by a stop, followed by a release, in music or speech

Doting love solos. . . . Arias of concupiscence. Choirs of asyncopatic, amatory, affricative, low-woodwind drone.
—Elkin, *George Mills*, p. 291.

AGELAST : *noun* one who never laughs

. . . a world of agelasts and executioners and cannibals who sat ready to spring.
—Theroux, *Darconville's Cat*, p. 478.

AGNATIC : *adj* related on the father's side. Compare antonym ENATIC

. . . for want of mothercare or some kind of agnatic pressure. . . .
—Theroux, *Three Wogs*, p. 58.

AGON : *noun* a public celebration consisting of competitions and games

. . . I was caught up in more than anyone knew, some grandiose ultimate agon.
—Gardner, *Jason and Medeia*, pp. 144,146.

But the Spartans do not like a game in which the

defeated concedes that he has lost. It seems to them to be giving up, even though there are four more agons.
—Davenport, "The Daimon of Sokrates," *Eclogues*, p. 76.

AGONAL : *noun* a tale of suffering and death or the agony of death itself

... [they knew] when to expect the irrumpent† flash of crazily wandering comets, could tell the agonals of stars no longer lit, old planets shogged† off course by accidents aeons old.
—Gardner, *Jason and Medeia*, p. 58.

AISTH : *noun* See quotation

... the bothersome word *esthetic* was nothing but a mutant of old Greek *aisthetes*, which meant "One who perceives...."

Aisth means *here to know,* including a whole underworld of underprized phenomena: the peccary, dandelion, crow, why the very pancreas itself, not in some Little League order of beauts but as a helping of equal *aisth.*
—West, *Out of My Depths,* pp. 90-91.

AITHOCHROUS : *adj* reddish-brown, ruddy

... a boy as splendid and aithochrous as the Cnossan striplings wrestling among blue flowers on Minos' walls....
—Davenport, "The Dawn in Erewhon," *Tatlin!,* p. 253.

AKROPOSTHION : *noun* the tip of the foreskin. Compare CARDIOID, POSTHION, STEGOCEPHALIC

... a waking randiness limbering in the sny† of his

cock, the akroposthion of which he adjusted as if modestly. . . .
> —Davenport, "The Dawn in Erewhon,"
> *Tatlin!,* p. 252.

ALBESCENT : *adj* whitened, faded, bleached

. . . Athens—beautiful, albescent as an aging virgin, irrational, tyrannical, deep-dreamed as a wife inexplicably wronged.
> —Gardner, *The Wreckage of Agathon,* p. 60.

ALDERMANIC : *adj* literally, "like an alderman"; dignified, stately

There were flat fish, silvered, aldermanic; slim, darting fish; palindromic† fish that peered foully out of crevices. . . .
> —Fowles, *The Magus,* p. 138.

ALEATORIC, ALEATORY : *adj* subject to the roll of a die; random. ALEATORICALLY, *adv*

She smiled, girlish, pretending to be flattered, but her eyes were as cold, as aleatory, as the Kyklops eye of Lykourgos.
> —Gardner, *The Wreckage of Agathon,* p. 57.

The novelist is still a god, since he creates (and not even the most aleatory avant-garde modern novel has managed to extirpate its author completely). . . .
> —Fowles, *The French Lieutenant's Woman,* p. 106.

The pianist, who seemed as drunk as his leader, was doing something atonal and aleatoric. . . .
> —Burgess, *Tremor of Intent,* p. 83.

. . . whistle the aleatoric music of license plates. . . .
> —Elkin, *George Mills,* p. 19.

He was mixing cocktails in big crocks, selecting the ingredients aleatorically.
> —Burgess, *Enderby,* p. 239.

ALFEAR : *noun* See quotation

A shiver of *alfear* (uncontrollable fear caused by elves) ran between his shoulder blades.

—Nabokov, *Pale Fire,* p. 143.

ALGEDONIC : *adj* pleasingly painful or painfully pleasing

For him even the most painful social confrontations . . . were stingless. Without significance except as vignettes, as interesting discords, as pleasurable because vivid examples of the algedonic polarity of existence.

—Fowles, *The Magus,* p. 178.

ALGO : *noun* a pain

. . . the old itch and algos crept back into his mind.

—Beckett, "Ding-Dong,"
More Pricks than Kicks, p. 43.

ALGOLAGNIAC : *noun* a masochist, a sadist, or both

She had the soft, pure, angelic sort of beauty that spoke to every fiber of his algolagniac's heart. With her it wasn't the mere momentary pleasure of sex, it was an ongoing process of erotic defilement, it was pissing in the pews, jerking off on the altar. She was made for him.

—Boyle, *Water Music,* p. 264.

ALIQUOT : *noun* 1) a sympathetic note in music; 2) a partial harmonic tone

A great major symphony of supply and demand, effect and cause, fulcrate† on the middle C of the counter and waxing, as it proceeded, in the charming harmonics of blasphemy and broken glass and all the aliquots of fatigue and ebriety.†

—Beckett, "Ding-Dong,"
More Pricks than Kicks, p. 42.

ALLELOMORPH : *noun* literally, "shaped for each other"; an alternative shape or form. Compare CATOPTRIC, ENANTIOMORPHIC

Next came the chain bicycle and its dread allelomorph the motorcycle.
> —Davenport, "The Dawn in Erewhon,"
> *Tatlin!,* p. 216.

ALLOPHONE : *noun* a different form of the same phoneme in linguistics

Love, for instance. Interesting, that collocation of sounds: the clear allophone of the voiced divided phoneme gliding to that newest of all English vowels which Shakespeare, for instance, did not know. . . .
> —Burgess, *The Doctor Is Sick,* p. 152.

ALLOTROPY : *noun* a variation in form, an alternative way or means

But now he was willing to wait, and take a closer and deeper look into the nature of things, into the homologies† and allotropies of relationships. . . .
> —Aczel, *Illuminations,* p. 18.

ALTILOQUENT : *adj* superior or lofty in speech

. . . they listened . . . to grandly romantic trash: bad poetry, stupid theology—altiloquent designs in the empty air.
> —Gardner, *Jason and Medeia,* p. 96.

AMAIN : *adv* with violent effort, vehemently

But Sir Hector ordered him to replace the blade in the stone, and Kay mounted the stage and so did. "Pull it out then," said Hector, and Kay tried amain and could not move it whatever.
> —Berger, *Arthur Rex,* p. 32.

AMARANTHINE : *adj* referring to the flower *Amarantus* which keeps its color to the end; hence, something unfading, usually used in reference to love

The amaranthine murmur of honey-makers. Culling from every flower the virtuous sweets.
　　　　　　　　　　—Nye, *Falstaff*, p. 164.

Every semirecluse has his amaranthine woman. Imaginary love-lies-bleeding.
　　　　　　　　　　—DeLillo, *Ratner's Star*, p. 202.

AMATION : *noun* the activity of love

Leo spoke of amation, of the importance of afters and the special role of the man in the boat. . . .
　　　　　　　　　　—Burgess, *The Doctor Is Sick*, p. 121.

AMAUROTIC : *adj* referring to an externally unobservable loss of eyesight; also to Amaurote, the city in Sir Thomas More's *Utopia* and to the Amaurots, the populace of Rabelais's Utopia. Compare CECITY, SCOTOMA

. . . and there, right in front of his amaurotic eyes. . . .
　　　　　　　　　　—Aczel, *Illuminations*, p. 175.

AMBAGE, AMBIAGE : *noun* roundabout or indirect speech

They read, still as tigers in their dusky rooms, and watch through the dark, rustling ambiage for some dire phrase to pounce on.
　　　　　　　　　　—Gardner, *The Wreckage of Agathon*, p. 32.

AMBISINISTROUS : *adj* literally, "both left"; clumsy, klutzy, maladroit; the opposite of "ambidextrous"

It is not a practice of mine to toast the memory of dead, ambisinistrous queens. . . .
　　　　　　　　　　—Theroux, *Darconville's Cat*, p. 313.

AMBIT : *noun* ambience. "Suggested by the cognate Spanish—*ambiente,* which besides meaning 'mood' also can have the sense of 'circle' or 'world' as, 'Me encuentro bien [o mal] en ese ambiente' " (Koster)

I came to know it first through her old lovers, this longing to enter and reenter Angela's ambit, to plumb her depths and swell within her, make her notice and acknowledge.

—Koster, *Mandragon*, p. 264.

. . . a riff of tender joy repeated indefinitely in the ambit of something that is next to nothing. . . .

—West, *Out of My Depths*, p. 95.

AMBLES, also UMBLES : *adj* referring to deer guts

. . . the Old Physician who cures the world by his
ambles pie;
the magician cook (Hamburger Mary), "Eternal
Verities". . . .

—Gardner, *Jason and Medeia*, p. 142.

AMBSACE : *adj* or *noun* literally, "snake-eyes on dice"; bad luck, misfortune; or, figuratively, hypnotized as if by a snake's stare. AMBSACED, *adj*

We hunch forward in our chairs, ambsaced. . . .

—Gardner, *Jason and Medeia*, p. 174.

She was my Great Bitch, my ambsace, my doom.

—Gardner, *The Wreckage of Agathon*, p. 55.

AMPHICLEXIS : *noun* an embracing speech

Real love to be successful, must move each to each equally, an amphiclexis of souls wherein the giving by one generates, not taking, but a natural impulse by the other to give in return.

—Theroux, *Darconville's Cat*, p. 227.

ANABATIC : *adj* 1) augmenting, increasing, as in a fever; 2) a movement upward, a march upcountry as in Xenophon's

9

Anabasis. Antonym, "Catabasis"

... I am he who will know no peace, no happiness until
he holds you in his arms again! ...
   This anabatic epistle was not arrived at until after
several drafts.
   —Fowles, *The French Lieutenant's Woman*, p. 382.

ANABLEPT : *noun* literally, "a look up"; a genus of fish with
   bifocal eyes, able to see above and below the surface

   ... his secretary, a blinking anablept with mis-mated
   eyes. ...
                              —Theroux, *Darconville's Cat*, p. 64.

ANACLITIC : *adj* term from psychology for being excessively
   dependent on the mother. Compare ENATIC

   I don't think I have to gloss the true anaclitic purport
   behind your need to humiliate a woman doctor symbolically.
                              —Fowles, *Mantissa*, p. 144.

ANACREONTIC : *adj* in the manner of the Greek poet
   Anacron; convivial, amatory, erotic

   In the modern and enlightened sunshine of Freud, in
   this Anacreontic milieu where we were all going to be
   absolved of guilt and its ensuing remorse, [Nathaniel]
   Hawthorne had seemed to me irrelevant and spurious.
                              —Exley, *A Fan's Notes*, p. 367.

ANAGNORESIS, ANAGNORISIS : *noun* the denouement of
   a drama

   P.: Here it comes. You down there: wake up for the
      anagnoresis!

                              —Barth, *Chimera*, p. 306.

   "You treacherous bloody bitch!"
   "But darling, this is what they called the anagnorisis."
                              —Fowles, *Mantissa*, pp. 191-192.

ANAPHRODISIAC : *adj* sexually de-appetizing

> . . . catering to her husband's pleasures had so defeminized her that her effect on men was anaphrodisiac. . . .
> —Barth, *Giles Goat-Boy,* p. 357.

ANCHYLOSIS, ANKYLOSIS : *noun* a stiffening, usually at an angle, of a human limb or other object. ANKYLOSE. *verb;* ANKYLOSED, *adj*

> I despaired at first of ever bending my leg again, and then, a little later, through sheer determination, did succeed in bending it, slightly. The anchylosis was not total!
> —Beckett, *Molloy,* p. 188.

> . . . it was a strange spot, this forest of dark petrifacts, this grove of ankylosed trees.
> —Durrell, *Monsieur,* p. 136.

> So process gets slowed down by cowardice and slowly ankyloses.
> —Durrell, *Monsieur,* pp. 278-279.

ANDROCRAT : *noun* one who believes in supremacy of the male

> . . . I am an anorchid,† an autotome,† an androcrat. Pedicating† is not my line.
> —Theroux, *Darconville's Cat,* p. 453.

ANFRACTUOUS : *adj* crooked, twisted, sinuous, tortuous

> . . . stammering to some extent represented the "curse" of verbal communication, the anfractuous blacktop route from the pure noise of infancy.
> —DeLillo, *Ratner's Star,* p. 397.

ANHELATE : *verb* to pant, to puff, to be short of breath. ANHELATING, *adj.* Compare DYSPNEAL

11

... the driver, the stoker, the guard and the station staffs all along the line, were anhelating towards their wives, after long hours of continence. ...
—Beckett, *Watt*, p. 30.

ANNUATED : *adj* back formation from "superannuated"; hence, slightly aged

... A's behaviour has been more a gentleman's and less an annuated adolescent's.
—Barth, *Letters*, p. 539.

ANNULATE : *adj* furnished or marked with a ring; ringing. Compare TORQUATED

... annulate tones moving out through the arch of distances.
—Gardner, *Jason and Medeia*, p. 45.

ANNULUS : *noun* a ring

Steam drifts into the glare of the gooseneck lamp, now and then becoming very bright, and the shadows of the men's gestures may pass through it, knife-edged, swooping very fast, but both faces are usually reserved, kept well back, in the annulus of night.
—Pynchon, *Gravity's Rainbow*, p. 47.

ANODYNIC : *adj* able to assuage pain, soothing to the sensibilities. Compare FEBRIFUGE

Mrs. Alloway explained to her that ladies were meant for hoops and finery, for accomplishment in verse and music and other anodynic arts, that ladies above all else were ladies, the fleece and plumage of society.
—Boyle, *Water Music*, p. 33.

ANORCHID : *noun* one without testicles. See ANDROCRAT

ANORECTIC : *adj* having no appetite, usually over a long period of time; severely skinny. Compare CACHECTIC,

DYSCRASE, INANITION, MARASMIC, MARCESCENCE, TABESCENT

... slim anorectic queans† with gamboge† complexions.
—Theroux, *Three Wogs,* p. 186.

ANTIMONY : *noun* the element stibium

... the alchemist who watched pigs grow fat on food containing stibium. . . .you tried it on some fasting emaciated monks and they all died. . . . And so they named it antimony, anathema to monks.
—Gaddis, *The Recognitions,* p. 384.

ANTINOAN : *adj* referring to Antinous, a companion of the Roman Emperor Hadrian; hence, having masculine beauty

A young sailor whose body is antinoan. . . .
—Davenport, "The Dawn in Erewhon,"
Tatlin!, p. 226.

ANTINOMIAN : *noun* one who refuses to accept moral laws or moral authority

Her name was Amy Sprue, a family renegade turned Antinomian at age 23 and running mad over the Berkshire countryside, ahead of Crazy Sue Dunham by 200 years, stealing babies, riding cows in the twilight, sacrificing chickens up on Snodd's Mountain.
—Pynchon, *Gravity's Rainbow,* p. 329.

ANTINOMY : *noun* literally, "against the law"; a conflict between two true statements, a paradox

... the Tragic View of Marriage and Parenthood ... to affirm it was to affirm the antinomy of the cosmos ... the pity and terror of the affirmation whereof effected in the human soul an ennobling catharsis.
—Barth, *Chimera,* pp. 148-149.

ANTIPLUVIAL : *adj* preventing precipitation

> ... Johnson has taken measures to insure against an untimely deluge: that is, he has concocted a potent antipluvial fetish consisting of the chucked scales of a small dune-dwelling lizard, a square inch of camel tripe, a pinch of sulfur and six lines of Milton's "L'Allegro."
> —Boyle, *Water Music,* p. 344.

ANTIVERBALITY : *noun* a disinclination if not outright distaste for using speech to communicate

> But one wonders ... whether that vague antiverbality proceeds from (I had almost said *bespeaks*) a mindless will or a mere vacuum. ...
> —Barth, *Letters,* p. 218.

APHELION : *noun* See APOCHEIR

APICAL : *adj* at the tip, point or apex. APICALLY, *adv*

> ... a lengthy brick improvisation, a Victorian paraphrase of what once, long ago, resulted in Gothic cathedrals—but which, in its own time, arose not from any need to climb through the fashioning of suitable confusions toward any apical God. ...
> —Pynchon, *Gravity's Rainbow*, p. 46.

> Apically, the white of the abdomen, brought out in frightening *repoussé*, with an ugliness never noticed before, a man's portable zoo. ...
> —Nabokov, *Look at the Harlequins!*, p. 31.

APOCHEIR : *noun* See quotation

> If you look from the side at a planet swinging around in its orbit, split the sun with a mirror and imagine a string, it all looks like a yo-yo. The point furthest from the sun is called aphelion.† The point furthest from the

yo-yo hand is called by analogy apocheir.
—Pynchon, *V.*, p. 35.

APOCOPE : *noun* a dropping of the last letter of a word

... a bar called the Palac (which might have been an English word in adventitious apocope or else Serbo-Croat for Thumb). . . .
—Burgess, *Earthly Powers*, p. 121.

APODICTIC : *adj* demonstrably certain, established as true

... as time passed, the apocryphal, simply by repetition, became the apodictic.
—Theroux, *Darconville's Cat*, p. 139.

APODOSIS : *noun* a conclusion

If only I could make an effort, an effort of attention, to try and discover what's happening, what's happening to me, what then, I don't know, I've forgotten my apodosis. . . .
—Beckett, *The Unnamable*, p. 560.

APORIA : *noun* perplexity, dubiety

... how proceed? By aporia pure and simple? Or by affirmations and negations invalidated as uttered. . . .
—Beckett, *The Unnamable*, p. 401.

APOSEMATIC : *adj* warning away

Crucifer's fat arms shot victoriously out of the red robe, an almost aposematic coloration, it seemed, warning of a frightful attack. . . .
—Theroux, *Darconville's Cat*, p. 469.

APOSIOPESIS : *noun* a sudden stopping of speech

This somewhat abrupt ending (or aposiopesis) is caused by a previous movement from the figure on the bed.
—Fowles, *Mantissa*, p. 92.

"Kick---!" The aposiopesis signified horror.
—Theroux, *Three Wogs*, p. 77.

APOSTROPHE : *noun* 1) an aside or digression in a speech; 2) a speech to someone not present. APOSTROPHIC, *adj*. See also PROSOPOEIC

He lay in the bunkhouse nights smoking in the dark and apostrophizing the glowing end of his cigarette butt.
—Pynchon, *V.*, p. 27.

. . . Rose addressed these apostrophes to our usual invisible ceiling cherubs, the unseen tribunal asked again to offer judgment. . . .
—DeVries, *Into Your Tent I'll Creep*, p. 136.

APOTROPAIC : *adj* turning away evil, exorcizing. Compare ABREACTION, DIABOLIFUGE

The Duce hurriedly withdrew his left hand from his crotch . . . the apotropaic gesture against the sacerdotal evil eye.
—Burgess, *Earthly Powers*, p. 303.

APTEROUS : *adj* wingless. Compare IMPENNOUS

He was dressed like some apterous mythological bird, in azure and gold and burnished black and scarlet, with barbaric golden earrings like those of Sardis, and though it should all have been lewd, bumptious, he brought it off: his smile and eyes were brighter than his garb.
—Gardner, *The Wreckage of Agathon*, p. 43.

APTERYX : *noun* a flightless bird, such as the penguin

. . . the old apteryx [the butler] would come puffing and snuffling along, looking into rooms.
—Davenport, "A Field of Snow on a Slope of the Rosenberg," *Da Vinci's Bicycle*, p. 167.

ARCHESPORIAL : *adj* literally, "original spore"; a biological term for cells from which spore mother cells originate

At no time did she look toward the sink or toward whatever was growing in the sink, whatever boneless archesporial horror.

—DeLillo, *Ratner's Star,* p. 131.

ARMSCYE : *noun* the armhole in clothing

... I saw the muscles bunched in his shoulders that had strained the threads of the armscye apart. ...
—Davenport, "A Field of Snow on a Slope of the Rosenberg," *Da Vinci's Bicycle,* p. 162.

ARTEMID : *adj* having the characteristics of Artemis, Diana the Huntress, goddess of chastity. Compare DRYAD, MAE-LID, NAIAD, OREAD

There were days when her body was artemid, an oread's,† the flat belly grooved and brown, butt, breasts, and hips strict and firm. ...
—Davenport, "The Dawn in Erewhon," *Tatlin!,* p. 257.

ASPERITY : *noun* a roughness, protrusion, or excrescence

... you ... have to drag yourself to the nearest plot of vegetables, using the tufts of grass and asperities of the earth to drag yourself forward. ...
—Beckett, *Malone Dies,* pp. 318-319.

ASPERSE : *verb* to sprinkle. ASPERSED, *adj*

Nameless until then, a small sentient creature ... was aspersed with water drops.
—Cozzens, *By Love Possessed,* pp. 329-330.

ASSOT : *verb* to make an ass of oneself or of someone else. ASSOTTED, *adj*

... but the dowry with which he filled the hold was only real gold and silver at the tops of the chests, being underneath cheap tinware of Irish tinkers, for he counted on King Mark to be so assotted with Isold that he would plunge his hands into her robe rather than deeply into the supposed treasure.

—Berger, *Arthur Rex*, pp. 127-128.

ASTRIVE : *adj* energetically struggling. "Adjective from verb by prefixing 'a,' a favorite of Nabokov's messings-around with English" (Koster)

My double sprawled on Angela's white breasts, his hips astrive between her lifted thighs.

—Koster, *Mandragon*, p. 271.

ASTUNOMOLOGIST : *noun* See quotation

"It [astunomologist] comes from the Greek for policeman. . . . Policeman sounds horrible, of course. O'Grady is highly skilled in techniques of pacification."
"That sounds horrible too."

—Burgess, *The End of the World News*, p. 268.

ASYMPTOTICALLY : *adv* getting closer but never quite meeting

Lovers move asymptotically toward the paradise. . . .

—Theroux, *Darconville's Cat*, p. 225.

ATRAMENTAL : *adj* inky, black. Compare ATROCIFY

Sometimes I had dinner with friends, shot pool, went to the aquarium, danced to a pulsing Latino beat in close atramental clubs; sometimes I felt like a bearded ascetic contemplating the stones of the desert.

—Boyle, *Budding Prospects*, pp. 3-4.

ATROCIFY : *verb* originally, "to blacken"; to perform a dark deed. Compare ATRAMENTAL

. . . the surviving Janissary is obligated . . . to atrocify and consummate even to the *n*th degree his chum's lewd scheme.

—Elkin, *George Mills,* p 381.

AUDACULOUS : *adj* slightly bold

We teach their audaculous hands the delicate tricks of love-making. . . .
—Gardner, *Jason and Medeia,* p. 50.

AUREATE : *adj* golden, gold-colored

Carol Doda's breasts are up there the way one imagines Electra's should have been, two incredible mammiform† protrusions, no mere pliable mass of feminine tissues and fats there but living arterial sculpture—viscera spigot—great blown-up aureate morning-glories.
—Wolfe, *The Pumphouse Gang,* p. 85.

AURICOME : *noun* golden hair. Compare FLAVICOMOUS

The light from the window seemed in love with his head: it polished its nudeness and was an auricome for the stubble above the folded nape.
—Burgess, *Honey for the Bears,* p. 64.

AURIFEROUS : *adj* gold-bearing or gold-producing

". . . Guiana would still be there if I did not think about it."
"And the gold?" Bacon asked, in a curiously detached and clinical voice.
"What do you mean?" I said.
"You believe Guiana to be highly auriferous?" he said.
—Nye, *Voyage of the Destiny,* p. 19.

AUSCULTATE : *verb* to listen to internal sounds, as with a stethoscope. AUSCULTATING, *adj*

By Christ! He did die! They had forgotten to auscultate him!
—Beckett, "Yellow," *More Pricks than Kicks,* p. 174.

. . . she . . . skips out to the long balcony and its tubular chairs, which also get her listening, auscultating them, like some convict receiving messages in stir.
—West, *Gala,* p. 45.

AUTOCHTHONIC : *adj* 1) native, indigenous; 2) primeval, primitive

. . . on long autochthonic legs that looked like flexible ducting. . . .
—Theroux, *Three Wogs,* p. 183.

AUTOFRUCTIFEROUS : *adj* self-productive, parthenogenic. Compare PARTHENIC

. . . before Osiris sported erection, before men knew of their part in generation, and regarded skirted women as autofructiferous.
—Gaddis, *The Recognitions,* p. 312.

AUTOPTIC : *adj* self-obvious

That concept of piacular† pollution, much diminished as the idea of the undressing Hope was entertained, received, with the autoptic fact of the undressed Hope, its *coup de grâce.*
—Cozzens, *By Love Possessed,* p. 128.

AUTOTOME : *noun* literally, "self-cut"; a self-pruned eunuch. See ANDROCRAT

AVULSION : *noun* a plucking out, a tearing away, a sudden separation

So once her father said to me with the same mad shine of the skin, "Get out of this house!" said it with such out-and-out avulsion that I would have done it. . . .
—Gardner, *The Wreckage of Agathon,* p. 64.

AXILLA : *noun* armpit hair. AXILLAE, *noun plural*

The urine [of a camel] is a powerful astringent, and serves to destroy vermin and other parasites. Indeed, I have had the opportunity to assess its efficacy personally as my pubes, axillae, sidewhiskers, and locks were infested with lice and desert mites. I found it refreshing, if somewhat mephitic†. . . .

—Boyle, *Water Music*, p. 55.

AXILLARY : *adj* having to do with the armpit. Compare OXTER

Another time a red-haired school girl hung over me in the *métro*, and a revelation of axillary russet I obtained remained in my blood for weeks.

—Nabokov, *Lolita*, p. 22.

B

BALANIC : *adj* having to do with the glans penis and/or the clitoris. BALANOS, *noun*. See also CARDIOID

> Sometimes he wondered what the phrase really meant . . . how did a "balanic plum" look. . . .
> —Nabokov, *Transparent Things,* p. 75.

BALATRON : *noun* an unintentional clown

> His fat body shook like a balatron. . . .
> —Theroux, *Darconville's Cat,* p. 32.

BALBUTIATE : *verb* to stammer or stutter. BALBUTIAT-ING, *adj*

> . . . the old cloudmonger
> stammered the state of the kingdom, stuttered his
> counsellors' thoughts,
> balbutiating the world to balls of spit.
> —Gardner, *Jason and Medeia,* p. 65.

BANAUSIC : *adj* mechanically contrived, utilitarian as opposed to artistic or aesthetic; a pejorative term to the Greeks. Compare DAEDALIAN, LOGODAEDALY, PAUCIPLICATE

He is enough of a writer to have isolated these true qualities in the city of the Soma. One could not expect more from an intruder of gifts who almost by mistake pierced the hard banausic shell of Alexandria and discovered himself.

—Durrell, *Justine,* p. 76.

I like to think of Our Saviour in terms of control, forgiving Him, of course, His one justified, but embarrassing, lapse with the banausic insurance agents squatting in the Temple of Jerusalem.

—Theroux, "Theroux Metaphrastes," *Three Wogs,* p. 26.

BANGLE : *verb* to flutter aimlessly, flap uselessly; also, to dangle, as with baubles, bangles, or beads. BANGLING, *adj*

... it was dangerous to have such stuff bangling there unprotected. Watch him flop to the wooden chair, jouncing his ballocks against the edge, mashing them between his left thigh and the seat.

—Koster, *The Dissertation,* p. 25.

BARDASH, BERDACHE : *noun* a male prostitute

... any males among themselves who happen to have been by nature underendow'd ... are ... advised, if they have not the womanly nature of a *berdache,* to take a girl-child to wife.

—Barth, *Letters,* p. 132.

BARGUEST : *noun* literally, "hill-ghost"; a portentous phantom usually in the form of a dog.

... the fat rolls of the generous-waisted barguests bulging. . . .

—Theroux, *Darconville's Cat,* p. 307.

BARRELASS : *verb* to tumble head-over-heels, ass-over-teakettle. BARRELASSING, *adj*

23

The rooster is in the doorway hollering Achtung, Achtung, discipline in his harem is shot to hell, noisy white tumbleweed hens are barrelassing all over the inside of the coop. . . .
—Pynchon, *Gravity's Rainbow*, p. 574.

BATE-BREEDER : *noun* troublemaker. See MOME

BATHYCOLPOUS : *adj* deep-chested, heavy-bosomed

. . . Mavis . . . six years older than Beatrice-Joanna, with the same cider hair, speck-brown eyes and lavish limbs, bathycolpous.
—Burgess, *The Wanting Seed*, p. 99.

BATHYSIDERODROMOPHOBIA : *noun* fear of subways, undergrounds, or metros. Compare CHTHONIC, TANNHAUSERISM, TERRENITY

—Well, I came up on the subway, and . . .
—Bathysiderodromophobia! What did I tell you!
—Gaddis, *The Recognitions*, p. 618.

BATRACHIAN : *adj* having to do with frogs

His batrachian lips pursed into a smile, and he dug again in to the honey.
—Fowles, *The Magus*, p. 160.

BATRACHOMYOMACHIA : *noun* literally, "the battle between frogs and mice"; a silly and trifling altercation. Compare FRATCH, QUISQUOUS, TIRRIT

Sex is merely lust—the batrachomyomachia of the bunghole and battery from which love, apparently, can do anything but shelter one.
—Theroux, *Darconville's Cat*, p. 562.

BAUBON : *noun* a variant of "bauble"; in this sense, a device for the stimulation of the female genitalia. Compare

DILDO, DOLICHOPHALLIC, HERMSPRONG, ITHY-PHALLIC, OLISBOS

At the quiet hour in the afternoon they were adepts of the olisbos,† baubon, and finger.
> —Davenport, "The Dawn in Erewhon,"
> *Tatlin!*, p. 234.

BEAST-WITH-TWO-BACKS : *noun* an expression for face-to-face sexual coupling. See also PALINDROME

Iago: I am one, sir, that comes to tell you your daughter and the Moor are now making the beast with two backs.
> —Shakespeare, *Othello,* I, i, 16-17.

. . . first he came upon a lady's clothing strewn on the earth and then that of a knight, and under the fruit-laden branches of this tree . . . this page saw the heaving of the beast-with-two-backs, and this being a domesticated breed and not savage except to its own constituent parts, he observed its antics for a while. . . .
> —Berger, *Arthur Rex,* p. 272.

. . . the now engendered beast of two backs of that acting androgyne whose he-half was excitedly prodding and probing, whose she-half was excitedly prodded and probed. The little life span of the beast soon sped, its death was died.
> —Cozzens, *By Love Possessed,* p. 414.

BEBELOGLYPHIC : *noun* profane, unholy writing

. . . the words themselves sank down into the ink-crimped paper and perversely seemed to have an existence only on the other side of the page: a bebeloglyphic of revolt and refusal, backwards in dead black.
> —Theroux, *Darconville's Cat,* p. 302.

BED-SWERVER : *noun* an adulteress. See also MOME. Compare SPOUSEBREACH

Leontes: . . . she's
A bed-swerver, even as bad as those
That vulgars give bold'st titles. . . .
—Shakespeare, *The Winter's Tale,* II, i, 92-94.

BEEBUCKLE : *noun* "Scottish-Irish-Caribbean term for dead rat" (Helprin)

"Now that you're armed, you're your own worst enemy. Why? I'll tell you why. Power is like a lion. It won't sit like a cat in a boudoir. Although the weak don't know this, when you have power you have to protect yourself from it. You're a strange little beebuckle, Marshall. But you've got a lot of growing up to do."
"What's a beebuckle?"
"That's just what I mean. You don't know anything. You're ignorant. Everyone knows what a beebuckle is."
—Helprin, *Refiner's Fire,* p. 130.

BENEPLACIT : *noun* literally, "a good pleasure"; a gift

HAIR: A beneplacit of God. Shode† at the center, it falls in fine burnished gold. . . .
—Theroux, *Darconville's Cat,* p. 106.

BIBLIOCLASM : *noun* a destruction of books or a biblical cataclysm

. . . house, garden, even part of the orchard was gone, or blasted and scorched, gone, all gone in that sudden infernal cataclysm, that biblioclasm.
—Lowry, *October Ferry to Gabriola,* p. 89.

BINT : *noun* from Arabic, British slang for girl, woman, or prostitute. See PERIPETEIA

BLAEDSIAN : *verb* See quotation

In the days when bless was *blaedsian,* it meant to smear with blood, as if to recombine things guided apart by

fear, the word for which was uggr,† or by indignation or even primitive good taste.
—West, *Out of My Depths,* p. 17.

BLAKE : *verb* to become pale, to blanch

. . . Medeia blaked with fury that had no possible vent. . . .
—Gardner, *Jason and Medeia,* p. 243.

BLEB : *noun* a bump, a blister. See PYKNIC

BLISSOM, BLISSOMING : *adj* in heat or rutting, usually in reference to sheep; copulating; bleating with sexual desire

Blissful Mr. Thimm danced blissom Miss Swint squealing over a ha-ha. . . .
—Theroux, *Darconville's Cat,* p. 214.

. . . soft-lipped blissoming maidens.
—Gardner, *Jason and Medeia,* p. 317.

BLORE : *noun* a blasting wind, a tempest

The daughter had a beauty which was, at that hour and mauger† the blore, wearying toward length in the tooth and a sharpness of nose.
—Davenport, "John Charles Tapner," *Da Vinci's Bicycle,* p. 47.

BOANTHROP : *noun* one who thinks he is, or acts like, an ox. Compare DODDIPOL, JOBBERNOWL, NUPSON, UNGULATE, VACCINE, VITULINE

. . . the electronic marketing-box . . . where grinning boanthrops . . . interrupt us every two minutes mumbling Party-Think. . . .
—Theroux, "Theroux Metaphrastes," *Three Wogs,* p. 17.

BOBBERY : *noun* from Hindi for "Oh, Father," an exclamation of excitement; signifies a brawl, contretemps, noisy altercation

. . . full of bobbery and griefs must be his heart. . . .
—Theroux, *Three Wogs*, p. 110.

BODACIOUS : *adj* a combination of "bold" and "audacious"; the OED defines it as "complete, thorough"

"Purpose number two," he said, "is the jolt it'll give the establishment. Man oh man, it'll be a bodacious blow to authority."
—Robbins, *Another Roadside Attraction*, p. 258.

BOLUS : *noun* lump, large pill. See also DIGLOT. Compare HOLUS-BOLUS

—Grandfather Hippagoras . . . was physicking the ass, sticking a turpentine and onion bolus down it.
—Davenport, "The Antiquities of Elis,"
Da Vinci's Bicycle, p. 144.

BORBORYGMIC : *adj* having to do with the noise produced by a rumbling stomach or gurgling guts

All the toilets and waterpipes in the house had been suddenly seized with borborygmic convulsions.
—Nabokov, *Ada*, p. 260.

BOREAL : *adj* northern. See TRAMONTANA. Compare SEPTENTRIONAL

BOUNCE : *verb* to bully, to talk big to. BOUNCING, *noun*

. . . by bounce I mean men always want to disconcert women and put them at a disadvantage; bouncing is genial, patronizing bullying and I won't put up with it.
—Davies, *The Rebel Angels*, p. 60.

BOUSTROPHEDON : *noun* literally, "as the ox turns." See quotation

The members of the inner Cabal corresponded frequently with one another, using the curious old form of writing, known as the *boustrophedon;* that is to say a writing which is read from right to left and from left to right in alternate lines.
—Durrell, *Justine,* p. 101.

BRACHIATE : *verb* to swing from limb to limb, usually in a tree

". . . climbing trees."
"Oh, I'm good at that, " said Van, "in fact, I can even brachiate."
—Nabokov, *Ada,* p. 51.

BRACHYCEPHALIC : *adj* short or broad-headed

—Herschel! . . . your head is brachycephalic. . . .
—It's the coming shape in heads.
—Gaddis, *The Recognitions,* p. 171.

BRINDIZE : *verb* to toast, to drink to the health of someone

I took the initiative in glass-clinking. "To the happy couple," I brindized.
—Burgess, *Earthly Powers,* p. 161.

BRONSTROP : *noun* a corruption of "Bawdstrot," a procuress, a madam. See PATIBULARY

BRUMMAGEM : *noun* originally a reference to cheap, tawdry goods manufactured in Birmingham, U.K.; now any such junk

. . . —the whole brummagem inventory of head-shop fetishes, countercultural gewgaws, radical fripperies. . . .
—Barth, *Letters,* p. 346.

BRUSTLE : *verb* portmanteau of "bustle" and "rustle"; to bustle about making a rustling noise

Sometimes he'd get up and go out on the porch to listen to the sounds of night—animals brustling about in the fallen leaves not far away, wind moving softly through diseased beeches and pines.
　　　　　—Gardner, *Mickelsson's Ghosts,* p. 486.

BUBUKLE : *noun* portmanteau of "buboe" and "carbuncle"; boil, pimple

His face was his misfortune. It was full of meteors. It was covered with bubukles, and whelks,† and knobs, and flames of fire.
　　　　　—Nye, *Falstaff,* p. 251.

BUGLE : *verb* 1) to blow on a horn of that name; 2) a "euphemism for 'suck' " (Koster)

To tour the provinces of her mind and body, swilling up deference all along the way. Angela received him and paid homage. Fugled† and bugled, that is. . . .
　　　　　—Koster, *Mandragon,* p. 335.

BUNGLE : *verb* to be poorly constructed or faultily fabricated. BUNGLED, *adj*

In the small, dark, messy universe described by *La Patria,* a coffin-shaped universe bungled together out of soft lumps of dog shit scraped from people's shoes, I am an impotent cuckold cripple. . . .
　　　　　—Koster, *The Prince,* p. 142.

BURDEL : *noun* variant of "bordel," French for "brothel"

I do not mean she joined the rum- and bum-vendors in the warren of cantinas, burdels, and impromptu assignation burrows on the Tinieblan side of Avenida Jorge Washington. Tinieblas had become an exporter of alcoholic glee and sexual euphoria, a transit zone for

Pediculis pubis, an importer of human semen. . . .
>—Koster, *The Dissertation,* p. 54.

BURGLARIOUS : *adj* in the manner of a burglar, surreptitious

The light of the full moon, burglarious, steals through the eagre† of dart-shaped clouds. . . .
>—Theroux, *Darconville's Cat,* p. 213.

BURKE : *verb* to murder by suffocation and/or strangulation; derived from an Edinburgh murderer executed in 1829 for securing cadavers for medical dissection before they were properly dead

. . . those bible-thumping wompsters† . . . of the American South, had for so long impunitively burked reason, honesty and truth. . . .
>—Theroux, *Darconville's Cat,* p. 21.

Something happened down there yesterday morning in the French front, a regiment failed—burked—mutinied, we don't know what and are not going to know what because they aren't going to tell us.
>—Faulkner, *A Fable,* p. 78.

C

CACAFUEGO : *noun* Spanish for "... a shitfire, for which English 'spitfire' may be a euphemism" (Koster)

Sir Francis Drake passed within sight of Mituco in March, 1579, some two weeks after his celebrated fight with the treasure galleon *Nuestra Señora de la Concepción* or "*Cacafuego.*"
—Koster, *The Dissertation*, p. 8.

CACHECTIC, CACHEXIC : *adj* 1) nutritionally deprived, often because of disease; 2) mentally depraved. Compare ANORECTIC, DYSCRASE, INANITION, MARASMIC, MARCESCENCE, TABESCENT

His horse has been restored to him (cachectic as ever, looking like one of the gutted nags the Druids used to impale for decoration). . . .
—Boyle, *Water Music*, p. 44.

But now I am old and cachexic, I need my nourishment.
—Gardner, *The Wreckage of Agathon*, p. 39.

He . . . ran a cachexic finger down a painted sign that listed the available treats.
—Theroux, *Three Wogs*, p. 56.

CACHINNATION : *noun* loud and/or immoderate laughter. CACHINNANT, *adj*

The house was crowded and noisy as the sea with party cachinnation. . . .
—Gardner, *The Wreckage of Agathon,* p. 44.

. . . the gaped crowding faces merely bayed at them again, the sound filling the alley and roaring from wall to wall until the reverberations had a quality not only frantic but cachinnant, recoiling and compounding as it gathered strength. . . .
—Faulkner, *A Fable,* p. 220.

CACOCHYMICAL : *adj* foul-humored, bad-tempered

. . . they had been almost to a man nothing but a bunch of lackeys, cacochymical scroyles,† and middle-brow merchants. . . .
—Theroux, *Darconville's Cat,* p. 304.

CACODAEMONIC, CACODEMONIC : *adj* possessed by or possessing an evil spirit. Compare DYBBUK, ECSTATIC, ENERGUMENICAL

But the airplane! . . . that streak of cacodaemonic extravagance sundering the very dome of heaven.
—Gaddis, *The Recognitions,* p. 322.

. . . whatever strange hold she had on me had relaxed a little; I might eventually free myself of her cacodemonic influence.
—Gardner, *The Wreckage of Agathon,* pp. 54-55.

CACODOXY : *noun* the wrong opinion or doctrine; heresy

The most outlandish cacodoxy can take on the seeming solidity of stone if its argument is given with sufficient flourish—a proper appeal to our delight in symmetry, with pedal tone notice of our universal dissatisfactions. . . .
—Gardner, *Jason and Medeia,* p. 296.

CADUCITY : *noun* tendency to fall; perishability, transitoriness. Compare DECIDUOUS, FUGACIOUS, FLUXION, LABILE

Religion, as I've said, was one of his fascinations. Sex and wine, sad proofs of life's caducity, were the others.
—Gardner, *The Wreckage of Agathon,* p. 45.

CAFARD : *noun* literally, "bug"; French slang for the madness produced by terminal boredom

To do India, cockroach by cockroach, for example, was beyond all imagining; the original *cafard* must have dwelt there in the plains.
—Durrell, *Constance,* p. 339.

Not infrequently men spent loving weeks and months preparing their own death in some complicated mechanical fashion. The occupation drove away the cafard by giving them something interesting to do and think about.
—Masters, *Bugles and a Tiger,* p. 156.

CALCINATE : *verb* to reduce to quicklime by burning; to refine or to purify by fire. CALCINATING, CALCINED, *adj*

I would hear Tuka at her practice. . . . She would work one phrase again and again, doggedly, her mind calcinating by patient violence the stubbornness of fingers and wires.
—Gardner, *The Wreckage of Agathon,* p. 61.

. . . the cumulative but hardly integrated smells of calcined sausages, overheated bodies and what seemed like a trace of fowlpest.
—Theroux, *Three Wogs,* p. 62.

CALCULUS : *noun* See quotation

"A calculus?"

"A stone. A urinary calculus. An abnormal mass in my
bladder."
—DeLillo, *Ratner's Star*, p. 349.

CALIGINOUS : *adj* misty, dim, murky, obscure, dark. Compare TENEBROUS, THESTRAL

Inside, the atmosphere was rank and caliginous: fumes
rose from puddles, groans sifted through shadows.
—Boyle, *Water Music*, p. 155.

. . . in one "caliginous" aspect . . . life was *like* this bar,
from which you could not see out. . . .
—Lowry, *October Ferry to Gabriola*, p. 263.

CALIGULAR : *adj* referring to the extravagant excesses perpetrated by Caligula, third Roman Emperor. See NEROTIC

CALLIBLEPHARY : *noun* makeup for the eyelids, eyeshadow

. . . a supply of calliblepharies for her eyes!
—Theroux, *Darconville's Cat*, p. 231.

CALLIPYGIAN : *adj* literally, "beautiful buttocks"

. . . those dusky Afro-Scandinavian buttocks, which
combine the callipygian rondure observed among the
races of the Dark Continent with the taut and noble
musculature of sturdy Olaf, our blond Northern cousin.
—Pynchon, *Gravity's Rainbow*, p. 69.

CAMARINE : *adj* from Camarina, a Sicilian town located
beside a notoriously noxious swamp; hence, mucky and
stinking with decayed matter

For all man's nature, save only his god-given mind,
is a fetid and camarine thing, unfit to fish or swim in.
—Gardner, *Jason and Medeia*, p. 295.

CAMBER : *verb* to arch in the middle

He felt the doctor, suspended on her arms, expertly lower her loins, camber, arch, adjust herself. Insertion.
—Fowles, *Mantissa*, p. 37.

I cambered my *queue* over the waistband of my briefs.
—Davenport, "On Some Lines of Virgil,"
Eclogues, p. 181.

CANESCENT : *adj* growing white, hoary; often confused with "candescent," which means dazzlingly white, glowing

An aureole of canescent hair fanned out round his head and his jaws collapsed on toothless gums: he could have been the first man on earth, father of us all. . . .
—Boyle, *Water Music*, p. 434.

There are doubtless envoys who would have scorned the canescent unrealities I manipulated like Sardinian pieces on a playing board. . . .
—Gardner, *The Wreckage of Agathon*, p. 124.

CANICULAR : *adj* from Latin for "little bitch"; refers to the rise of Sirius, the dog-star, in August and thus to the dogdays of insufferable heat and humidity

But, in the sudden storm, calculations went to the canicular devils.
—Nabokov, *Ada*, p. 403.

CANOROUS : *adj* swellingly melodic

Unfortunately Watt was thinking of birds at the time, their missile flights, their canorous reloadings.
—Beckett, *Watt*, p. 144.

CANTILENA : *noun* from Latin for "little song"; a melody or ballad

He clung, riding her, fearful of being dislodged, then, as

the honeyed cantilena broke and flowed, he was ready
to sink with her. . . .
—Burgess, *Tremor of Intent,* p. 90.

CANTRIP : *noun* Scottish for a "spell" or "charm"

. . . the unarmed and diseagled battalion of the Fourth
went speeding off in retreat, crazy, panicky, panting
Long Live The Emperor as though that were a cantrip
solvent of crazed panic and cowardice.
—Burgess, *Napoleon Symphony,* p. 334.

CARDIOID : *adj* heart-shaped. See also BALANIC. Compare
AKROPOSTHION, POSTHION, STEGOCEPHALIC

He drew his foreskin back. He liked the Greek words:
posthia† drawn back from the *balanos,* the acorn. The
curve was cardioid.
—Davenport, "The Dawn in Erewhon,"
Tatlin!, p. 155.

CARIOUS : *adj* rotten, decayed

He found streets wide enough . . . but carious, cracked,
in cynical disrepair. . . .
—Burgess, *Honey for the Bears,* p. 56.

CAROTEEL : *noun* from Arabic, a measure of dried fruit in
a basket, 700 hundred weight. See PATIBULARY

CARUS : *noun* heavy sleep, torpor, comatose state

. . . the lady might lie in this deathlike carus
for days. . . .
—Gardner, *Jason and Medeia,* p. 106.

CASEATION : *noun* the process of making cheese

. . . a stinking anthology of Italian caseation. . . .
—Burgess, *Earthly Powers,* p. 365.

CATAMENIA : *noun* literally, "monthly descent"; menstruation

> . . . the air stale and close and rancid with the heavy tang of perspiration and catamenia.
>
> —Aczel, *Illuminations,* p. 167.

CATAPLASM : *noun* a compress, a poultice

> Yet how interested would the doctor have been in one who felt himself being shattered by the very forces of the universe? What cataplasms have laid on his soul? What did even the hierophants† of science know of the fearful potencies of, for them, unvintageable evil?
>
> —Lowry, *Under the Volcano,* p. 145.

> . . . that is arctium lappa; a good cataplasm of fresh roots cicatrizes skin eczemas.
>
> —Eco, *The Name of the Rose,* p. 139.

CATASTASIS : *noun* See quotation

> "The object of meta-theatre is precisely that—to allow the participants to see through their first roles in it. But that is only the catastasis. . . what precedes the final act, or catastrophe, in classical tragedy." He added, "Or comedy. As the case may be."
> "The case depending on?"
> "Whether we learn to see through the roles we give ourselves in ordinary life."
>
> —Fowles, *The Magus,* pp. 408-409.

CATENARY : *noun* a chain, a curve formed by a chain hanging freely from two fixed points not in the same vertical line

> A smile to you; to me the truth behind the catenary: locus of the transcendental: $y = a/2(e^{x/a} + e^{-x/a})$.
>
> —Pynchon, *V.,* p. 326.

> "A bridge," he proclaimed, "is a very special thing. Haven't you seen how delicate they are in relation to

their size? They soar like birds; they extend and embody our finest efforts; and they utilize the curve of heaven. When a catenary of steel a mile long is hung over a river, believe me, God knows."

> —Helprin, *Winter's Tale*, pp. 66-67.

CATENATE : *verb* to connect like the links of a chain. CATENATING, *adj*

... like a string of firecrackers or the chains of orgasms that Shahryar could sometimes set my sister catenating.
> —Barth, *Chimera*, p. 24.

CATENATION : *noun* a chain, a series

History is a catenation of disasters, redeemable only (and imperfectly) by the Tragic View.
> —Barth, *Letters*, p. 94.

CATOPTRIC : *adj* mirroring. Compare ALLELOMORPH, ENANTIOMORPHIC

... the intimacies of catoptric communion were by now as strange to him as any other. . . .
> —Gaddis, *The Recognitions*, p. 673.

CECITY : *noun* blindness. Compare AMAUROTIC, SCOTOMA

... my love for you ... induces a cecity to your inefficiency and your bad behavior.
> —Burgess, *Earthly Powers*, p. 479.

CELADONY : *noun* "[Charles, the utopian] Fourier's word for Lesbian (sexual sense)" (Davenport)

They were skilled in celadony and the sapphic kiss.
> —Davenport, "The Dawn in Erewhon,"
> *Tatlin!*, p. 234.

CELEUSMA : *noun* Greek for the timing call to rowers

> . . . the rowing cry, unholy celeusma ringing on the
> cliffs. . . .
> —Gardner, *Jason and Medeia,* p. 213.

CELOSTOMY : *noun* speaking with a hollow voice

> . . . the oracular celostomies of a midget concealed
> in an echo chamber?
> —Gardner, *Jason and Medeia,* p. 191.

CENAL : *adj* referring to the midday or afternoon meal

> For it is not enough to carouse, it is not enough to sit
> long over the cenal or prandial ambrosia, it is not, for
> that matter, enough to swoop down on hapless nymphs
> in zoomorphic† disguises.
> —Burgess, *Napoleon Symphony,* p. 261.

CENTRIPETAL : *adj* toward the center, unifying

> With Rossini, the whole point is that lovers always get
> together, isolation is overcome, and like it or not that is
> the one great centripetal movement of the World.
> —Pynchon, *Gravity's Rainbow,* p. 440.

CERVINE : *adj* having to do with deer

> What *is* it about short-sighted men that I find so
> attractive? And these long cervine heads. . . .
> —Durrell, *Constance,* p. 263.

CETACEAN : *adj* pertaining to whales

> It was in the sunrise that the cetacean majesty of the
> highest mountain on the island, of Mount McCabe,
> made itself known to me. It was a fearful hump, a blue
> whale. . . .
> —Vonnegut, *Cat's Cradle,* p. 172.

CHAOGENOUS :   *adj*   arising out of chaos

> . . . chaogenous dreams of revenge
> were fuming in his serpent brain. . . .
> —Gardner, *Jason and Medeia,* p. 222.

CHEMURGY :   *noun*   the use of organic materials in industrial processes. Compare IMMACHINNATION

> They were infantrymen, and know how to snooze between footfalls—at some hour of the morning they will fall out by the side of the road, a moment's precipitate out of the road chemurgy of these busy nights, while the invisible boiling goes on by, the long strewn vortices. . . .
> —Pynchon, *Gravity's Rainbow,* p. 550.

CHICHIVACHE :   *noun*   See quotation

> Chichivache, that French monster, the sorry cow that lives only on the flesh of good women, and is consequently all skin and bone. . . .
> —Nye, *Falstaff,* p. 193.

CHIMEROMACH :   *noun*   one who fights mythical monsters or she-goats

> Your fame as a Chimeromach seems secure, judging by your fanmail. . . .
> —Barth, *Chimera,* p. 139.

CHORDEE :   *noun*   an inflamed, erect penis that curves downward, usually as a result of gonorrhea

> Enderby . . . was emboldened by morning chordee to say, "Oughtn't you to come back to bed for a while?"
> —Burgess, *Enderby,* p. 137.

CHRONOSYNCLASTIC INFUNDIBULUM :   *noun*   (singular), INFUNDIBULA (plural). See quotation

These places are where all the different kinds of truths fit together as nicely as the parts in your Daddy's solar watch.
Chrono (kroh-no) means time. Synclastic (sin-class-tick) means curved toward the same side in all directions, like the skin of an orange. Infundibulum (in-fun-dib-u-lum) is what the ancient Romans like Julius Caesar and Nero called a funnel.

—Vonnegut, *The Sirens of Titan*, pp. 14-15.

CHRYSAL : *adj* golden, yellow. Compare FULVOUS

Calyxa was neither white, like most other nymphs of my acquaintance, cinnamon-dark like Ethiopish Cassiopeia, nor high-chrysal like my handsome widow . . . but sun-browned as a young gymnasiast through her gauzy briefs.

—Barth, *Chimera*, p. 67.

CHRYSOSTOMATIC : *adj* from Greek for "golden-mouthed"; richly eloquent. Compare TURPILOQUENCE

. . . the unpremeditated chrysostomatic utterance.

—Burgess, *Enderby*, p. 221-222.

CHTHONIC : *adj* of, in, or beneath the earth. Compare BATHYSIDERODROMOPHOBIA, TANNHAUSERISM, TERRENITY

Rancho Merced . . . the building was not large but its lowness made it look far-flung. One almost looked down upon it: you got down into it like a sports car and with the same expectation of the chthonic dividends of living close to the ground.

—Percy, *The Last Gentleman*, p. 341.

Eating and defecating at once they remained blind and

earthbound—were carried into the chthonic darkness of
unreason.

> —Durrell, *Monsieur*, p. 305.

After a fortnight with the odors of bunker fuel, chthonic
plumbing vapors, and human sweat, the pasture smells
of dirt and grass that came rolling off the Devon fields
were welcome and tantalizing and worked a gaiety on
the crew.

> —C. Buckley, *Steaming to Bamboola*, p. 121.

CHUNNERING : *adj* muttering, murmuring

The red-lit underground station entrance milled with
people, re-lit like devils of the old mythical hell, silent,
chunnering, giggling, sped singly or in pairs down the
grumbling escalator

> —Burgess, *The Wanting Seed*, p. 92.

CICISBEO : *noun* an acknowledged escort (and perhaps
lover) of a married lady, from an inversion of the Italian
belcecce, "beautiful chick pea"

I was outraged. This faceless cicisbeo, this panting lover,
schmuck, male—this shithead was going to walk into
Grace and Rubie's just like that?

> —Boyle, "A Women's Restaurant,"
> *Descent of Man*, p. 89.

"Look here," he said, "you are beginning to be noticed.
Of course a *cicisbeo* is a normal enough figure in
Alexandrian life, but things are going to become very
boring for you if you go out with those two so much."

> —Durrell, *Justine*, p. 63.

CIRCUMFLUENT : *adj* flowing around

He consulted his watch: still only a quarter to seven.
Time was circumfluent again too, mescal-drugged.

> —Lowry, *Under the Volcano*, p. 364.

CISATLANTIC : *adj* on this, the nearer, side of the Atlantic, whichever that happens to be

... it was called *Confrontation,* a cisatlantic quarterly transatlantically financed. ...
—Burgess, *Enderby,* p. 226.

CLAM : *verb* to make or to become damp and cold. CLAMMED, *adj*

I allowed myself to entertain hopes of a hot breakfast, for I was clammed near to death by this time. ...
—Caine, *Heathcliff,* p. 16.

CLAVIGEROUS : *adj* literally, "key-bearing"; guarding, custodial

Twenty-five drawings of a clavigerous lion guarding a rather imbecilic teenage Britannia.
—Burgess, *Enderby,* p. 230.

CLERISY : *noun* a group of scholars; a contemptuous term for the intelligentsia

Composers, artists, or architects in a compound began to have the instincts of the medieval clergy, much of whose activity was devoted exclusively to separating itself from the mob. Once inside a compound an artist became part of a clerisy, to use an old term for an intelligentsia with clerical presumptions.
—Wolfe, *From Bauhaus to Our House,* p. 19.

CLINQUANT : *adj* tinkling, clinking; glittering with gold or silver

... the clinquant possible of profit tomorrow.
—Gardner, *Jason and Medeia,* p. 243.

CLIP : *verb* 1) to embrace; 2) to have to do with sexually

I pronged Ophelia well, and clipped and kissed her.
—Nye, *Falstaff*, p. 101.

Clip and tumble as they might, dine on shellfish, ply the uterine thermometer, she went to her grave unfructified.
—Barth, *Letters*, p. 153.

CLIPSOME : *adj* eminently embraceable

WAIST: Clipsome, sized to Love's wishes.
—Theroux, *Darconville's Cat*, p. 106.

CLOACAL, CLOACINAL : *adj* having to do with sewers and sewage. CLOACA, *noun*. See also CLONIC, CREPITOUS

. . . the Consul was also saying something cloacal very quietly to himself over and over again.
—Lowry, *Under the Volcano*, p. 191.

. . . setting finally on top of the mess like a cloacal overflow, the sugary buttocks of a meringue.
—Burgess, *Earthly Powers*, p. 191.

. . . he slurped and chewed until the rest of the beef followed in with a loud cloacinal suction. . . .
—Theroux, *Three Wogs*, p. 154.

CLONIC : *adj* convulsing, having a spasm

. . . the echo murmuring in their hearts . . . of past passion, ancient error, warning them not to sully not to trail, in the cloaca† of clonic gratification, a flower so fair, so rare, so sweet, so frail. . . .
—Beckett, *Watt*, p. 141.

Nervous about everything from poison oak to pot poachers to detection and arrest by the DEA, FBI, IRS and the Willits Sheriff's Department, he was practically clonic, every facial muscle twitching, fingers drumming

the tabletop, legs beating like pistons. In a word, he was wired.
> —Boyle, *Budding Prospects,* p. 130.

. . . the boy's own muscles staying fiercely tight for what seems hours, as if he intends to kill, but not a word, only the long, clonic, thick slices of night that passes over their bodies.
> —Pynchon, *Gravity's Rainbow,* p. 100.

CLOSE : *verb* to come together in sexual contact or union

Now, though Arthur had not previously known a woman, he soon discovered how to close with one, in the which procedure the lady lent much aid.
> —Berger, *Arthur Rex,* p. 63.

CLOU : *noun* French for "nail"; the main attraction of an event. See EPHEBE

COCKAROUSE, COCKEROUSE : *noun* a title of honor among the Indians of seventeenth-century Virginia. See also quotation

. . . a tobacco-planter ("cockerouse" in the argot of the time, & a naughty pun too). . . .
> —Barth, *Letters,* p. 113.

COCKET : *adj* from French "coquette"; saucy, lively, flirtatious

. . . Kaatje's arched back and jumping breasts, pritch-kempt† and cocket.
> —Davenport, "The Dawn in Erewhon,"
> *Tatlin!,* p. 243.

COCKSHUT : *noun* or *adj* the time of day when fowl are shut in; twilight. Compare CREPUSCULAR, VESPERTINE

. . . in the cockshut sky. They lighted the torches, for
> the day had gone dark

prematurely, grown sullen as a nun full of grudges.
—Gardner, *Jason and Medeia,* p. 314.

It was that early span of twilight his father had called "cockshut," back in that lost age when every slightest flicker of reality had a name—birds, grasses, weathers, times of day and season.
—Gardner, *Mickelsson's Ghosts,* p. 22.

COENAESTHESIS : *noun* a.general numbness or paralysis

Whereupon she was without thought or feeling, just a slush, a teary coenaesthesis.
—Beckett, "Draff," *More Pricks than Kicks,* p. 175.

COG : *verb* to cheat at cards, dice, etc. COGGING, *adj.* Compare FUGLE

I dub thee, dear Frog, a swinking,† cogging, jadish prattler; a bescabbed, fart-shotten, monastical fustilug;† a flogging, surfeited, whore-hunting piece of carnal concupiscence. In fact, not a bad fellow at all!
—Lloyd-Jones, *Lord of the Dance,* p. 47.

COLLOGUE : *verb* to flatter, fawn, and/or cajole. See DEIPNOSPHIST

COLLUCTATION : *noun* a struggle, a wrangle. Compare DIGLADIATION, RENCOUNTER

You were not in love with her, only with the desire to win her, for colluctation grows out of concupiscence as quickly as the stricken hydra of old did sprout another head.
—Theroux, *Darconville's Cat,* p. 551.

COLLUVIA : *noun* a mixed mess of rocky material at the base of a slope or cliff

. . . the "avalanche" nightmares at the rush of awakening when their imagery turned into the movement of

verbal colluvia in the valleys of Toss and Thurn. . . .
—Nabokov, *Transparent Things,* p. 60.

COLLYWOBBLES : *noun* upset tummy, bellyache

Colleens, they called them. Not to be confused with
collywobbles.
—Nye, *Falstaff,* p. 222.

COLUBRINE : *adj* relating to snakes, generally nonpoison-
ous; hence, snakey, sneaky, cunning. Compare HERPE-
TINE, OPHIDIAN

Impotent, wily, colubrine, you'd buy and sell
all man's history, if it lay in your power.
—Gardner, *Jason and Medeia,* p. 178.

COMMINATION : *noun* a threat of divine punishment

Manning had gone off somewhere, perhaps to deliver
a telephonic commination to *The Times* bureau in
Washington.
—Burgess, *Earthly Powers,* p. 570.

COMMISSURE : *noun* a seam, an interstice, a joint

By day the shepherd would have raised his pipe in vain,
towards the long clear-cut commissure of earth and sky.
—Beckett, *Molloy,* pp. 216-217.

COMPRADOR, COMPRODOR : *noun* from Portuguese for
the native head of a household or business staff in China.
See PATIBULARY

CONARIUM : *noun* the pineal gland

"God bless my soul," said Murphy.
"Just so," said Neary. "I should say your conarium has
shrunk to nothing."
—Beckett, *Murphy,* p. 6.

CONATION : *noun* the conscious drive to do something. Compare antonym VELLEITY

One day I took counsel of an Israelite on the subject of conation. That must have been when I was still looking for someone to be faithful to me, and for me to be faithful to.

—Beckett, *Malone Dies,* p. 297.

CONFRICATE : *verb* to rub

"Hey, Mr. Park," rumbles the voice of Johnson, "don't you know enough to come in out of the sand? . . . You coulda had the hide confricated right off you, you know that? I mean a sandstorm is nothin' to fuck around with."

—Boyle, *Water Music,* p. 67.

CONGENERIC : *adj* of the same race or origin

. . . technically the two sets [of confessions] were congeneric since both were affected by the same stuff (soap operas, psychoanalysis and cheap novelettes) upon which I drew for my characters and she for her mode of expression.

—Nabokov, *Lolita,* p. 82.

CONGRESS : *noun* a coming together in a sexual sense

. . . she listened with furious concentration to the silence which from time to time blurred into the small sounds of congress which they made.

—Durrell, *Constance,* p. 38.

Freud smiled. "No, I mean that nature intended semen to be discharged in the healthful, life-giving, loving, normal way of companionate congress.

—Burgess, *The End of the World News,* p. 41.

CONGRUE

CONGRUE : *verb* to come together, to coincide, to agree

> . . . his soul congrued in triteness with the public's to the immense enrichment of his producer, his publisher, and himself. Money is when you never have to say you're sorry.
> —Koster, *The Dissertation,* p. 277.

CONSENTANEOUS : *adj* with the consent of all, unanimous

> . . . affirming in sharp consentaneous silence, the illusion of motion. . . .
> —Gaddis, *The Recognitions,* p. 398.

CONSILIENT : *adj* literally, "to leap together"; 1) reaching a single logical conclusion from different inductive sources; 2) jumping to a single conclusion for different reasons; 3) here used to suggest the agreeably mixed fluids of two different people

> Kaatje lay back. Adriaan sliddered† to the divergence of her thighs and sank his tongue into the consilient melt, roving his hands from thicket to breasts.
> —Davenport, "The Dawn in Erewhon,"
> *Tatlin!,* p. 242.

CONSTATATION : *noun* a certainty, a verification

> I now call upon my dear friend and colleague and whilom† mistress, Madame Germaine de Staël, bluestocking extraordinary, to amplify these considerably unconstellated† constatations.
> —Burgess, *Napoleon Symphony,* p. 246.

CONSUETUDE : *noun* a social custom or jointly held habit

> I . . . learned the meaning of words like . . . whilom,† terraqueous,† consuetude. . . . I have by now forgotten the meanings of most of them, and though actual occasions for their use were all but inconceivable, they

gave me a sense of security, like a gun kept loaded just in case.
—DeVries, *Consenting Adults,* p. 4.

CONTRAVALLATIONS : *noun* siegeworks, fortifications erected to protect the besiegers

The critic straightened up, unprepared for this sally; without time to recover his own walls, he withdrew instantly behind contravallations of mistrust.
—Gaddis, *The Recognitions,* p. 602.

CONTRECTATION : *noun* fondling, foreplay. Compare DACTYLIC, EUTRIPSIA, HAPTIC

C is for Contrectation. Their love-play lasted long.
—Theroux, *Darconville's Cat,* p. 340.

COPROCRAT : *noun* "Democracy is the rule of the people; coprocracy is the rule of the shits, the prevailing form of government in Central America" (Koster)

If, by the way, one cares to fit the [Fuertes] scale [of Human Worth] to the contemporary Republic of Tinieblas, General Genghis Manduco, arch-mediocrity and coprocrat, squats at the bottom while I, Camilio Fuertes, arranger of the past and guide into the future, stand at the top.
—Koster, *The Dissertation,* p. 288.

COPROLALIA : *noun* fecal chatter, dirty language. Compare DYSPHEMISM, TURPILOQUENCE

When you have Tourette's disease you go around repeating dirty words all the time. Coprolalia.
—Gaddis, *The Recognitions,* p. 531.

COPROPHAGOUS : *adj* shit-eating. Compare EXCRE-MENTIVOROUSLY, MERDIVOROUS

He fell in love with Dédé, that kind of love whose gratification is injury and humiliation, a coprophagous

love engendered by its object's foulness.
—Koster, *The Dissertation*, p. 119.

COPULA : *noun* a connection, a link

The younger and less experienced, driven mad with the delicious copula of their lust, clambered anything that presented itself, alive or dead, male or female.
—Durrell, *Constance*, p. 366.

We know that the little copula "is" is a very late comer in the evolution of languages. Many languages contain no form of the verb "to be."
—Percy, *The Message in the Bottle*, p. 156.

CORIACEOUS : *adj* resembling leather, tough, durable

"Women don't make such a fuss," said Kelleher . . .
"All things considered," Gallagher remarked, chewing his oily fish, "their skin's tougher than ours."
"It must be admitted," said MacCormack, "that when they put their minds to it, they can be more coriaceous."
—Queneau, *We Always Treat Women Too Well*,
p. 151.

. . . to pry open the hidden receptacles of Mr. Macmillan's coriaceous cunning that, on the small screen, appeared astonishingly as wide-eyed, boyish innocence. . . .
—Aczel, *Illuminations*, p. 295.

CORNUTE : *verb* literally, "to furnish with horns"; to cuckold. CORNUTING, *noun*

Will you cooperate with me in cornuting your husband? It's a must!
—Nabokov, *Ada*, p. 456.

CORUSCATE : *verb* to sparkle, to glitter, to flash. CORUSCATING, *adj*

They confirmed that Mr. Essanjee was indeed dead. His suit and jacket were soaking with blood, rendered all the more coruscating by the contrast it made to the patches of gleaming white.

—Boyd, *An Ice Cream War,* p. 134.

CORYBANTIC : *adj* referring to wild, noisy dancing, from the Corybantes, the priests of Cybele, a goddess of fertility and mountains

Toby gorged on corybantic Cambridge Sausages. Marsupial dons bellying out like sails. Galleons of furry gowns.

—Durrell, *Monsieur,* p. 276.

CORYPHÉE : *noun* the chief dancer in a ballet

Almost instantly the crowd picks up the refrain ... "me, me, ooh, take me!" From here on it is chaos. The sick throw away their crutches and dance like coryphées, the enfeebled strain to lift logs and boulders, the fevered recite recipes and the lyrics of popular songs to demonstrate their perspicuity.

—Boyle, *Water Music,* p. 305.

COSMOPSIS : *noun* See quotation

It is the malady *cosmopsis*, the cosmic view, that afflicted me. When one has it, one is frozen like a bullfrog when the hunter's light strikes him full in the eyes, only with cosmopsis there is no hunter and no quick hand to terminate the moment—there's only the light.

—Barth, *The End of the Road,* p. 69.

COUN : *noun* variant of "cunt." Compare COUNTRY MATTERS, COYNTE, DELTA, ESCUTCHEON, FOTZE-POLITIK, FURBELOW, MERKIN, QUIM, QUIMTESSENCE

He was fascinated with eighteenth-century dirty words. Perhaps he would whisper "coun," "cullion,"† "crack," (for "cunt," "testicles," "pussy") in my ear as we screwed?

—Jong, *Fear of Flying,* p. 213.

COUNTRY MATTERS : *noun* an archaic pun on "cunt." Compare COUN, COYNTE, DELTA, ESCUTCHEON, FOTZEPOLITIK, FURBELOW, MERKIN, QUIM, QUIMTESSENCE

Hamlet : Lady, shall I lie in your lap?
Ophelia: No, my lord.
Hamlet : I mean, my head upon your lap?
Ophelia: Ay, my lord.
Hamlet : Do you think I meant country matters?
Ophelia: I think nothing my lord.
Hamlet : That's a fair thought to lie between maid's legs.

—Shakepeare, *Hamlet,* III, ii, 119-126.

What he wanted to tell her but could not think quite how was that he did not propose country matters. He did not propose to press against her in an elevator. What he wanted was both more and less. He loved her. His heart melted. She was his sweetheart, his certain someone. He wanted to hold her charms in his arms. He wanted to go into a proper house and shower her with kisses in the old style.

—Percy, *The Last Gentleman,* p. 68.

COYNTE : *noun* archaic variant of "cunt." Compare COUN, COUNTRY MATTERS, DELTA, ESCUTCHEON, FOTZE-POLITIK, FURBELOW, MERKIN, QUIM, QUIMTESSENCE

You find the Middle English form *coynte.*Earlier forms have a more definite initial *kw.* Cognate with quim† . . .

the quimtessence† of womanliness. . . .
—Burgess, *The Doctor Is Sick,* p. 107.

COZEN : *verb* to cheat, deceive, defraud. See DEIPNOSOPHIST

CRAPULA : *noun* a hangover

The scientific approach to life is not really appropriate to states of visceral anguish. . . . The cold deflation of crapula perhaps made him see himself as temporarily empty of a future. . . .
—Burgess, *Tremor of Intent,* p. 16.

CRAPULENT, CRAPULOUS : *adj* intoxicated, inebriated, drunk

Mr. Slump was late and crapulous.
—Waugh, *The Loved One,* p. 28.

There was a crapulous trembling of lips and cheeks. . . .
—Cozzens, *By Love Possessed,* p. 365.

The explorer has begun to wonder about some of his choices—especially Bird and M'Keal, both of whom have been consistently crapulent since they left Goree.
—Boyle, *Water Music,* p. 335.

CRATERIFORM : *adj* in the form of an inverted crater, bowl, saucer, or frisbee

The crateriform brisket, lipped with sills of paunch, cowers ironically behind a maternity tunic.
—Beckett, "A Wet Night,"
More Pricks than Kicks, pp. 50-51.

CRENULATED : *adj* marked by many small rounded indentations; distinguished from "crenated," marked by larger toothmarks. Compare MACHICOLATED

. . . and those puerile hips on which I had kissed the

crenulated imprint left by the band of her shorts. . . .
—Nabokov, *Lolita*, p. 41.

CREPITATING : *adj* 1) crackling; 2) rasping; 3) clattering.
CREPITATION, *noun*

Crepitating waves of ecstasy, tongue-lolling satiation, mine-shaft glimpses into their hearts' cores that tinged the drabbest physical sensation with all the heady hues of guilt and horror.
—Koster, *Mandragon,* p. 263.

It was her inability to come to rest anywhere inside plausible extremes, her nervous, endless motion, like the counter-crepitation of the ball along its roulette spokes, seeking a random compartment. . . .
—Pynchon, *V.,* p. 256.

. . . like the sizzling crepitation of a lightning bolt. . . .
—Gardner, *Jason and Medeia,* p. 47.

"Hello, hello," he said. "Who's there?" But there came only the sound of breathing and of the crepitation of skin on plastic.
—Percy, *The Last Gentleman,* p. 86.

CREPITOUS : *adj* farting

I . . . blundered out of the caravanserai, through streets of cloaca† and crepitous ordure. . . .
—Lloyd-Jones, *Lord of the Dance,* p. 99.

CREPUSCULAR : *adj* relating to twilight, dusk. Compare COCKSHUT, VESPERTINE

. . . the tall exotic plants, livid† and crepuscular through his dark glasses, perishing on every hand of unnecessary thirst, staggering, it almost appeared, against one another, yet struggling, like some dying voluptuaries in a vision to maintain some final attitude of potency, or of

a collective fecundity. . . .
—Lowry, *Under the Volcano*, p. 65.

But then suddenly the cavern blooms with light (a brown crepuscular light, it's true, but light just the same). . . .
—Boyle, "The Big Garage," *Descent of Man*, p. 123.

The two figures lie embraced on the crepuscular bed, their eyes closed, a charming picture of sexual concord. . . .
—Fowles, *Mantissa*, p. 184.

CRESCENT : *verb* to grow, to increase, to develop

Now I wanted all the world to acknowledge Mandragon, and even as this strange craving came upon me, the world narrowed into Angela, Angela crescented till she encompassed all the world.
—Koster, *Mandragon*, p. 264.

CRESSET : *noun* a fire basket, a beacon. CRESSETED, *adj*

Glendower: . . . at my nativity
The front of heaven was full of fiery shapes,
of burning cressets. . . .
—Shakespeare, *Henry IV, Part I*, III, i, 13-14.

. . . the one big final identification . . . was of glory, a dayspring to his former dimness, a crimson-cresseted east, entirely and satifactorily enthroned and crowned. . . .
—Burgess, *Napoleon Symphony*, p. 349.

CRETACEOUS : *adj* literally, "chalky," referring to the geological period when chalk beds were laid down; therefore, very old

In the middle of the bed he saw a small, jellylike blob on the dark-blue craziness of the quilt, cretaceous, motionless. . . .
—Aczel, *Illuminations*, p. 165.

CRETINIZE : *verb* to turn into an especially deformed idiot dwarf

". . . I fear even more that a sociologist will get ahold of it. Then my ideas will cretinize in the news magazines. I'd have to go some place where they don't have *Time* or *Newsweek*."
"Doesn't exist," said Marshall.
—Helprin, *Refiner's Fire*, p. 208.

CRIBRIFORM : *adj* full of small holes, sieve-like

. . . with a glare through a cribriform veil she had just pulled over her face. . . .
—Theroux, *Three Wogs*, p. 149.

CROTCHET : *noun* a peculiar and whimsical perversion; a nonsensical notion

"Everyone *else* in the Firm packs a Sten, you know. The Mendoza weighs three times as much, no one's even *seen* any 7mm Mexican Mauser bullets lately. . . ."
"Am I going to let the extra weight make a difference? It's my *crotchet*. . . ."
—Pynchon, *Gravity's Rainbow*, p. 107.

CROTELS, CROTTELS : *noun* See quotation

. . . in the Middle Ages, how concerned people who lived close to the world of nature were with the faeces of animals. And what a variety of names for them: the Crotels of a Hare, the Friants† of a Boar, the Spraints† of an Otter, the Werderobe† of a Badger, the Waggying† of a Fox, the Fumets† of a Deer.
—Davies, *The Rebel Angels*, p. 113.

CRYPTOCHROMISM : *noun* secret color, camouflage

. . . grays, however, remained his favorite cryptochromism, and, in agonizing nightmares, I tried in vain to sort out properly such ghosts as Chrysler's Shell Gray,

Chevrolet's Thistle Gray, Dodge's French Gray. . . .
—Nabokov, *Lolita*, pp. 229-230.

CTENOPHILE : *noun* one who has great affection for a comb

. . . making a show of looking for his comb which is, as usual, lost, suspect is known as a notorious ctenophile. . . .
—Pynchon, *Gravity's Rainbow*, p. 123.

CUCKQUEAN : *noun* a female cuckold

It was as if the archangel Gabriel had suddenly visited earth and married a ravening cuckquean.
—Theroux, *Darconville's Cat*, p. 467.

CUCUMIFORM : *adj* shaped like a cucumber, squash, or muskmelon

She was there, tumbling the marvelous cucumiform weights down upon a chest which looked as though it would cave in under such manna.
—Gaddis, *The Recognitions*, p. 329.

CULLION : *noun* testicle. See also COUN. Compare OR-CHIDACEOUS, STEREODIDYMOUS

. . . the cullions hang like barnacles on a ship just beached, dark tumorous growths.
—Gardner, *Jason and Medeia*, p. 112.

. . . Pappos crinkled his eyes, which is his way of laughing when his mouth is full, and Pappas asked how, by the cullions of Hermes.
—Davenport, "The Wooden Dove of Archytas,"
Da Vinci's Bicycle, p. 38.

CUNCTATION : *noun* procrastination, delaying

"No room for cunctation in any line of work."

... Cunctation. ...
Something about that word implied a threat.
—DeLillo, *Ratner's Star,* p. 6-7.

CURKLING :   *adj*   crying as a quail. Compare RUCKLE

I ... watched him when he came to call with his
curkling retinue. ...
—Gardner, *Jason and Medeia,* p. 65.

CUSTUS :   *noun*   a scullion, dishwasher; a menial servant. See
TARANTULOUS

CUTWATER :   *noun*   1) the most forward part of a ship; 2) a
projecting sharp portion of a bridge or pier abutment
designed to reduce the force of flowing water

... her flattened mammae, in sympathy with this tor-
mented eructation† of countenance, had put forth cu-
twaters and were rowelling her corsage.
—Beckett, "A Wet Night,"
More Pricks than Kicks, p. 61.

CYCLAMEN :   *adj*   the dark reddish-purple color of "a flower
of the Vienna woods" (Aczel)

... the cyclamen-colored bedspread.
—Aczel, *Illuminations,* p. 51.

D

DAB : *adj* skillful. Compare DARB

Perhaps my dear dad was one of the soldiers? Junker
Wagner? A pikeman? A dab hand with the halberd?
　　　　　　　　　　　　　　—Nye, *Faust,* p. 9

DACRYOPYOSTIC : *adj* tear-producing, lachrymal

. . . .dacryopyostic onion patches and citizens with faces
like leeks!
　　　　　　　—Theroux, *Darconville's Cat,* p. 373.

DACTYLIC : *adj* having to do with fingers. Compare CON-
TRECTATION, EUTRIPSIA, HAPTIC

Knott was also addicted to solitary dactylic ejaculations
of extraordinary vigour, accompanied by spasms of the
members.
　　　　　　　　　　　—Beckett, *Watt,* p. 209.

DAEDALIAN : *adj* ingeniously made; having to do with
Daedalus, the first aeronautical engineer. Compare BA-
NAUSIC, LOGODAEDALY, PAUCIPLICATE

The Daedalian plan simplified by a look from above—
smeared out as it were by the splotch of some master

thumb, that made the whole involuted, boggling thing one beautiful straight line.
> —Nabokov, *Pale Fire*, p. 261.

DAGSWAIN : *noun* a coarse bedspread of rough material. See PATIBULARY

DARB : *noun* something wonderful. Compare DAB

... I melted back into sleep as I tried to recapture a darb of an eye, Jonquille's, a long kiss.
> —Davenport, "On Some Lines of Virgil," *Eclogues*, p. 180.

DAVEN, DAVVEN : *verb* from Hebrew, to sway to and fro rapidly while praying. DAVENING, *adj*

Then, sober again, he *davvens* his own introduction.
> —Elkin, *George Mills*, p. 67.

The sun began to rise. Marshall found himself swaying back and forth, davening, moved by waves of energy which swept past the dawn in a great crackling storm.
> —Helprin, *Refiner's Fire*, p. 295.

DEASIL, DEISEAL : *noun* towards the right, clockwise (an auspicious way to move in many cultures). See also and compare antonym WIDDERSHINS. Compare antonym SINISTRAL

But on the grand old yaller wall [a clock] ... a pillar of higher tone, representing the sun, was spinning out its placid deiseal.
> —Beckett, "Yellow," *More Pricks than Kicks*, p. 167.

DECALCOMANIC : *adj* from French for "copy by tracing"; later, "fascinated by decals"; also the root for "cockamamy"

... the two rocky ruin-crowned hills that I have retained

for seventeen years in my mind with decalcomanic romantic vividness. . . .
—Nabokov, *Ada*, p. 551.

DECIDUOUS : *adj* shedding, falling off. Compare CADU-CITY, FLUXION, FUGACIOUS, LABILE

Katje's always there, slipped by Them into his bed like nickels under the pillow for his deciduous Americanism, innocent incisors 'n' Momworshipping molars just left in a clattering trail back down these days at the Casino.
—Pynchon, *Gravity's Rainbow*, p. 211.

DECOLLATED : *adj* cut off at the neck

. . . instead of turning on the lights, he would illuminate his ranting face with a pocket-torch, a decollated saint's head brave above a kind of hell-glow.
—Burgess, *Tremor of Intent*, p. 6.

DECORTICATED : *adj* deprived of bark; skinned, flayed

He looked around him, noticed Gallagher and Caffrey dozing beside a little castle of empty Guinness bottles and decorticated tins.
—Queneau, *We Always Treat Women Too Well*, p. 92.

DECUSSATED : *adj* intersected, crossed like an "X"

The philonoetic† Greeks sat with legs crossed, feet decussated. . . .
—Theroux, *Darconville's Cat*, p. 223.

DEFALCATION : *noun* a lopping off, a defection

. . . earth itself had faltered, rapacity itself had failed, when regardless of whatever had been the nephew's old defalcation from his family's hope or dream seven or eight or ten years ago even that uncle and that godfather had been incapable of saving him. . . .
—Faulkner, *A Fable*, p. 253.

DEFENESTRATE : *verb* "to toss out of a window, as in the Defenestration of Prague, May 23, 1618, when Bohemian rebels tossed the imperial regents out a window, precipitating the Thirty Years War" (Koster). Compare antonym ADFENESTRATE

"Anybody who continues to live in a subculture so demonstrably sick has no right to call himself well. The only well thing to do is what I am going to do now, mainly, jump out this window."
So speaking Winsome straightened his tie and prepared to defenestrate.

—Pynchon, *V.*, p. 361.

DEHISCENCE : *noun* a gaping open. Compare DISSILIENT, ERUMPENT, GURN, IRRUMPENT, RINGENT

. . . their advance was at once rapid and sullen, for Una had become aware of an uncontrollable and ill-placed dehiscence in the stuff of her gossamer.

—Beckett, "What a Misfortune,"
More Pricks than Kicks, p. 139.

DEINOSIS : *noun* See quotation. DEINÓS, *adj.* Compare EFFED, INFANDUM

Maybe theirs was the only way of defusing horror, of coming to terms with what makes us gag, or bellow with commonsense indignation. By contemplating things in their most hideous aspect (what the Greeks called *deinosis*), you could learn to get along, even if with only slightly lessened aversion, even if only your mind said O.K. while your senses still recoiled.

—West, *Out of My Depths*, p. 19.

—To us she said it was wild and awful, *deinós*.

—Davenport, "The Antiquities of Elis,"
DaVinci's Bicycle, p. 144.

DEIPNOSOPHIST : *noun* literally, "dinner demagogue"; someone skilled at across-the-table chitchat

"The Deipnosophists"
He was wined and dined at every turn by little jellybones and psychobiological suckeggs who, never missing a chance, scraped, climbed, snatched, glozed,† cozened,† and collogued.†
　　　　　—Theroux, *Darconville's Cat,* pp. 190-191.

DELIQUESCE : *verb* to melt away, dissolve, disappear. DELIQUESCING, *adj*

A cord stands out in his neck as his head lolls to the side: no other muscle stirs. He looks as if he's deliquescing, sinking into the earth.
　　　　　—Boyle, *Water Music,* p. 351.

DELPHINET : *noun* young dolphin

. . . —you cannot demand pudicity† on the part of a delphinet!
　　　　　—Nabokov, *Ada,* p. 416.

DELTA : *noun* the Greek letter "D"; "the dark triangle" — pudendum or cunt. Compare COUN, COUNTRY MATTERS, COYNTE, ESCUTCHEON, FOTZEPOLITIK, FURBELOW, MERKIN, QUIM, QUIMTESSENCE

I can think of another portion of your anatomy that would have summed you up a damned sight better. They called it *delta* in Ancient Greek.
　　　　　—Fowles, *Mantissa,* p. 150.

DEMIURGIC : *adj* cosmically creative. DEMIURGE, *noun.* See also SUFFLAMINANDUS

　　　　　　　　　Each eyelid-flicker

of the Unnamable marks the decease of a demiurgic mind.
—Gardner, *Jason and Medeia*, p. 41.

DEODAND : *noun* a thing forfeited or given to God

. . . I would propitiate
the gods, my surest foe, with prayers and deodands.
—Gardner, *Jason and Medeia*, p. 59.

DEORSUMVERSION : *noun* a downward motion, a descent

"The Deorsumversion"
Then night fell like a guillotine blade.
—Theroux, *Darconville's Cat*, p. 473, 478.

DERACINATE : *verb* to uproot, to tear out by the roots.
DERACINATED, *adj*. Compare DERADICATE, antonym
ENRACINATE

Deracinated. Which of them is not. Which of this Crew
couldn't pick up tomorrow and go off to Malta, go off
to the moon. Ask them why and they'll answer why not.
—Pynchon, *V.*, p. 382.

. . . a bear. Tooth, sinew and muscle, four hundred
pounds of raging hirsute flesh, claws the size of fingers,
jaws that could deracinate limbs and pulverize bone.
—Boyle, *Budding Prospects*, p. 141.

DERADICATE : *verb* to uproot, to tear out by the roots.
Compare DERACINATE, antonym ENRACINATE

A solitary gum tree for which he had an especial
affection seemed likely to withstand the tempestuous
disruption, but that too was at length deradicated and
sent wildly hurling and thrashing like a dog maddened
with the pain of the whip.
—Burgess, *Napoleon Symphony*, p. 338.

DEROGATION : *noun* the removal of something from a
larger entity, thus causing harm to the whole. DEROGATE,
adj

The derogation of her gentle Belacqua from one whom she had loved in all the shadows and tangles of his conduct to a trite spy of the vilest description. . . .
—Beckett, "Walking Out,"
More Pricks than Kicks, p. 110.

Darconville . . . was by no means so derogate from the common run of human emotions as not to share . . . a derivative feeling of loneliness. . . .
—Theroux, *Darconville's Cat,* p. 10.

DESIPIENCE : *noun* foolishness, silliness

Half by desipience, half by proclivity, he had come to live in a world where the only significant leisure activities were coupling and consuming. . . .
—Fowles, *The Magus,* p. 160.

DESMESURE : *noun* See quotation

. . . the common ground of all Marie's [de France] stories (what she herself would have termed *desmesure,* or passionate excess) is remarkably akin to the later novelist's view of sense and sensibility [Jane Austen].
—Fowles, "Eliduc," *The Ebony Tower,* p. 120.

DESSIATINA : *noun* a Russian land measure equivalent to 2.7 acres

. . . the sweeping dessiatinas of grasses of mullein stalks, rippling out of sight, green and gray in the wind.
—Pynchon, *Gravity's Rainbow,* p. 339.

DEVENUSTATION : *noun* the condition or process of being reduced from Venus-status

LEGS :
The one devenustation. . . .They are "filled" legs, in the tradition of the round goblet which wanteth not liquor. . . .
—Theroux, *Darconville's Cat,* p. 106.

DEVOLUTION : *noun* See quotation

> "Devolution." . . .I take it to be some Irishism to do with a rolling motion in a bog, from the Latin *devolutionem,* to descend or fall like a ball.
> —Nye, *Falstaff,* p . 220.

DIABOLIFUGE : *noun* something that drives off the devil (a coinage of Oliver Wendell Holmes). Compare ABREACTION, APOTROPAIC

> I wished that I could administer a diabolifuge as easily as a vermifuge† for the expulsion of worms.
> —Lloyd-Jones, *Lord of the Dance,* p. 56.

DIANOETIC : *adj* intellectual, pertaining to thought. Compare PHILONOETIC

> I felt outside time, as if all things merely temporal, coldly dianoetic, were of no importance. . . .
> —Gardner, *The Wreckage of Agathon,* p. 63.

> . . . he might be arguing with passionate Jean-Jacques or dianoetic Immanuel about the virtue and liberty of olden times. . . .
> —Aczel, *Illuminations,* p. 103.

> But the mirthless laugh is the dianoetic laugh, down the snout—Haw!—so.
> —Beckett, *Watt,* p. 48.

DIAPHORETIC : *adj* sweaty, perspiring, sweat-producing. Compare SUDORIFEROUS

> . . . one tedious and diaphoretic afternoon. . . .
> —Theroux, *Darconville's Cat,* p. 455.

DIASTASIS : *noun* a separation, a setting apart

> Looking into the diastasis of her wide grey eyes, their

cadence a fire delicious as crushed honeycomb. . . .
> —Davenport, "The Dawn in Erewhon,"
> *Tatlin!*, p. 181.

DICLESIUM : *noun* a dried fruit. See PATIBULARY

DIGHT, DIGHTE : *verb* to have to do with sexually, to maltreat, to abuse, to deal with in a severe manner. Compare FER, FIG, FIRK, SCROG

"But be assured that I shall take you into my black pavilion, strip you naked, and then I shall dighte you soundly." And the lady wept piteously.
> —Berger, *Arthur Rex,* p. 241.

DIGLADIATION : *noun* a duel, a combat. Compare COLLUCTATION, RENCOUNTER

Those luminous digladiations gave at first the impression of taking place in sinister silence. . . .
> —Lowry, *October Ferry to Gabriola,* p. 159.

DIGLOT : *noun* one with two tongues or two languages, a bilingual

"Marry! Le Blonde and his men are here, asking the village to divvy its piscaries† among diglots holus-bolus.†
> —Helprin, *Winter's Tale,* p. 424.

DILDO : *noun* 1) a cylindrical or "sausage" curl on a wig; 2) a device for the stimulation of the female genitalia. Compare BAUBON, DOLICHOPHALLIC, HERMSPRONG, ITHYPHALLIC, OLISBOS

His wig was a campaigner, full but not extremely long, its tight curls terminating before either shoulder in pendulous corkscrewed dildoes. . . .
> —Barth, *The Sot-Weed Factor,* p. 72.

DIMERIC :   *adj*   a compound formed from two simpler ones (chemistry)

> This was a bedtime routine he'd lately developed not only for the common monkey sport of fingering those boiled orbs (dimeric witness to virility) but also in earnest celebration of the fact that his left testicle had fully emerged at last. . . .
> —DeLillo, *Ratner's Star,* p. 38.

DIMIDATE :   *verb*   to be cut in the middle, to halve

> . . . those bank ads where limited little employees dimly dimidated by more fortunate shoulders. . . .
> —Nabokov, *Ada,* p. 407.

DIOPHTHALM :   *noun*   something with two eyes

> . . . eyes pulled from their sockets and knotted neatly into a grotesque single diophthalm by a tugging and then twisting of their stalks?
> —Burgess, *Napoleon Symphony,* p. 173.

DISCALCED :   *adj*   barefooted, without shoes

> . . . Miss Gibletts was now handspringing naked and discalced through the shrubbery. . . .
> —Theroux, *Darconville's Cat,* p. 216.

DISEMBOGUE :   *verb*   to leave a river by its mouth; debouch

> . . . he came out coughing to the central living space into which all the rooms of the bungalow disembogued. . . .
> —Burgess, *The End of the World News,* p. 25.

DISEMBOSOM :   *verb*   literally, "to get something off one's chest"; to release from an embrace

> . . . the Frauenkirche disembosomed impartial welcome from twin and towering domes. . . .
> —Gaddis, *The Recognitions,* p. 68.

DISLIMNING : *adj* rubbing out, blotting out

> ... even the light, the sea outside, now due to an accident of sun and dislimning cloud looking like a luminosity between two darknesses. ...
> —Lowry, *October Ferry to Gabriola,* p. 252.

DISQUIPARANT : *adj* having a different name from one's own

> ... a social class disquiparant to her own. ...
> —Theroux, *Darconville's Cat,* p. 94.

DISSENTIENT : *adj* disagreeing in feeling or thought

> I take it that there will be no dissentient voices raised to this proposal.
> —Burgess, *The End of the World News,* p. 233.

DISSILIENT : *adj* literally, "leaping apart"; bursting open or out. Compare DEHISCENCE, ERUMPENT, GURN, IRRUMPENT, RINGENT

> It was written in a stiff, old-mannish hand, and signed, with a sudden dissilient flourish, *Michael Nugent.*
> —Gardner, *Mickelsson's Ghosts,* p. 26.

DIVAGATE : *verb* to wander about, to take a sidetrip. DIVAGATION, *noun.* Compare NOCTIVAGANT

> The railway—a double track but of narrow gauge—now divagated away from the grove, for no apparent reason, then wandered back again parallel to it.
> —Lowry, *Under the Volcano,* p. 115.

> You might tuck in a little Proustian divagation here. ...
> —DeVries, *Consenting Adults,* p. 100.

DIZENED : *adj* decked out, dolled up, attired tackily

> ... little near imbeciles often not much past puberty,

dizened with fake jewelry and dime-store make-up. . . .
—Cozzens, *By Love Possessed,* p. 150.

DODDIPOL : *noun* a hornless cow; hence, a fool. Compare BOANTHROP, JOBBERNOWL, NUPSON. See LOOBY.

DOITED : *adj* aged, decrepit

. . . there on the doited and chewed shelves, merchandise that had been around for years. . . .
—Theroux, *Three Wogs,* p. 21.

DOLICHOPHALLIC : *adj* long-penised. Compare BAUBON, DILDO, HERMSPRONG, ITHYPHALLIC, OLISBOS

His neck rising dolichophallic from his blue singlet. . . .
—Davenport, "The Dawn in Erewhon,"
Tatlin!, p. 230.

DOWELLING : *adj* fastening together by means of a cylindrical connecting peg. "Hence we manage another euphemism for 'fuck,' one that rhymes with 'prowling' and so allows the prose to bounce along jauntily" (Koster)

. . . a night-prowling, tart-dowelling petty hustler, addicted to tobacco and afflicted with the clap, with, to the common view, no higher prospects in this life than crime and vice.
—Koster, *The Dissertation,* p. 67.

DOWSET, DOUCET : *noun* from French for "little sweet"; the testicles of a deer. Compare CULLION, ORCHIDACEOUS, STEREODIDYMOUS

. . . his ounce† pelt, hermsprong,† and gowpen† of dowsets. . . .
—Davenport, "The Dawn in Erewhon,"
Tatlin!, p. 253.

DRACULARITY : *noun* the condition or state of being like Dracula; a vampire, a blood-sucker

... dialectics, matrices, archetypes all need to connect, once in a while, to some of that proletarian blood, to body odors and senseless screaming across a table, to cheating and last hopes, or else all is dusty Dracularity, the West's ancient curse. . . .
—Pynchon, *Gravity's Rainbow,* pp. 262-263.

DRAGOMACHY : *noun* dragon duel

... like that gentlest of dons, Quijote, they were wont at the very least to damage useful windmills in the name of dragomachy. "Heroes, bah," he said.
—Barth, *Giles Goat-Boy,* p. 90.

DRAGONATE : *adj* having the qualities of a dragon; fierce, powerful, fire-breathing

He took as models men like Professor Berry and Ariosto Ben Haifa, his professor of Jewish History—dragonate and of genius, and often quite nasty, as geniuses and dragons tend to be.
—Helprin, *Refiner's Fire,* p. 173.

DREICH : *noun* Scottish for something tedious or dreary

"Tell our friend the Ambassador of our dear brother of Spain that we're feeling just a little *dreich* after a day when we had momentous decisions to make. . . ."
"What's that dreich?" George Villiers asked idly.
"Fucked out and far from home," replied King James.
—Nye, *The Voyage of the Destiny,* p. 70.

DRUGGEL, DRUGGLE : *noun* a dull, fat coward. Compare FERBLET, GORP, MEACOCK, NESH

... I might add that you are a slabberdegullion† druggel, a doddipol† jolthead, a blockish grutnol,† and a turdgut.
—Burgess, *The End of the World News,* p. 59.

DRYAD : *noun* a wood nymph. See NAIAD. Compare AR-TEMID, MAELID, OREAD

DUCTILE : *adj* tractable, pliable

What rot, the old female itch to be . . . not *mastered,* God forfend, but ductile, polar to the male, intensely complemental.
—Barth, *Letters,* p. 247

DUMFUSION : *noun* portmanteau of "dumb" and "confusion"

. . . her asinine dumfusion.
—Beckett, "A Wet Night,"
More Pricks than Kicks, p. 75.

DUPRASS : *noun* See quotation. Compare GRANFALLOON

They were love birds. . . .They were, I think, a flawless example of what Bokonon calls a *duprass,* which is a *karass†* composed of only two persons.
—Vonnegut, *Cat's Cradle,* p. 78.

DYADIC : *adj* involving two elements

His own life then was a bitter contradiction of that dyadic principle of thought in which an element comple-ments its opposite.
—DeLillo, *Ratner's Star,* p. 392.

DYBBUK : *noun* Hebrew for a dead soul or evil spirit which takes possession of one of the living. Compare CACODAE-MONIC, ECSTATIC, ENERGUMENICAL

. . . Recent Reincarnations, in whom the dybbuk of past antagonists had recently, if inarticulately entered. . . .
—Theroux, *Three Wogs,* p. 86.

. . . he expected some kind of illumination in exchange, as it were, from a mighty and just God for the horrors

of petty tyrants and malevolent dybbuks. . . .
>—Aczel, *Illuminations*, p. 260.

DYSCRASE : *verb* to put the body in a bad state. DYSCRA-
SIA, *noun*. Compare ANORECTIC, CACHECTIC, INANI-
TION, NARASMIC, MARCESCENCE, TABESCENT

. . . to disgrace is to dyscrase.
>—Theroux, *Three Wogs*, p. 97.

Straining, my fingers trembling with alcoholic dyscrasia,
monkeys shrieking and war drums thumping in my
head, I managed to make contact with and knock over
the glass, and I lay there gasping like some sea creature
carried in with the tide and left to the merciless sun and
the sharp probing beaks of the gulls.
>—Boyle, *Budding Prospects,* pp. 160-161.

DYSPHEMISM : *noun* an offensive expression as opposed to
a pleasant one; the antonym of "euphemism." Compare
COPROLALIA, TURPILOQUENCE

. . . a *friend*—the commonest dysphemism in an affair
of the heart—is always a member of the opposite sex.
>—Theroux, *Darconville's Cat,* p. 100.

DYSPHORIA : *noun* anxiety, vexation; the antonym of
"euphoria"

. . . when he was forced to remember something he
really preferred to forget—Feldheimer was hit by the
dysphoria of recognition.
>—Aczel, *Illuminations*, p. 52.

DYSPNEAL : *adj* short of breath. Compare ANHELATE

It was an eroded dyspneal voice.
>—Burgess, *Enderby*, p. 348.

E

EAGRE : *noun*   a tidal wave, flood. See BURGLARIOUS

EBRIETY : *noun*   drunkeness. See ALIQUOT

ECOUTEUR : *noun*   from French for an eavesdropper

> Behind him he heard someone enter the room and
> Hedwig begin to moan. Chains tinkled in the heavy
> sickroom air, something whistled and impacted with a
> loud report against what might have been flesh. Satin
> tore, silk hissed, French heels beat a tattoo against the
> parquetry. Had the scurvy changed him from voyeur to
> écouteur, or was it deeper and part of a general change
> of heart?
>
> —Pynchon, *V.*, p. 274.

ECSTATIC : *noun*   literally, "put out of place"; someone
subject to fits of frenzy, rapture, mystical transports. EC-
STATICI, *noun plural*. Compare CACODAEMONIC, DYB-
BUK, ENERGUMENICAL

Yet there are many boys and men, religiosi of a sort in
Los Angeles, Oakland, Chicago, Cleveland, who know
of it. They know of this *ecstatic* in Columbus, Tom
Reiser—the stud who rides a motorcycle with an auto-

76

mobile engine on it.
—Wolfe, *The Pumphouse Gang*, p. 115.

Depressing to him were the various ecstatici and trancists howling for universal repentance from soap-boxes. . . .
—Theroux, *Three Wogs*, p. 157.

ECTOPHONY : *noun*   an external sound

Pfffrrrp. And then Brrrrrr. But that, he realised, after surprise at his stomach's achievement of such metallic ectophony, that, he heard with annoyance, was the doorbell.
—Burgess, *Enderby*, p. 42.

ECTOPLASMIC : *adj*   referring to a spiritual emanation, the visible manifestation of soul. See PARVIS

ECTROPY : *noun*   the development of matter and energy, form and diversity; the antonym of "entropy"

Then I Got To Thinking about negativism, how it would be positive in the antiworld, where entropy would be ectropy. . . .
—Barth, *Letters*, p. 108.

EDACIOUS : *adj*   hungry, voracious, devouring

. . . his edacious continental yens were delightfully and indulgently satisfied by graceful continental Yins. . . .
—Aczel, *Illuminations*, p. 79.

EDENTULOUS : *adj*   having lost the teeth one once possessed

It would not do if he dug up old poems, or wrote new ones, celebrating the glory of fair hair or pegs like margarite† if she should chance to be black, grey, edentulous.
—Burgess, *Enderby*, p. 37.

EFFED : *noun* the apocope of "effable"; utterable, speakable, explainable. Compare DEINOSIS, INFANDUM

... an emblem for the undiscerned, the un-effed, the latent. ...
... for instance, the etymology of a thing's name, evoking within its name's sound the successive ways in which humans try to *utter* it. ...
—West, *Out of My Depths,* pp. 115-116.

EFFLORIATE : *adj* blooming, flowering. Compare FIORI-TURA, FLORIFEROUS

One of the things he liked best about his business was the grand tradition of ornate formulations, the effloriate rhetoric of a Goethe, Santayana, Collingwood, or Russell. ...
—Gardner, *Mickelsson's Ghosts,* p. 18.

EFFULGENCE : *noun* a splendid radiance. EFFULGENT, *adj*. Compare FULGENT

—I see it [atheism] as a divinely bestowed state of utter emptiness, a sort of dark night of the soul, into which the ultimate effulgence will rush unaware and the un-faith become faith.
—Burgess, *Napoleon Symphony,* p. 116.

... the armour, the intricate chain mail like net or metal scrim, being's effulgent Maginot line. ...
—Elkin, *George Mills,* p. 1.

ELLIPSIS : *noun* an omission, a leaving out

Either we didn't mean to lose her—either it was an ellipsis in our care, in what some of us will swear is our love, or someone has Taken her, deliberately, for reasons being kept secret. ...
—Pynchon, *Gravity's Rainbow,* p. 218.

EMBER : *adj* referring to the three-day vigil of fasting each quarter; a period of time. See quotation

End of May, Ember day; full moon come 'round again. My calendar dubs it the Invasion Moon, no doubt because a quarter-century ago it lit the beaches of Normandy. . . . But *ember* as in Ember days means recurrent, not burnt to coals: what's waned will wax, waxed wane. . . .

—Barth, *Letters*, p. 251.

EMPASM : *verb* to sprinkle perfume or powder on someone

The handmaids pounced upon them like pards† and, having empasmed them with not unlesbian zest. . . .

—Nabokov, *Ada*, p. 354.

EMPRISE : *noun* 1) an undertaking; 2) a glorious effort; 3) a preoccupation of the mind

. . . he was somehow, actually, well, *inside his own cock*. If you can imagine such a thing. Yes, inside the metropolitan organ entirely, all other colonial tissue forgotten. . . .Everything is about to come, come incredibly, and he's helpless, here in this exploding *emprise*. . . .

—Pynchon, *Gravity's Rainbow*, p. 470.

EMPYREAN : *noun* or *adj* the highest heaven, the home of light; heavenly. See also REVERBERATE, WELKIN

Hail to the sea gull, in the empyrean!
Who man's head useth as a spare latrine.

—Lowry, *October Ferry to Gabriola*, p. 307.

The Seagull—pure scavenger of the empyrean, hunter of edible stars. . . .

—Lowry, *Under the Volcano*, p. 151.

He walked on, steely eyes surveying some empyrean of higher thought; or else the problem of paying a bill or

ridding himself of a mistress no longer wanted.
—Burgess, *The End of the World News*, p. 231.

But he loved her with a pure, empyrean love, all passion
and vileness purged, and all that she did was beautiful.
—Masters, *Coromandel*, p. 248.

EMUNCTION : *noun* the act or process of picking or blow-
ing the nose. Compare MUNGENCY

. . .parading in public certain habits such as the finger in
the nose, the scratching of the balls, digital emunction
and the peripatetic piss. . . .
—Beckett, *Molloy*, p. 28.

ENANTIOMORPHIC : *adj* having the opposite form, a mirror image. Compare ALLELOMORPH, CATOPTRIC

. . . the Greek *e*, after some refinement, turned out to be
the reverse, graphically of the Phoenician *e*. . . .these *e*'s
are enantiomorphic, unable to be superimposed because
one mirrors the other.
—DeLillo, *Ratner's Star*, p. 153.

ENATE, ENATIC : *adj* See quotation. Compare ANACLITIC

And little *n* is as well the abbreviation of the Latin
natus, meaning 'born,' which returns us full-belly to the
word 'enate,' growing outward, and to its fetal twin,
'enatic,' related on the mother's side.
—DeLillo, *Ratner's Star*, p. 153.

ENCHARNELLED : *adj* having had the body disposed of,
usually in a charnel house rather than in a cemetery or
mausoleum. Compare INHUME

I shall be encharnelled (good, romantic word) before
anybody thinks to look under the carpet.
—Davies, *The Rebel Angels*, p. 296.

ENDOSMIC : *adj* osmosing inwardly as opposed to "exosmic." See PATIBULARY

ENERGUMENICAL : *adj* possessed by an evil spirit, demoniacal, zealous, fanatic. Compare CACODAEMONIC, DYBBUK, ECSTATIC

... the steady energumenical force of the engines, filling his heart to a shape rising from his chest. ...
—Gaddis, *The Recognitions*, p. 855.

ENRACINATE : *verb* to be rooted in. ENRACINATED, *adj.* Compare antonyms DERACINATED, DERADICATED

It wasn't sufficiently enracinated, sufficiently powerful, the strain. ...
—Durrell, *Monsieur*, p. 186.

ENTELECHY : *noun* the complete and/or perfect realization of a concept

... above Watt, or about Watt, a shade uncast, a light unshed, or the grey air aswirl with vain entelechies?
—Beckett, *Watt*, p. 220.

I had to take into account all things bright and beautiful *and* all things their exact opposite. The fancy word for this was "entelechy," which meant not only something's is-ness, but how its is-ness had evolved and was evolving. ...
—West, *Out of My Depths*, p. 89.

EOAN : *adj* having to do with dawn, sunrise, or the east

... a young actor with handsome Irish features ... pressed upon me what he called a Honolulu Cooler, but at the eoan stage of an attack I am beyond alcohol, so could only taste the pineapple part of the mixture.
—Nabokov, *Look at the Harlequins!*, p. 145.

EPHEBE : *noun* Greek for an adolescent, a young man. EPHEBIC, *adj*

81

I felt lacquered from head to foot, like that naked
ephebe, the bright *clout*† of a pagan procession, who
died of dermal asphyxia in his coat of golden varnish.
> —Nabokov, *Look at the Harlequins!*, p. 206.

EPHECTIC : *adj* skeptical, unconvinced, dubious

Can one be ephectic otherwise than unawares?
> —Beckett, *The Unnamable*, p. 402.

EPICLIMACTICALLY : *adv* after the climax

. . . (these conversations were all post coitally, anyhow
epiclimactically, couched). . . .
> —Barth, *Chimera*, p. 77.

EPIDICTIC, EPIDEICTIC : *adj* showing off, ostentatiously
displaying. Compare VENDITATE

. . . Bals the god of beauty and intelligence, a callisthenic
pentathlete stereodidymous† and epidictic of genitalia. . . .
> —Davenport, "The Dawn in Erewhon,"
> *Tatlin!*, p. 219.

EPINASTIC : *adj* bent out and down. Compare EVAGINATE

. . . and they stood there motionless as plants, Valentine
in epinastic curve as the expression on his face unfolded
to immediacy. . . .
> —Gaddis, *The Recognitions*, pp. 544-545.

EPIPHYTE : *noun* a plant which grows upon another plant

. . . The Measles all wore green-suede cavalier boots and
long red underwear, which made them appear like some
undiscovered insect of some unreported sex, some an-
drogynous epiphyte, symbiotic to orchids or flame
trees—flamboyant and freak.
> —Eastlake, *Dancers in the Scalp House*, p. 156.

EPITHELIAL : *adj* literally, "on the nipple"; referring to the tissue forming the outer layer of a mucous membrane: lips, nipples, etc.

No more grubby epithelial embraces in dogbane thickets, followed by accusing phone calls.
—Percy, *The Last Gentleman*, p. 159.

EPITOMISTIC : *adj* tersely cogent, condensed

Half my thinking is epitomistic blazes amid a linear mosaic of the not-me. . . .
—West, *Gala*, p. 26.

EPIZOOTIC : *noun* 1) animal disease; 2) misery, ailment. "A generation or two ago people had uncles who said humorously at the dinner table, when asked whether they would like another helping, 'No, thank you. My epizootic is sagatiating.' Or they would just say it out of a clear sky as an expression of glut, perhaps patting their stomachs.
I was surprised to find there is a legitimate word 'epizootic.' Of course the uncles only gave it four syllables, not separating the two 'o's as one does in the legitimate usage about animals and diseases" (DeVries)

. . . the conversation he disbursed with his own big words, such as remarking after dinner that his epizootic was sagatiating†. . . .
—DeVries, *Consenting Adults*, p. 4.

EPONYMY : *noun* See quotation

"Eponymy?"
"That properly refers to the derivation of place-names from personal ones. . . ."
—Burgess, *Earthly Powers*, p. 469.

ERISTIC : *adj* enjoying argument for its own sake

. . . an eristic jawing of bottomless fart-gas, messianic

rant, bilk and boozy guffaws. . . .
—Theroux, *Three Wogs*, p. 85.

ERUCT, ERUCTATE : *verb* to burp, to belch. ERUCTA-TION, *noun*. See also CUTWATER

Enderby put down his glass, gave the dart-man a glassy but straight look, then eructed strongly and without malice.
—Burgess, *Enderby*, p. 70.

Stalin eructates, Bolgin thought. Lesser phenomena, like volcanoes, merely erupt.
—W. Buckley, *Stained Glass*, p. 46.

There are some eructations that sound like cheers—at least, mine did.
—Nabokov, *Lolita*, p. 75.

ERUMPENT : *adj* bursting forth, breaking out. Compare DEHISCENCE, DISSILIENT, GURN, IRRUMPENT

. . . on his head—pressing down his erumpent red hair— the vaguely Westernish broad-brimmed hat that signalled his difference from other philosophers (as if any such signal were needed), aligning him more nearly with the Southern or Western poets who came, every week or so, to read their flashy junk to the Department of Anguish.
—Gardner, *Mickelsson's Ghosts*, p. 19.

ESCULENT : *adj* edible, suitable for oral consumption. Compare INESCULENT, SAPOROUS

The honey-hued hair of the Walewska lady—positively esculent.
—Burgess, *Napoleon Symphony*, p. 219.

ESCUTCHEON : *noun* the crotch of a quadruped animal. Compare COUN, COUNTRY MATTERS, COYNTE, DELTA,

FOTZEPOLITIK, FURBELOW, MERKIN, QUIM, QUIMTESSENCE

I turned to the red-faced lady I was complimenting and touched my stick lightly to her crotch. "Do you have a special name for it, ma'am? What we call the escutcheon?"
>—Barth, *Giles Goat-Boy*, p. 158.

ESEMPLASTIC : *adj* unifying disparate things, synthesizing

. . . the poor woman added her frenzied bellows, making the whole one esemplastic miserere, wailings from heaven and earth commingling in a single howl. . . .
>—Lowry, "Elephant and Colosseum," *Hear us O Lord from heaven thy dwelling place*, p. 144.

ESPLUMOIR : *noun* See quotation

I am in my esplumoir, the cage of the moulting hawk.
>—Nye, *Merlin*, p. 12.

ESTELLATION : *noun* the act or process of becoming a star or constellation

Estellation . . . was as natural a fate for mythic heroes as coronation was for princes, death in battle for combat soldiers, oblivion for ordinary men.
>—Barth, *Chimera*, pp. 171-172.

ETIOLATE : *verb* from French for "to bleach"; to pale, to weaken

. . . a silk dress of screaming scarlet that would have etiolated a white woman to bled veal.
>—Burgess, *Earthly Powers*, p. 438.

EUDEMONISTIC, EUDAEMONISTIC : *adj* in contrast to "hedonistic," pursuing the good life by reason rather than by pleasure

. . . I did it and avoided it, all unsuspecting that one day,

much later, I would have to go back over all these acts and omissions, dimmed and mellowed by age, and drag them into the eudemonistic slop.
—Beckett, *Molloy*, p. 71.

EUHEMERISTIC : *adj* interpreting myth as history; named for Euhemerus, fourth-century B.C. mythographer

. . . a mystery of euhemeristic proportions. . . .
—Gaddis, *The Recognitions*, p. 861.

EUPEPTIC : *adj* 1) cheerful; 2) having a good appetite, digestion

Rained flesh and blood, eh? Strong appetite and something or other health. Hm. A bit too eupeptic for my taste, Thoreau.
—Burgess, *Earthly Powers*, p. 437.

EUPHROSYNE, EUPHRASY : *noun* cheerfulness, joy

Eros, always explicit and always rich in *euphrosyne*, survives best in the sensuality of the French.
—Davenport, "The Dawn in Erewhon,"
Tatlin!, p. 174.

EUPHUISTIC : *adj* speaking or writing in an elevated, affected style. From Euphues, the central character of two works by the sixteenth-century English writer, John Lyly.

"The court's decision in favor of Count Wintergrin," said Himmelfarb, imitating the tired, tiresome archness of Razzia and his euphuistic style, "is a tergiversation† for the German people."
—W. Buckley, *Stained Glass*, p. 68.

EUTRIPSIA : *noun* felicitous fondling. Compare CONTRECTATION, DACTYLIC, HAPTIC

They were erudite and sensual about the orectic,† the

synchronous, the vellicative,† about eutripsia, salacious aromas, amplitudes.
—Davenport, "The Dawn in Erewhon,"
Tatlin!, p. 256.

EVAGINATE : *verb* to unsheath; to turn out. Compare EPINASTIC

"A turning outward. Not that I'd say the word. I'd rather commit the act than say the word. Particularly in front of a lady."
"What word?"
"Evaginate."
—DeLillo, *Ratner's Star*, p. 242.

EXCREMENTIVOROUSLY : *adv* shit-eatingly. Compare COPROPHAGOUS, MERDIVOROUS

Phantom Liz entered from the bath, surveilled him lovingly, then dropped her head to graze. Phantom Sig groaned, fluttered his eyelids, closed them, smiled excrementivorously, and drew a pillow over his face.
—Koster, *The Dissertation*, p. 350.

EXCURSIVE : *adj* desultory, digressive, erratic

Though the storm had passed and it was mild and dry outside in the dark, with the sound only of a few taxis, they felt again the excursive cracks of thunder and lighting which had rolled down from Eagle Bay.
—Helprin, *Refiner's Fire*, p. 145.

EXIGUOUS : *adj* in small measure, meager. Compare FILLIP, MANTISSA, PARVIS

His list of literary achievements was exiguous. . . .
—Burgess, *Earthly Powers*, p. 20.

. . . my second journey to Florida. It was a trip for which I felt exiguous warmth. . . .
—Exley, *A Fan's Notes*, p. 358.

EXOGAMIA : *noun* the custom of taking wives from outside the clan or group

The First Consul as fertility god, a wandering Priapus. But it was true: a great man was expected to scatter bastards abroad. . . .war might be an instrument of . . . *exogamia.*
—Burgess, Napoleon Symphony, p. 84.

EXOLETE : *noun* someone obsolete, out of use. Compare PARACHRONIC, PRETERIST

. . . all the exoletes, dunces, procumbents†, and unpal-teringly† ugly bagmen she called her councillors. . . .
—Theroux, Darconville's Cat, p. 235.

EXORDIUM : *noun* the beginning of something. EXOR-DIA, *noun plural*

. . . she collaborated in the exordia of the act—the baring of her arms and shoulders and breasts. . . .
—Burgess, The End of the World News, p. 136.

EXOTERIC : *adj* suitable for public consumption; antonym for "esoteric"

. . . we may be guilty of trying to render exoteric the intrinsically esoteric, which, while seeming the most human, is the essential proliferating folly of man.
—Lowry, October Ferry to Gabriola, p. 84.

All this is an exoteric scale of reference, an explanation. . . .
—Durrell, Monsieur, p. 134.

EXTRAVASATED : *adj* pumped out, drained, usually in reference to blood, lava, or toothpaste

His eyes closed slowly; and when he thought, he fastened his hand on his extravasated heart, glad if only of recognition and familiarity, proof against Reason, and

EXTRAVASATED

the cries of the mendicant Past.
—Gaddis, *The Recognitions*, p. 564.

F

FACIES : *noun* overall aspect, appearance

... nowadays whole tourist caravans come through to look at him, usually while he's Under The Influence....They all stand peering into his dreamstruck facies. ...
—Pynchon, *Gravity's Rainbow*, p. 346.

FADGE : *noun* a bundle of leather, a bale of goods

... a lord and lady whose love was a fadge of guilt and scorn. ...
—Gardner, *Jason and Medeia*, p. 46.

FAINÉANT : *adj* French for "do nothing"; idling, indolent, lazy, or weak. Compare FRANION

A strong, wooden box, just big enough to hold both legs, the *brodequin* was a rather fainéant Gallic answer to the more spirited Anglo-Saxon *boots*. ...
—Aczel, *Illuminations*, p. 281.

FAITERY : *noun* hypocrisy, fraud, imposture

Faitery throttled faith.... as that magic-muttering, instinct-bound piece of pawkery† called Christianity

vanished I knew I had learned Fadi's lesson with a vengeance.
—Theroux, *Darconville's Cat*, p. 467.

FANTOD : *noun* a state of acute anxiety, fidgets

... it was always easy, in open and lonely places, to be visited by Panic wilderness fear, but these are the urban fantods here, that come to get you when you are lost, or isolate inside the way time is passing. ...
—Pynchon, *Gravity's Rainbow*, p. 303.

FARADIC : *adj* operating on inductive electricity; a term derived from its discoverer, Michael Faraday, English scientist

Anxious about his impotence in this land of sexual gargantuans, he could have sent to a degenerate mail-order house for a faradic device which attached to the genitals helps stimulate with electrical charges a more rapturous sexual act, only to have the device miscue and electrocute him, frying off his balls in the process.
—Exley, *A Fan's Notes*, p. 297.

FARINACEOUS : *adj* having the odor of ground wheat flour

A cloying, oddly farinaceous smell came from her body.
—Boyd, *An Ice Cream War*, p. 26.

FARL : *noun* a wedge—often a quarter—of an oatmeal cake; a chunk of bread

He tore a farl from his *baguette* ... munched it. ...
—Davenport, "The Dawn in Erewhon,"
Tatlin!, p. 233.

FAROUCHE : *adj* sullen, shy, antisocial

... there was nothing *farouche* in her telling of the story, and ... she seemed as mystified as a child while she related it.
—Bunting, *The Advent of Frederick Giles*, p. 104.

FASHED : *adj* bothered, inconvenienced

The bonnet and frogged cape behind him was his wife, fashed and tottering, flapping like a sea mew.
—Davenport, "John Charles Tapner,"
Da Vinci's Bicycle, p. 46.

FATA MORGANA, FATAMORGANA : *noun* a mirage, an illusion; term derived from King Arthur's sister, Morgan Le Fay

. . . chased down whatever fatamorganas could be found. . . .
—Theroux, *Darconville's Cat*, p. 179.

. . . a mirage named after Morgan Le Fay, a fairy who lived at the bottom of a lake. It was famous for appearing in the Strait of Messina, between Calabria and Sicily. Fata Morgana was poetic crap, in short.
—Vonnegut, *Cat's Cradle*, p. 75.

FATIDIC : *adj* prophetically portentous, fateful. Compare MANTIC, VATIC

. . . the event had been stupidly unforeseen, yet had been bound to happen and was the representation of a fatidic problem which had to be solved lest I perish. . . .
—Nabokov, *Look at the Harlequins!*, p. 16.

FAVONIAN : *adj* referring to the west wind; hence favorable, auspicious, pleasant, mild

Sunday. Heat ripple still with us; a most favonian week.
—Nabokov, *Lolita*, p. 44.

FEATOUS : *adj* handsome, good-looking

I wasn't a featous boy.
—Theroux, *Darconville's Cat*, p. 458.

FEBRIFUGE : *noun* a fever reliever. Compare ANODYNIC

And there appeared to be no febrifuge against this

double sickness. . . .
　　　　—Lowry, *October Ferry to Gabriola*, p. 116.

FEBRILE : *adj* feverish, fevered. Compare PYRETIC

. . . ships, I imagined, full of lovers and revelers, men and women in staterooms thick with perfume and the febrile heat of sex. . . .
　　　　—Bunting, *The Advent of Frederick Giles*, p. 4.

. . . his vocal cords, quite independently of anything he was willing, were attempting the impossible feat of staying attuned to his acutely febrile cerebrum.
　　　　—Exley, *Pages from a Cold Island*, p. 231.

FER : *verb* a nonsense word, apparently echoic on the character's name. See and compare FIG, FIRK. Compare DIGHT, SCROG

Pistol:　Master Fer: I'll fer him, and firk him, and ferret him. . . .
　　　　—Shakespeare, *Henry IV, Part 2*, IV, iv, 28-29.

FERBLET : *noun* an effeminate male. Compare DRUGGEL, GORP, MEACOCK, NESH

. . . every last ferblet . . . had the distinct impression he was a born gentleman. . . .
　　　　—Theroux, *Darconville's Cat*, p. 303.

FERIAL : *adj* referring to a nonfeast day

. . . those graceful and tiny observances that somehow connote aspiration and make every ferial act festal.
　　　　—Theroux, *Darconville's Cat*, p. 96.

FERROUS, FERRUGINOUS : *adj* containing iron

"A hairpin," suggested Charlie. "If this one won't nothing will," said Leo Stone. A heavy ferrous noise

ensued, a rape of the lock.
—Burgess, *The Doctor is Sick*, p. 160.

Beginning with some harsh and ferruginous clanging of pans in the kitchen, to which the Counselor snapped, "quiet, hon, you'll wake the baby," the scene ballooned to encompass a flashing butcher knife, a broken kitchen window, the wail of a police siren.
—Exley, *A Fan's Notes*, pp. 363-364.

He dug deeper down the well-shaft and came back with a dribble of foul ferruginous liquid.
—Chatwin, *Viceroy of Ouidah*, p. 55.

FIANCHETTO : *verb* from Italian, for "little flank movement"; in chess, to move the Knight's pawn to clear the way for the bishop

. . . to compile an annotated record of my best games . . . six thousand M-2 carbines fianchettoed from their New Orleans warehouse to a hardware deposit in Tinieblas. . . .
—Koster, *The Prince*, p. 14.

FIDIMPLICITARY : *adj* having implicit faith in the ideas, feelings, etc., of another. Compare SEDULOUSLY, SEQUACIOUS

It had grown later and later when Dr. Dodypol,† fidimplicitary no more, burst into a crazy fit of laughter. . . .
—Theroux, *Darconville's Cat*, p. 286.

FIG : *verb* 1) a euphemism for "fuck"; 2) a reference to a tale from Rabelais involving the oral extraction of a fig from the vulva of a mule; 3) in the second quotation below, "I have Sir John rely on supplies of figs as a supposed aid to his performance as a sexual athlete. Consequently when on page 335 he refers to having 'figged her' he is inventing a verb based on his little aphrodisiac" (Nye). Compare DIGHT, FER, FIRK

Pistol: When Pistol lies, do this, and fig me like
the bragging Spaniard.
—Shakespeare, *Henry IV, Part 2*, V, iii, 117.

Fixed her and foxed her and fetched her and fexed her.
Figged her and firked† her and ferred† her and fired
her. Forked her, all frosty, and brought her to fruition.
—Nye, *Falstaff*, p. 335.

FILLIP : *noun* 1) the act of thwacking something by releasing
a tensioned forefinger from the thumb; 2) a trivial addition;
3) an arousing agent, a stimulus. Compare EXIGUOUS,
MANTISSA, PARVIS

"Hush," he heard, and a low laugh. And his father's
hammer, the loud crack of steel on steel undiminished,
if anything quickened, lending a kind of fillip of assent
like a rimshot under a joke.
—Elkin, *George Mills*, p. 109.

FINNEGANSWAKE : *verb* to write or speak in the style
employed by James Joyce in *Finnegans Wake*; especially to
combine words and use elaborate puns

... the intermittent drone was finneganswaked by lightly
sleeping Enderby into a parachronic† lullaby chronicle,
containing Constantine the grandgross and battlebottles
fought by lakes which were full of lager.
—Burgess, *Enderby*, pp. 143-144.

FIORITURA : *noun* a flowering, a blooming. Compare EF-
FLORIATE, FLORIFEROUS

The majesty of the eagles in their gold, the arms raised
in salute, the cries of obeisance, praise, and glory, the
rise of the horns falling in fioritura. . . .
—Davenport, "C. Musonius Rufus,"
Da Vinci's Bicycle, p. 10.

FIRK : *verb* from German "ficken," to fuck; in English,
euphemism for "fuck" with the sense of "to pound or beat";

used in the passage below because it is "alliterative, equivalent in length and consonants, and particularly nice for the suggestion of friction, since 'r' and 'i' sometimes reverse (as in 'brid' to 'bird'—the first is usual in Chaucer)" (Koster). See also FIG. Compare DIGHT, FER, SCROG

Phil clomps by the door, calling for Marta. Godspeed. Find her, firk her, fork her, and fangle her so she'll give me some peace.
>   —Koster, *The Prince*, p. 288.

FLAVESCENT, FLAVID : *adj* yellow, yellowing. Compare FULVOUS

. . . sprayed on her flavescent skin a heady perfume. . . .
>   —Theroux, *Three Wogs*, p. 148.

. . . spitting into his heavy-lidded eye
ripping his flavid toga. . . .
>   —Nabokov, *Lolita*, p. 302.

FLAVICOMOUS : *adj* yellow-headed. Compare AURICOME

. . . the back of his flavicomous male secretary.
>   —Burgess, *The Wanting Seed*, p. 104.

FLIMMERING : *adj* a portmanteau of "flicker" and "glimmer"

. . . only flimmering dreams of plans, intentions dark
as the lachrymal† flutter of corpse-candles.
>   —Gardner, *Jason and Medeia*, p. 183.

FLOCCILLATE : *verb* to twitch aimlessly. Compare VELLICATION

. . . floccillating his hard hat (Mr. Graves always took off his hard hat, even in the open air, when in speech with his betters). . . .
>   —Beckett, *Watt*, p. 144.

FLORIFEROUS : *adj* bearing or producing flowers. Compare EFFLORIATE, FIORITURA

. . . the same touched-up prints of extravagantly floriferous brides. . . .
>—Lowry, *Under the Volcano*, p. 54.

FLUE : *adj* fluffed, flocked, covered with down. Compare LANUGO, PLUMULACEOUS

. . . her gold-flued arms apparently insensitive to the untimely winter. . . .
>—Burgess, *Napoleon Symphony*, p. 347.

FLUXION : *noun* a flowing, a continual state of change. Compare CADUCITY, DECIDUOUS, FUGACIOUS, LABILE

I was, I must explain, an attractive and witty young man. This furfuraceous†, and fucoid† mop that now shatters my brow and spatters obscenely at the world from my chin was an august brown; my eye was auroraborealic; my every speech was delicately perfumed. I had not yet succumbed to the fluxion of the world.
>—Gardner, *The Wreckage of Agathon*, p. 40.

FOCATIVE : *adj* referring to the activities of a concubine

The lovely focative sucking over, just this side of emission, she'd let my engine out of her spiced trap. . . .
>—Nye, *Falstaff*, p. 201.

Evans: Remember, William; focative is caret.
Quickly: And that's a good root.
>—Shakespeare, *The Merry Wives of Windsor*,
>IV, iv, 45-47.

FOIN : *verb* from French, to thrust with a trident or other pointed instrument, and used in the quotation below as a double entendre involving the thrust of a penis and a devil's pitchfork. Compare GANCH

In good faith, he cares not what mischief he does, if his weapon be out! He will foin like any devil! He will

spare neither man, woman, nor child!
> —Shakespeare, *Henry IV, Part 2*, II, i, 16-19,
> and Nye, *Falstaff*, p. 205.

FOISONED, FOYSENED : *adj* nourished, fattened

Bateless in our hunger ... we ... went after the foysened cluckers when their heads were under wing. . . .
> —Rooke, *Shakespeare's Dog*, p. 135.

FOLIUM : *noun* a piece of paper folded in half; also the largest size of book. See LEMNISCATE

FOMA : *noun* See quotation

Nothing in this book is true. Live by the *foma** that makes you brave and kind and healthy and happy.
> —*The Books of Bokonon* II:5

**Harmless untruths*
> —Vonnegut, *Cat's Cradle*, epigraph

FORELAY : *verb* to ambush, to waylay

. . . for these various reasons I found it easy to forelay and squelch the commercial allurements and knew that all I really wanted was to produce another book. . . .
> —Exley, *Pages from a Cold Island*, p. 12.

FORMICATING : *adj* crawling like an ant; having an sensation of ants crawling on the skin; or, acting as ants in mindless, continous activity

. . . And if this man Opiskin can get you formicating little peasants into such a lather there must quite *definitely* be a lot of good in him. . . .
> —Burgess, *Honey for the Bears*, p. 11.

FORNICATORY : *adj* referring to fornication

. . . a long night given over to listening for sounds of

padding fornicatory feet. . . .
—Burgess, *Earthly Powers*, p. 145.

FOTZEPOLITIK : *noun* from Bavarian and Austrian slang for "cunt"; therefore, "cuntocracy" or "pussy politics." Compare COUN, COUNTRY MATTERS, COYNTE, DELTA, ESCUTCHEON, FURBELOW, MERKIN, QUIM, QUIMTESSENCE

Christine Keeler and Mandy Rice-Davies. . . .Much more than just whores. They put the English-speaking world back into the grand tradition of *Fotzepolitik*.
—Koster, *The Dissertation*, p. 282.

FRAMPOLD : *adj* boisterous, rambunctious; peeved, agitated

        . . . all but frampold devils are shackled
in chains.
—Gardner, *Jason and Medeia*, p. 289.

FRANGIBLE : *adj* capable of being broken, breakable. Compare INDEFEASIBLE, INFRANGIBLE, IRREFRAGABLE

. . . fibers that clot and draw a wound together like fingers, fibers inextricably bound up in the calculated weave of the fabric. Dried blood. Frangible, no more than dust—and yet the stain will persist through half a dozen washings.
—Boyle, *Water Music*, p. 244.

FRANION : *noun* inveterate idler, a dilettante. Compare FAINEANT

Who was this franion? There was a *grivoiserie†* about him that smacked of Berlin. . . .
—Davenport, "A Field of Snow on a Slope of the Rosenberg," *Da Vinci's Bicycle*, p. 168.

FRASS : *noun* the dung of insect larvae

. . . Miss Dessiquint, with eyes like frozen frass. . . .
— Theroux, *Darconville's Cat*, p. 69.

FRATCH : *noun* a squabble, a quisquous quarrel, contretemps. Compare BATRACHOMYOMACHIA, QUISQUOUS, TIRRIT

—What fratch! Sint Anton said, tickling his pig on the tummy.
— Davenport, "The Dawn in Erewhon,"
Tatlin!, p. 219.

FREIT : *noun* anything to which superstition attaches

People shied away from him as if he were a leper, dogs snarled at him, his coevals kept him at a distance with sticks and stones. He was a toad, a worm, a freit—not fit for human company.
— Boyle, *Water Music*, p. 215.

FREMITUS : *noun* dull roar, murmur, continuous noise. FREMESCENT, *adj*. See also PATIBULARY

All at first was the fremitus of things, the jigget† of gnats, drum of the blood, fidget of leaves. . . .
— Davenport, "C. Musonius Rufus,"
Da Vinci's Bicycle, p. 10.

FRESHEN : *verb* to renew or revive sexually

It's your sex-life I had in mind, sir. I believe you should freshen Mrs. Sear.
— Barth, *Giles Goat-Boy*, p. 477.

FRIANTS, FIANTS, FEANCE: *noun* fox or badger's dung. See CROTELS

FRICATIVE : *adj* rubbing. Compare EUTRIPSIA, FROTTAGE, TRIBADISM

His fricative finger has stopped all the same. "She is

wet," he says, grinning to conceal distaste.
—Nye, *Merlin*, p. 19.

FRISSON : *noun* a little thrill

There were risks involved, sure, but that was what made the project so enticing—the frisson, the audacity, the monumental pissing in the face of society.
—Boyle, *Budding Prospects*, p. 9.

FRITINANCY : *noun* the buzzing, chittering sound made by insects such as cicadas. Compare STRIDULATE

Unsupported libels and slanders whizzed all day long through the offices of the great, a sort of gnat-fritinancy, disregarded.
—Burgess, *The Wanting Seed*, p. 104.

FROTTAGE, FROTTING : *noun* rubbing, caressing, stroking especially with a sexual connotation. Compare FRICATIVE, TRIBADISM

... the frottage of a conjuror's thumb dissolving a coin. ...
—Nabokov, *Ada*, p. 420.

... while Alex and Anna occupied the bed, he had not yet heard anything which sounded like cheerful frotting, the old springs zithering away.
—Burgess, *Honey for the Bears*, p. 147.

FRUGIVOROUS : *adj* fruit-eating

Comparative anatomy teaches us that man resembles frugivorous animals in everything, and carnivorous in nothing; he has neither claws wherewith to seize his prey, nor distinct and pointed teeth to tear the living fibre.
—Burgess, *The Wanting Seed*, p. 166.

FUBSY : *adj* short and fat. Compare PUDSY, PYKNIC

. . . she was nothing but a fubsy pig-pink whorelet. . . .
—Nabokov, *Ada*, p. 33.

As for Callinan, who was a bachelor, he knew little of the blandishments preliminary to the radical act, never having hunted anything other than fubsy totties†, or slatterns harvested on piles of hay or tavern tables still greasy with everything.
—Queneau, *We Always Treat Women Too Well*,
p. 86.

FUCOID : *adj* having to do with seaweed. See FLUXION

FUGACIOUS : *adj* short-term, ephemeral, evanescent. Compare CADUCITY, DECIDUOUS, FLUXION, LABILE

Why should he be interested in an early specimen of something so fugacious that it barely lived a day, an hour?
—Aczel, *Illuminations*, p. 37.

FUGLE : *verb* to cheat, to trick actively, especially in "the sense of extra-marital action" (Koster). FUGLING, *noun.* See also BUGLE. Compare COG

. . . all the world knew of Irene's flagrant fuglings. . . .
—Koster, *Mandragon*, p. 324.

FULCRATE : *adj* having a fulcrum, acting as a fulcrum. See ALIQUOT

FULGENT : *adj* glittering, dazzling. Compare EFFULGENT

I tell him with fulgent rhetoric things of no interest, the nature of his doom. . . .
—Gardner, *The Wreckage of Agathon*, p. 21.

FULGURATE : *verb* to flash vividly like lightning. FULGUR-ANT, *adj*

Gallagher's eyes abandoned their examination of the face and activity of his compatriot and transferred themselves to the feminine object lying beneath him, and very precisely to its long, white thighs, on which fulgurated the outline of a garter.
—Queneau, *We Always Treat Women Too Well,*
p. 118.

. . . he could make out for an instant the exact color values of the fulgurant ingots. . . .
—Elkin, *George Mills,* p. 108.

FULIGINOUS : *adj* sooty, smoky

"I shall linger behind a turning or two, for to evade besmirchment by your fuliginous torch." For a draught came from below, and the enclosed staircase performed as a chimney for the smoke from King Arthur's light.
—Berger, *Arthur Rex,* p. 50.

The two one-eyed men yelled and gesticulated, and exchanged fuliginous stares.
—Durrell, *Monsieur,* p. 153.

FULVOUS : *adj* yellowish, tawny, yellow tinged with red and/*or* brown. Compare FLAVESCENT

. . . his robed arms like angular fulvous wings. . . .
—Theroux, *Darconville's Cat,* p. 549.

FUMETS : *noun* excrement of a deer or other animal hunted for sport. See CROTELS

FUNEST : *adj* fatally flawed; portending doom

. . . Flora. . . .an irory-pale, dark-haired funest beauty. . . .
—Nabokov, *Ada,* p. 340.

FURBELOW : *noun* 1) a flounce, pleat or border on a gown or dress, often referring to unnecessary, frivolous decoration; 2) the pudendum. "The line referred to I think was a catch (or glee) of Purcell's: 'Adam caught Eve by the fur below/And that is the oldest catch we know' " (Gaddis). Compare COUN, COUNTRY MATTERS, COYNTE, DELTA, ESCUTCHEON, MERKIN, QUIM, QUIMTESSENCE

If she is only a woman (but a good cigar is a smoke) with Eve caught by the furbelow, Hae cunni (the oldest catch we know). . . .
—Gaddis, *The Recognitions,* p. 392.

FURCATING : *adj* forking

He now noticed, however, that furtive, furcating cracks kept appearing in his physical well-being. . . .
—Nabokov, *Ada,* p. 569.

FURFURACEOUS : *adj* covered with small scales, like bran or dandruff. See FLUXION

FURIBUND : *adj* incensed, enraged

Beside himself, furibund, the ridiculous frenzied mouse. . . .
—Cozzens, *By Love Possessed,* p. 424.

Furibund, the speaker thought he sniffed a whiff of complacent jackass.
—Theroux, *Three Wogs,* p. 82.

FURUNCULAR : *adj* afflicted with boils, carbuncles. Compare BLEB, BUBUCKLE

He remembered the inspector's pipe studded with Bohemian gems (in harmony with its owner's furuncular nose). . . .
—Nabokov, *Transparent Things,* p. 88.

FUSIFORM : *adj* shaped like a spindle, tapering to a point at both ends

. . . to wind bandages . . . with the crazy little hand-

windlass that she provided was no easy matter. The roll
would become fusiform.

—Beckett, "Yellow,"
More Pricks than Kicks, p. 168.

FUSTILUG : *noun* a fat sloppy woman. See COG. Compare
DRUGGEL, FUBSY.

FUTTER : *verb* from French "foutre," to fuck. "Burton uses
it throughout his Arabian Nights" (Koster)

Then she would have me futter Mrs. Ford, while the
two of them wriggled about poking their fingers up
each other's arses.

—Nye, *Falstaff,* p. 7.

. . . he took the steel coffer out of its casket, unlocked
the seven locks with seven keys, fetched out and futtered
the girl he'd stolen on her wedding night. . . .

—Barth, *Chimera,* p. 43.

FYLFOT : *noun* a swastika, grammadion, a cross with right
angle turns

The trouble with that damned swastika was that it was
a very satisfying symbol and very ancient. . . . Medieval
scribes filled in spaces with it and called it a fylfot.

—Burgess, *Earthly Powers,* p. 343

G

GALINGALE : *noun* an East Indian aromatic root with medicinal and culinary applications. See PATIBULARY

GALLIARD : *adj* 1) lively, vivacious; 2) stouthearted; 3) gallivanting

Thank you, my galliard friend, let's go and drink.
　　　—Burgess, *The End of the World News,* p. 59.

. . . the galliard Captain Wynne.
　　　　　　　—Davenport, "A Field of Snow
on a Slope of the Rosenberg," *Da Vinci's Bicycle,* p. 170.

GALLIMAUFREY : *noun* a hash, a confused jumble. Compare SYNCHYSIS

. . . our [English] love of conforming is so all-pervasive, so ideal a culture for a fascist takeover, that we've had to evolve the whole constitutional gallimaufrey (one of his odd words) and God knows how many other public safeguards against our real natures.
　　　—Fowles, "The Cloud," *The Ebony Tower,* p. 272.

I had . . . MacBeth and his minions running up and down the steps of the cellar with gallons and gallipots

and general gallimaufries of sack, and burnt brandy. . . .
—Nye, *Falstaff*, p. 225.

GALLINACEOUS : *adj* 1) having the characteristics of a domesticated bird; 2) "treading like a cock" (Davenport)

Bruno, gallinaceous, mounted. Kaatje gripped him in with her heels.
—Davenport, "The Dawn in Erewhon,"
Tatlin!, p. 199.

GAMAHUCHE : *noun* cunnilingus or fellatio, but usually the former

. . . I was Doll Tearsheet's alchemist that night, and by gamahuche turned her base metal into gold.
—Nye, *Falstaff*, p. 384.

GAMBOGE : *noun* a bright yellow pigment. See also ANORECTIC

. . . a sumptuous sky of mauve and gamboge and smashed eggs. . . .
—Burgess, *Earthly Powers*, p. 206.

GANCH : *verb* to impale, usually as a torture; often has a sexual connotation. Compare FOIN

"You can sit for a minute in my lap."
"No—unless we undress and you ganch me."
—Nabokov, *Ada*, p. 464.

GASTER : *noun* the abdomen of ants, bees, wasps, and other Hymenoptera

We littles, whose pizzles are no bigger than the gaster of a wasp. . . .
—Davenport, "The Wooden Dove of Archytas,"
Da Vinci's Bicycle, p. 38.

GELID : *adj* frozen, cold

> We sat in gelid amiability. Our cheeks ached from smiling.
>> —Percy, *The Moviegoer*, p. 121.

GEN : *noun* British slang for "General Information"; U.S. equivalents—"poop," "the word." See PUKKA

GENETICODRAMATIC : *adj* having to do with the theatrical aspects of reproduction and genetics. Compare SEMIDEMIGOD

> ... the coupling of a demi-goddess and myself [a demi-god], for example, [is] a good deal richer in genetico-dramatic potential than the coupling of you [a mortal] and me, don't you think?
>> —Barth, *Chimera*, p. 183.

GIBBOUS : *adj* humpbacked, arched

> ... lying in the smelly dark, her long Astra Nielsen upper lip gibbous that night as the moon that ruled her....
>> —Pynchon, *Gravity's Rainbow*, p. 415.

GIMMAL, GEMEL : *adj* literally, "twin"; referring to a twin or triple ring for the finger

> ... a gimmal ring, consisting of three gold links, turning upon a sly pivot, which when pressed clicked shut in a solid circle, representing eternity.
>> —Nye, "A Portugese Person," *Tales I Told My Mother*,
>>> p. 19.

GITANILLA : *noun* variant of "gypsy"

> "Incidentally, I want all my clothes," said the gitanilla....
>> —Nabokov, *Lolita*, p. 246.

GLABROUS : *adj* bald

> At twelve I knew the difference between glaucous† and glabrous, though again, their respective meanings, once cathartic, totally escape me now.
>
> —DeVries, *Consenting Adults*, p. 7.

> Adriaan rose, pulling out his limbering glabrous cock, his eyes happy.
>
> —Davenport, "The Dawn in Erewhon,"
> *Tatlin!*, p. 190.

> The light given off by the radar's scanner arm playing over his glabrous features. . .gave him the look of a galactic navigator.
>
> —C. Buckley, *Steaming to Bamboola*, p. 123.

GLAMOUR : *noun* 1) instruction, spell; 2) see Davies quotation

> The word glamour has been so battered and smeared that almost everybody has forgotten that it means magic and enchantment.
>
> —Davies, *The Rebel Angels*, p. 279

> The ultimate illusion . . . that cannot be *inflicted* upon the good by the devil. . . .the direct removal of their male organs by some glamour.
>
> —Nye, *Merlin*, p. 36

GLANDES, GLANS : *noun* literally, "acorn"; the head of the human penis

> And in acorns in their involucra† he saw glandes malic† and red.
>
> —Davenport, 'The Dawn in Erewhon,"
> *Tatlin!*, p. 205.

GLAUCOUS : *adj* bluish-green, greyish-green, grey; a dull or pale color. See also GLABROUS

... gulls, glaucous and raucous, wheeled and sailed overhead. ...
—Lowry, "The Bravest Boat,"
Hear us O Lord in heaven thy dwelling place, p. 24.

GLENDOVEER : *noun*   a type of Hindu fairy, apparently beautiful, used by Robert Southey in *The Curse of Kehama*

My own sweeting, my best, my jewel, my dove, my princess, my glendoveer, my apotheosis, I worship you with all my blood.
—Foxell, *Carnival,* p. 87.

GLIM : *verb*   to glimpse, to glance, to look at

Glim me close up while I'm fresh, and lots of time to settle round the TV screens before I start dancing.
—Koster, *Mandragon,* p. 90.

GLOCKAMOID : *adj*   shaped like an arrow point. Compare HASTATE. See PATIBULARY

GLODE : *noun*   1) a clearing, open area; 2) a bright place in the sky, a flash of light

He clutched my shoulder, pointed at a glode
where blue burst through with a serenity like violence.
—Gardner, *Jason and Medeia,* p. 244.

GLOM : *verb*   1) to grab; 2) to understand; 3) to look at

I wanted him less romantic, less besotted with words' double-turning, less in conspiracy with what his epoch glommed was man and dog's natural configuration.
—Rooke, *Shakespeare's Dog,* p. 35.

GLOSSOEPIGLOTTIC : *adj*   having to do with the root of the tongue

... the sun bowled up over Quinsyburg—which Spell-

vexit, somersaulting, always greeted with a glossoepiglottic gurgle of joy, something like: "Gleep!"
—Theroux, *Darconville's Cat*, p. 48.

GLOZING : *adj* interpreting, commenting on. GLOZE, *verb*.
See also DEIPNOSOPHIST

Those whom the old Puritan sermons denounced as
"the glozing neuters of the world" have no easy road to
haul down. . . .Glozing neuters are just as human as
heroes and villains.
—Pynchon, *Gravity's Rainbow*, p. 677.

GLUTINOUS : *adj* sticky, gluey

Moths whirled around a glutinous patch of lamplight.
—Chatwin, *The Viceroy of Ouidah*, p. 27.

GLYPTIC : *adj* having to do with stone-carving, inscribing
on stone

. . . observe him in his trances . . . his eyes rolled back
into his head reading old, glyptic old graffitti on his
own sockets. . . .
—Pynchon, *Gravity's Rainbow*, p. 14.

GNOMIC : *adj* commonly known, aphoristic, epigrammatic

They were all traditional verses, mostly on cloacal†
subjects, but it was somehow warming to find that verse
was still in regard for its gnomic or mnemonic properties.
—Burgess, *Enderby*, p. 231.

GOETIC : *adj* invoking evil spirits

. . . diabolical rules likely to be broken by the other
party as soon as we come to understand them. That is
why goetic magic does not always work.
—Nabokov, *Pale Fire*, p. 226.

GORBELLY : *adj* big-gutted. Compare GOTCH-GUT

... the now dozen arid, wrung-out, flame-cured, behe-moth gorbelly trees. ...
—Elkin, *George Mills*, p. 17.

GORP : *noun* See quotation. Compare DRUGGEL

... *gorp*, a freakishly obese person who eats constantly because he achieves a kind of erotic splendor when sitting on the throne.
—Exley, *A Fan's Notes*, p. 300.

GOTCH-GUT : *adj* potbellied. Compare GORBELLY

... the stench of gotch-gut wealth, how it feeds
on children's flesh.
—Gardner, *Jason and Medeia*, p. 179.

GOWPEN : *noun* hands held to form a bowl; a handful. See also DOUCET

... cupping a guinea pig in his gowpen (hollowed hands). ...
—Nabokov, *Ada*, p. 402

GOZZARD : *noun* a goose-herder

Martyi, clever gozzard of the folk tale. ...
—Aczel, *Illuminations*, p. 26.

GRABEN : *noun* German for "ditch"; a valley formed by geologic uplift along fault lines. Compare antonym HORST

Your body is a horst† and mine is a graben, because horst is the opposite of graben.
—Burgess, *Enderby,* p. 279.

GRACILESCENT : *adj* growing skinny, slim, lithe

The students, ah yes!—the soft, lazy, unchangeable, gracilescent, sweet-scented nixies-from-Dixie. ...
—Theroux, *Darconville's Cat*, p. 344.

GRANFALLOON : *noun* See quotation. See also DUPRASS.

Hazel's obsession with Hoosiers around the world was a textbook example of a false *karass†,* of a seeming team that was meaningless in terms of the ways God gets things done, a textbook example of what Bokonon calls a *granfalloon.*

—Vonnegut, *Cat's Cradle,* pp. 81-82.

GRAVEOLENT : *adj* strongly fetid, heavily odoriferous

. . . Aphrodite—

sitting graveolent in her royal hebetation,†

surrounded by all

her holouries †. . . .

—Gardner, *Jason and Medeia,* p. 180.

GRIMP : *verb* from the French *grimper,* to climb

They went by sections, grimping their way up, ploying† beneath their pack loads, hindered by slung rifles and soggy bedrolls, pattered by dirt kicked down by those above.

—Koster, *The Dissertation,* p. 143.

GRIMPEN : *noun* on a mountain, a difficult and dangerous section for climbing, with the sense of requiring the use of all hands and feet at once

On the edge of a grimpen, where is no secure foothold,
And menaced by monsters, fancy lights,
Risking enchantment.

—T.S. Eliot, "East Coker,"
Four Quartets, II, 41-43.

. . . his grotesque shoes, which looked like they'd been built especially for participation in some sport, possibly one on snow, or in marshland, or some such sodden surface, that grimpen, perhaps, where is no secure foothold. . . .

—Gaddis, *The Recognitions,* p. 678.

GRIVOISERIE : *noun* French for a kind of licentiousness. See FRANION

GROUTNOLL, GRUTNOLL : *noun* someone whose head is filled with grout, hence a "blockhead." See LOOBY

GUDDLE : *verb* to use a fishing technique involving the use of only the hands, to grope

—You can guddle a spracker† spadger† there than in any bath in town, Diogenes said in his best, and wickedest imitation of the Athenian dialect. . . .
—Davenport, "Mesoroposthonippidon,"
Eclogues, p. 117.

GULES : *verb* from the heraldric term for "red"; to color red. Compare MINIATE, RUBESCENT

. . . he gouged his nails deep in his palms or, better yet, gobbled a fold of cheek between his molars and chewed it so bloody that her tongue depressor would emerge all gulesed. . . .
—Koster, *The Dissertation*, p. 114.

GULOUS : *adj* greedy for food, gluttonous

. . . Mrs. Walters urging further helpings on her dim but gulous husband.
—Burgess, *Tremor of Intent*, p. 70.

GURN, GIRN : *verb* to snarl, to show the teeth in anger. Compare RINGENT

". . . you haven't brought down many *rockets* lately have you, haha!" gurning his most spiteful pursed smile up against wrinkled nose and eyes. . . .
—Pynchon, *Gravity's Rainbow*, p. 38.

GURRY : *adj* relating to fish guts, fish oil, some slimy substance

. . . warm in the gurry odors of sex, the grassy sweet of hair, the fodderish smell of crotches, and the winey buckreek of armpits. . . .

—Davenport, "On Some Lines of Virgil,"
Eclogues, p. 203.

GYNAIKOPOINARIAN: *adj* woman-punishing

. . . I shall kick open the gates—stand aside!—and loose the gynaikopoinarian dogs, for a woman always respects a word she cannot spell.

—Theroux, *Darconville's Cat*, p. 551.

GYNECIC : *adj* having to do with women, feminine. Compare GYNECOMORPHOUS, MULIEBRIA

All that gynecic crowd . . . the fine, fair furniture of flesh. Prone, how like the Persian couch—the flufféd pillows of their breasts, the long soft bolster of their thighs. . . .

—Elkin, *George Mills*, p. 24.

GYNECOMORPHOUS : *adj* formed or characterized as a female. Compare GYNECIC, MULIEBRIA

There is something disturbing about this gathering of women, this classless convocation, this gynecomorphous melting pot. I think of Lysistrata, Gertrude Stein, Carry Nation.

—Boyle, "A Women's Restaurant,"
Descent of Man, p. 85.

GYNOTIKOLOBOMASSOPHILE : *noun* someone who loves to fondle (usually, nibble) women's earlobes

EARS: A gynotikolobomassophile's delight.

—Theroux, *Darconville's Cat*, p. 105.

H

HALITOTIC : *adj* having bad breath

Enderby . . . was aware of himself as gross, sweating, halitotic, his viscera loaded like a nightsoil-collector's bucket.

—Burgess, *Enderby*, p. 59.

HAMESUCKEN, HAMESUCN : *noun* an archaic legal term for an assault on a person in his own home

. . . you are welcome to Barbet House as those adept at hamesucn and sneakbudging† call my establishment.

—Davenport, "John Charles Tapner,"
Da Vinci's Bicycle, p. 52

HAPTERIC : *adj* fastening, usually in reference to the holdfast which anchors seaweed to the ocean floor

. . . she was attempting to dislodge her husband from the shoal of furniture where his hapteric glass anchored him.

—Gaddis, *The Recognitions*, p. 628.

HAPTIC : *adj* having to do with touching, tactile. Compare CONTRECTATION, DACTYLIC, EUTRIPSIA

She ... let loose ... a not-uncommon antagonism, syncopated with hot flashes: party bigotry, part haptic bias.
—Theroux, Three Wogs, p. 15.

HARUSPEX : *noun* a Roman entrail inspector, forecaster, or market analyst

Somehow, plastic cheaters and all, he had the charisma of a haruspex, the irresistable certitude of the monomaniac.
—Wolfe, The Pumphouse Gang, p. 137.

HASTATE : *adj* shaped like a spearhead or arrowhead. Compare GLOCKAMOID

... the pod of Bruno's *broekje* humped to a pommel which Kaatje with a blind hand freed from its strain hastate and nodular.
—Davenport, "The Dawn in Erewhon,"
Tatlin!, p. 199.

HATCHEL : *noun* a hackle, an erect hair or feather

... Lord Lindsay pollskepped† with the hatchels of a cassowary. ...
—Davenport, "A Field of Snow on a Slope of the
Rosenberg," DaVinci's Bicycle, p. 170.

HEBEPHRENIA : *noun* a condition of adolescent silliness. HEBEPHRENIC, *adj*

The hunt ... a merciless hacking through the damp growths of our historic hebephrenia.
—Coover, "Morris in Chains,"
Pricksongs and Descants, pp. 46-47.

... a difference of opinion in which seemed mingled in equal parts patience, ferocity, and complete futility, if not actual hebephrenic dilapidation.
—Lowry, October Ferry to Gabriola, p. 297.

HEBETATION : *noun* lethargy, torpidity. See GRAVEOLENT

HELOT : *noun* a serf of the Spartans. See MACHICOLATED

HEMATIC : *adj* having to do with blood; bloody

... his spacious, elegant office with the red Bukhara and Louis XV escritoire, yet so far from everything, a green, mossy island in the middle of a hematic ocean. ...
—Aczel, *Illuminations*, p. 140.

HEMATOSE : *adj* literally, "full of blood"; hence, with the blood up

... the hematose conspiracy of night when they shout gfckyrslf. ...
—Gaddis, *The Recognitions*, p. 394.

HEMIPYGIC : *adj* having only one buttock, half-assed

... an ellipsoid that wobbles through a period of hemipygic asymmetry to the beauty of a pear.
—Davenport, "The Dawn in Erewhon,"
Tatlin!, p. 238.

HERMETIC : *adj* from Hermes Trismegistus or Thoth: 1) mysterious, occult; 2) sealed airtight

She was not going to make any explanation, and something about her hermetic expression made it, yet once again, infuriatingly, seem vulgar to be curious.
—Fowles, *The Magus*, p. 630.

"Calm yourselves, gentlemen. And be humble." Purcell spoke with the hermetic theatricality of John Paul Ziller. "You are in the presence of Mon Cul, prince of baboons."
—Robbins, *Another Roadside Attraction*, p. 32.

HERMSPRONG : *adj* "from Richard Cumberland, wearing a phallos, as of Hermes" (Davenport). See DOUCET. Compare BAUBON, DILDO, DOLICHOPHALLIC, ITHYPHALLIC, OLISBOS

HERPETINE : *adj* reptilian, snakelike. Compare COLUM-
BRINE, OPHIDIAN

... Medusa's face, unaccountably, was but for the
herpetine coiffure, a lovely woman's!
—Barth, *Chimera*, p. 66.

HESYCHASTIC : *adj* keeping quiet, maintaining silence

... long hesychastic vigils. ...
—Theroux, *Darconville's Cat*, p. 460.

HETEROLOGY : *noun* See quotation. HETEROLOGICAL,
adj

Heterology refers to lack of correspondence between
bodily parts, as in structure, arrangement, or growth.
An adjective is heterological if it denotes something that
doesn't apply to the adjective itself.
—DeLillo, Ratner's Star, p. 302.

HETERONOMIC : *adj* functioning under externally con-
trolled or imposed rules

Mrs. Gamely had taken him aside and dictated it to
him, making him promise to deliver it personally,
because, as she said, "Coheeries mail is heteronomic
and ludibund.†"
—Helprin, *Winter's Tale*, p. 288.

HIERATIC : *adj* having to do with priestly purposes, sacred
activities

As she grew up the only language she knew expressed
fewer and fewer of her ripening needs; the facts which
littered her memory grew less substantial; the figure she
saw in the looking-glass seemed less recognizably herself. Aimee withdrew herself into a lofty and hieratic
habitation.
—Waugh, *The Loved One*, p. 135.

... he raised both his arms in an outlandish hieratic gesture, one foot slightly advanced, as if in some kind of primitive blessing.
—Fowles, *The Magus,* p. 88.

HIEROPHANT : *noun* a priest, an interpreter of holy mysteries. See also CATAPLASM

The clerks ... the vice-presidents ... the tellers ... these are the only hierophants left whose rites are unquestioned and unquestionable. ...
—Davenport, "A Field of Snow on a Slope of the Rosenberg," *Da Vinci's Bicycle,* p. 174.

HIEROPHANY : *noun* a manifestation of the sacred

... a universe of reverberating hierophanies and theophanies† that elevated them into a reality far above the miseries of their mud huts or the glitter of their palaces.
—Aczel, *Illuminations,* p. 297

HIPPIC : *adj* relating to horses

One day we shall all grow up, when the hippic and the reptilian brains have withered away, then solve everything with nothing but the fairly recent neo-cortex.
—West, *Gala,* p. 25.

HOLOURIES : *noun* fornicators and debauchees, usually female. See GRAVEOLENT

HOLUS-BOLUS : *adv* literally, "whole lump"; in one gulp. See DIGLOT. Compare BOLUS

HOMOLOGY : *noun* likeness produced by similar or same cause or origin. See ALLOTROPY

HORRENT : *adj* 1) bristling, raising the hackles; 2) feeling or expressing horror. Compare HORRIPILATING

And for good measure, chin and jaws bristling. Horrent, Milton might say.
> —Burgess, *Enderby,* p. 13.

Their language, uninhibited and horrent,
Is mercifully swallowed by the torrent.
> —Burgess, *Napoleon Symphony,* p. 90.

HORRIPILATING : *adj* bristling, particularly in reference to goose bumps or creeping flesh; shuddering. Compare HORRENT

. . . an inconceivable anguish of horripilating hangover thunderclapping about his skull, and accompanied by a protective screen of demons gnattering in his ears. . . .
> —Lowry, *Under the Volcano,* p. 126.

. . . the horripilating detail of the upper-lip writhing up and away in a kind of a duck or a cobra sneer. . . .
> —Beckett, "A Wet Night,"
> *More Pricks than Kicks,* p. 75.

HORST : *noun* German for "thicket"; a geological term for an upraised block of rock between two faults. See GRABEN

HORTATIVE : *adj* encouraging, urging, cheering on. Compare PROTREPTIC

Chiefy, at the other end of the mess, was yelling in a hortative frenzy at two oilers who shovelled seawater with dustpans toward the open end of a buzzing, sucking portable pump.
> —C. Buckley, *Steaming to Bamboola,* p. 51.

HOUGHMAGANDY : *noun* fucking as a pastime

. . . she would have preferred him to have gone through

a bit of wholesome houghmagandy with the wench.
—Nabokov, *Pale Fire,* p. 212.

People will put up with anything for the old Houghma-gandy. . . .man is also in the whole of Nature, the only creature to turn sex into a hobby.
—Davies, *The Rebel Angels,* p. 186.

HURDIES : *noun* the buttocks. Compare NATES, PRAT

. . . he with his dancing light behind her hurdies and calves and mobile shoulders and streaming hair. . . .
—Nabokov, *Ada,* p. 209.

HYALESCENCE : *noun* glassiness. HYALINE, *adj*

. . . the murky, cold hyalescence of a dried up aquarium.
—Aczel, *Illuminations,* p. 214.

. . . the cold waves, green hyaline swells. . . .
—Davenport, "The Dawn in Erewhon," *Tatlin!,* p. 244.

HYDRANTH : *noun* one of the colonial polyps

The full reach of his instroke tamped hydranths papil-lary† and marine in her myxoid† deep.
—Davenport, "The Dawn in Erewhon,"
Tatlin!, p. 243.

HYDROPHILIA : *noun* the love of water

Time was when she'd spend half of every day in the bath, tootling and warbling in rapt hydrophilia, the water ice cold.
—West, *Gala,* p. 43.

HYETOLOGIST : *noun* a rainmaker

At sundown, when the moon is a bloody eye on the horizon, the women gather to strip naked and haul plows through the crusted fields while the local hyetologist chants his rain song in a piercing clamorous falsetto. . . .

Boyle, *Water Music*, p. 313.

HYMENEAL : *adj* virginal, still possessing a maidenhead

Hymeneal still it lay, the thing so soon to be changed. . . .
—Beckett, *Watt*, p. 42.

HYPAETHRAL : *adj* uncovered, exposed to heaven

There was a dignity in their hypaethral presence. . . .
—Davenport, "The Dawn in Erewhon,"
Tatlin!, p. 216.

HYPERCATHEXIS : *noun* excessive concentration of desire upon a particular object, monomania

. . . language itself, on the one hand, originated in "infantile, pregenital erotic exuberance, polymorphously perverse," and that conscious attention, on the other, was a "libidinal hypercathexis". . . .
—Barth, *Chimera*, p. 24.

HYPEREMIAN : *noun* someone who vomits excessively

. . . theatrically erudite Episcopal hyperemians. . . .
—Theroux, *Darconville's Cat*, p. 311.

HYPERESTHESIA : *noun* oversensitivity, touchiness, excessive concerned with emotions

. . . the genre . . . of Hoodoo, Hackwork, and Hyperesthesia. . . .
—Theroux, *Darconville's Cat*, p. 73.

HYPERTROPHIA : *noun* excessive growth or complexity. Compare ACROMEGALIC

There were several levels of noise, people in shifting groups, rotary units turning, a sense of hypertrophia,

something growing outward toward a limit.
> —DeLillo, *Ratner's Star,* pp. 60-61.

HYPNOPIASIS : *noun* a mesmerized, hypnotized state

In the hypnopiasis of fatigue, they marched to a drill field in the pouring rain. It was as if stagehands on scaffolds were throwing buckets of water at them.
> —Helprin, *Refiner's Fire,* p. 312.

HYPOTYPOSIS : *noun* vivid description

" . . . a special talent for the sceptical hypotyposis."
"Mmmm . . . ?"
"The brainy over-view or the chilling put-down or whatever you like. . . . But he did it with such a grand sweep and such a light touch that you felt you had been illuminated."
"Until you got sick of it."
> —Davies, *The Rebel Angels,* p. 99.

The list could surely go, and there is nothing more wonderful than a list, instrument of wondrous hypotyposis.
> —Eco, *The Name of the Rose,* p. 73.

HYSTERESIS : *noun* the influence of previous actions on subsequent events, The Historical Process

The people will find the Center again, the Center without time, the journey without hysteresis where every departure is a return to the same place, the only place . . . .
> —Pynchon, *Gravity's Rainbow,* p. 319.

HYSTERICAL : *adj* concerning, related to, or coming from the womb

. . . they did an ectomy. It's what they do to quiet a woman when they get to a bad age. Take out the hysterical organs.
> —DeLillo, *Ratner's Star,* p. 248.

I

IANTHINE : *adj* violet-colored

> ... who sees in the mackled† crimsons upon hectic yellow leaves ianthine eyes.
> —Davenport, "The Dawn in Erewhon," *Tatlin!*, pp. 204-205

ICHTHYOFRAGE : *noun* See quotation

> The lesser sturgeon will then go sliding to the floor in a flaky fishwreck. *Ichtyofrage* [*sic*]—may one use such a neologism?
> —Burgess, *Napoleon Symphony*, p. 222.

ICTUS : *noun* in poetry, stress on one syllable, a stroke

> ... the steady, long-drawn hammering of the Vickers floated up the hill to make a tenor under the irregular staccato of my light automatics. A few riflemen who thought they saw someone and fancied their skill as marksmen joined in with single ictus taps.
> —Masters, *Bugles and a Tiger*, p. 209.

IDYLATRY : *noun* nature worship

> All possible cause for panic will be eradicated. . . . We

shall put an end to idylatry.
> —Coover, "Morris in Chains,"
> *Pricksongs and Descants*, p. 48.

IGNAVIA : *noun* laziness, torpor. Compare NESCIENCE, NIHILISCIENT

. . . a place sunk in blind ignavia. . . .
> —Theroux, *Darconville's Cat*, p. 163.

ILLATION : *noun* an inference, a conclusion drawn from premises

The tiger's rays are my mind's illations, his tectonics†
the hum of my braincells.
> —Gardner, *Jason and Medeia*, p. 296.

IMBRICATED : *adj* 1) overlapped like rooftiles; 2) relating to the overlapping of the calyx of flower (botanical). IMBRICATION, *noun*

. . . the low white house . . . was roofed with imbricated flower-pot-colored tiles resembling bisected drainpipes.
> —Lowry, *Under the Volcano*, p. 66.

He stopped speaking for a moment, like a man walking who comes to a brink; perhaps it was an artful pause but it made the stars, the night, seem to wait, as if the story, narration, history, lay imbricated in the nature of things; and the cosmos was for the story, not the story for the cosmos.
> —Fowles, *The Magus*, pp. 149-150.

He swallowed some of the oloroso sherry, and its warm course sent an imbrication of chills over his back.
> —Gaddis, *The Recognitions*, p. 399.

IMMACHINATION : *noun* the act, process, or state of becoming part of a plan or machine

Vectors in the night underground, all trying to flee a center, a force, which appears to be the Rocket: some immachination, whether of journey or of destiny, which is able to gather violent political opposites together in the Erdschweinhöhle [aardvark's hole] as it gathers fuel and oxidizer in its thrust chamber: metered, helmsmanlike, for the sake of its scheduled parabola.
—Pynchon, *Gravity's Rainbow*, p. 318.

IMMANENT : *adj* dwelling inside, remaining within

Vogelsang's voice rattled on. Immanent, inescapable, like beat of blood and thump of heart, the little creatures of house and wood saturated the auditory spectrum with clicks, rattles, hisses and grunts.
—Boyle, *Budding Prospects*, pp. 222-223.

IMMUREMENT : *noun* placed within a wall. See INSARCOPHAGUSEMENT.

IMPENNOUS : *adj* wingless. Compare APTEROUS

Certain fools thought that this was chemical engineering, a studious necessity, an obvious alacrity, a logical linkage. It was nothing of the kind, but rather a portrait by complications, an abstract of humor from above as impennous necessities were snared by thematic joking.
—Helprin, *Refiner's Fire*, p. 253.

IMPERSEVERANT : *adj* not constant in persistence. See MOME

IMPLEACH : *verb* to entwine, to interweave, to fold together. IMPLEACHMENT, *noun*

Her robe was bridal white impleached with gold. . . .
—Gardner, *Jason and Medeia*, p. 10.

An amorous impleachment. This was some husbandry.
Some pricking usury.
                                        —Nye, *Falstaff*, p. 333.

IMPUBERAL : *adj* literally, "without pubic hair"; not adult,
prepubescent

Another revelation of impuberal softness . . . was afforded by a photo of her in which she sat in the buff on
the grass. . . .
                        —Nabokov, *Transparent Things*, p. 41.

INANITION : *noun* a starved condition, a wasting away due
to malnutrition. Compare ANORECTIC, CACHECTIC,
DYSCRASE, MARASMIC, MARCESCENCE, TABESCENT

. . . not only must he contend with the sun, sandfleas,
dysentery and fever, but with inanition as well. The
Moors have . . . apparently decided to put him on a
stringent diet.
                                —Boyle, *Water Music*, p. 8.

The vagina starts to die of inanition, to falter from
hunger; a hundred men with inferior sperm cannot feed
it.
                                —Durrell, *Constance*, p. 302.

INCONCINNITY : *noun* unsuitability, incongruity

. . . a voyage in a hot-air balloon . . . could precipitate
no new shiver from my paraphenomenal and kithless
epistemology except the vastation† of brooding on the
sweep of inconcinnity displayed below me like a map
and perhaps acrophobia.
                        —Davenport, "A Field of Snow on a Slope
                of the Rosenberg," *Da Vinci's Bicycle*, p. 149.

INCONDITE : *adj* unpolished, crudely composed

... I might digress. ... But my tale is sufficiently incondite already.

—Nabokov, *Lolita,* p. 72.

INDEFEASIBLE : *adj* that which cannot be undone

... when this indefeasible urge of the flesh presses them, few men of normal potency prove able to refrain their foot from that path.

—Cozzens, *By Love Possessed,* pp. 236-237.

INDISCERPTIBILITY : *noun* inseparability. See SPISSITUDE

INENARRABLE : *adj* unspeakable, lacking describability

The inenarrable, inconceivably desolate sense of having no right to be where you are. ...

Lowry, "Through the Panama," *Hear us O Lord in heaven thy dwelling place,* p. 31.

Besides this took up very little room in the inenarrable contraption I called my life. ...

—Beckett, *Molloy,* p. 153.

INENUBILABLE : *adj* literally, "not uncloudy"; incapable of being made clear

Our blue inenubilable Zembla. ...

—Nabokov, *Pale Fire,* p. 288.

INESCULENT : *adj* tasteless, inedible. Compare ESCULENT, SAPOROUS

... the ragout de bully? So *gray,* just like dear summoning Bernard, and quite as inesculent.

—Burgess, *Earthly Powers,* p. 191.

INFANDUM : *noun* See quotation. Compare DEINOSIS, EFFED

Nothing stirred except their detestable jolly faces, and I felt I'd seen that for which there was no word: the

abominable, the unspeakable which the Romans called *infandum.*
—West, *Out of My Depths,* p. 9.

INFRANGIBLE : *adj* unbreakable, inviolable. Compare FRANGIBLE, INDEFEASIBLE, IRREFRAGABLE

... her privitie was that nice, and the tympanum therein so surpassing stowt, as to render it infrangible.
—Barth, *The Sot-Weed Factor,* p. 154.

INFUNDIBULIFORM : *adj* shaped like a funnel. See also CHRONOSYNCLASTIC INFUNDIBULA

... the two cunts ... the one for ever accursed that ejected me into this world and the other, infundibuliform, in which, pumping my likes, I tried to take my revenge.
—Beckett, *The Unnamable,* pp. 446-447.

INHUME : *verb* to bury in the ground. INHUMEMENT, *noun.* Compare ENCHARNELLED. See also INSARCOPHAGUSMENT.

... he could escape to his study, where he sank, inhumed until her voice struck with the sharpness of a gravedigger's pick.
—Gaddis, *The Recognitions,* p. 27.

INQUINATED : *adj* polluted, contaminated

... I feel my little body positively *inquinated.*
—Burgess, *Earthly Powers,* p. 558.

INSARCOPHAGUSMENT : *noun* the act of placing a body in a sarcophagus

Normal disposal is by inhumement,† entombment, inurnment or immurement,† but many people just lately prefer insarcophagusment.
—Waugh, *The Loved One,* p. 43.

INSESSORIAL : *adj* perching

Bars have made us insessorial—the term for birds that perch.
Five or six of us sat hunched in a semicircle like fowl silently killing time on a wet promontory over whose rocks the jukebox boomed like a steady surf. . . .
—DeVries, *Into Your Tent I'll Creep,* p. 151.

. . . his cock snub and insessorial in the codpiece of his curt briefs.
—Davenport, "The Dawn in Erewhon,"
Tatlin!, p. 242.

INSPISSATE : *verb* 1) to thicken, to condense; 2) to permeate. INSPISSATED, *adj.* Compare SPISSITUDE

Scents of noxious herbs alight arose to inspissate the air. . . .
—Burgess, *Earthly Powers,* p. 242.

Church bells inspissated the air, dropping it in sharp fragments
—Gaddis, *The Recognitions,* p. 399.

After that, I stared at her face for a good five minutes, knowing she'd said none of it; but she'd never said none of it at such intimidating, inspissated, length.
—West, *Gala,* p. 188.

. . . about holes. . . .But it is with the black as with the grey, the black proves nothing either, as to the nature of the silence which it inspissates (as it were).
—Beckett, *The Unnamable,* p. 507.

INSUFFLATE : *verb* to blow or breathe in

She must have beached and insufflated me; when I came to we were mouth to mouth under her cowl.
—Barth, *Chimera,* p. 99.

INTERCALATED : *adj* literally, "inserted in the calendar"; inserted, placed between layers

... narrow dim valleys with intercalated cotton-wool bits of cloud that seemed placed between the receding sets of ridges to prevent their flanks from scraping against one another.
—Nabokov, *Pale Fire,* p. 144.

INTERCLUTCHMENT : *noun* a grabbing together, an interlocking

... they clapped and coupled, buggered and bit; also sniffed and fiddled and fingered and shat, thrust out their tongues and forth their pudenda—a rare interclutchment it was of appetites.
—Barth, *Giles Goat-Boy,* p. 206.

INTROMITTER : *noun* the male organ of copulation

... the old Intromitter when thoroughly applied will look, even hours later, recognizably Applied.
—Barth, *Letters,* p. 448.

INVOLUCRUM : *noun* literally, an "envelope"; a sheath. See GLANDES

IPSEDIXITIST : *noun* or *adj* literally, "he himself said it"; a dogmatic doctrinarian

... medievally sworn in the old ipsedixitist tradition. . . .
—Theroux, *Darconville's Cat,* p. 11.

IRACUND : *adj* easily angered

His iracund, muscle-bound face was like a child's—it made me remember my own poor son Kleon, back in Athens.
—Gardner, *The Wreckage of Agathon,* p. 35.

IRIDAL : *adj* literally, "rainbow"; referring to the iris of the eye

The iridal dark-brown of her serious eyes had the enigmatic opacity of an Oriental hypnotist's look. . . .
—Nabokov, *Ada,* p. 58.

IRIDULE : *noun* "an iridescent cloudlet" (Nabokov, *Pale Fire,* p. 116)

> The iridule—when, beautiful and strange
> In a bright sky above a mountain range
> One opal cloudlet in an oval form
> Reflects the rainbow of a thunderstorm.
> —Nabokov, *Pale Fire,* pp. 36-37.

IRREALIST : *noun* fictionalist, a storyteller

At that time, as a budding irrealist, I took seriously the traditional publisher's disclaimer—"Any resemblance between characters in this novel and actual persons living or dead," etc.—and would have been appalled at the suggestion that any of my fictive folk were even loosely "drawn from life": a phrase that still suggests to me some barbarous form of capital punishment.
—Barth, *Letters,* p. 187.

IRREFRAGABLE : *adj* unbreakable, irrefutable. Compare FRANGIBLE, INDEFEASIBLE, INFRANGIBLE

Did they clip by some labor-saving device to the sterilized rubber privacies above? Did they come from the same department as the light irrefragable plastic head?
—Waugh, *The Loved One,* pp. 86-87.

IRRUMPENT : *adj* bursting inward or breaking in. See AGONAL. Compare DEHISCENCE, DISSILIENT ERUMPENT

ITERATION : *noun* a repetition

> It hasn't yet been a fortnight, but there is already something of ritual to this, of iteration. Each room will hold a single unpleasantness for him: a test he must pass.
>
> —Pynchon, *Gravity's Rainbow,* p. 231.

ITHYPHALLIC : *adj* penilely erect. ITHYPHALLI, ITHYPHALLUS, *noun.*Compare BAUBON, DILDO, DOLICHOPHALLIC, HERMSPRONG, OLISBOS

> "My God." He looks down at his ithyphallic self again. "It's revolting."
>
> —Fowles, *Mantissa,* p. 192.

> It was his organ of copulation her body craved, the Latinate folds between her legs that stirred him to ithyphallic meter.
>
> —DeLillo, *Ratner's Star,* p. 331.

> Could I distinguish a wild huntsman, and men mutilating themselves? Ithyphallic demons. The souls of warriors slain in fight.
>
> —Foxell, *Carnival,* p. 85.

> I swathed my ithyphallus in hand towels. . . .
>
> —Burgess, *Earthly Powers,* p. 282.

> . . . the Dionysian processions in which Greek boys dressed as women carried the ithyphalli through the streets, amid sounds of rejoicing from all sexes present. . . .
>
> —Gaddis, *The Recognitions,* p. 311.

J

JACTATION : *noun* a throwing, either of proud words or something else

... the immediate frenzy of jactation before a spinfit or conniption. . . .
—Theroux, *Three Wogs,* p. 59.

JEROPIGIA, GEROPIGIA : *noun* a mixture used to adulterate port wine; or port, so adulterated. See PATIBULARY

JIGGET : *noun* a juggling, a fidgeting. See FREMITUS

JOBBERNOWL : *noun* a blockhead, clodpate. Compare BOANTHROP, DODDIPOL, NUPSON

The jobbernowl approved this incredible plan (if you want the impossible done, always suggest an improbable manner of doing it.)
—Nye, *Falstaff,* p. 345.

K

KAKOPYGE : *noun* someone who has ugly buttocks

. . . a dark-haired kakopyge with fat hands, an insipid smile, and the morals of a muskcat.
> —Theroux, *Darconville's Cat,* p. 308.

KALEIDOGYN : *noun* a beautiful woman

Awkwardness is the prerogative of kaleidogyns.
> —Theroux, *Darconville's Cat,* p. 94.

KARASS : *noun* See quotation. Compare DUPRASS, GRANFALLOON

We Bokononists believe that humanity is organized into teams, teams that do God's Will without ever discovering what they are doing. Such a team is called a *karass* by Bokonon. . . .a karass ignores national, institutional, occupational, familial, and class boundaries.
> —Vonnegut, *Cat's Cradle,* p. 14.

KINABRA : *noun* See quotation

The *kinabra* of the goat. . . .It is the Greek word for the *stank* of a billy goat. There is no smell like it, and the Greeks had a separate word, because it really isn't a

stink. It is his glory and pride.
                    —Davenport, "The Dawn in Erewhon,"
                                        Tatlin!, p. 161.

KOOSH : *verb* See quotation

... fire—purring and snapping, a bloodshot terminal
moraine unto itself—was as familiar as Christmas morning. It said hello, come in and *koosh,* which is Manx for
warm your loins.
                    —West, *Out of My Depths,* p. 49.

L

LABILE : *adj* liable to fall; slippery, changeable. LABILITY, *noun.* Compare CADUCITY, DECIDUOUS, FLUXION, FUGACIOUS

The maddening thing, of course, is that they all lie, waiting to spring or be sprung into charming life and labile reality. . . .
>   —Fowles, *Mantissa,* p. 185.

. . . weep at words like *greatness.* It was called emotional lability, a disease of the senile.
>   —Burgess, *Earthly Powers,* p. 9.

. . . the terrible Face That Is No Face, gone too abstract, unreachable: the notch of eye socket, but never the labile eye, only the anonymous curve of cheek, convexity of mouth, a noseless mask of the Other Order of Being. . . .
>   —Pynchon, *Gravity's Rainbow,* p. 222

LACHRYMAL : *adj* tearful, weeping. See FLIMMERING

LACUSTRINE : *adj* having to do with lakes

. . . . three ample-haunched Ledas swapping lacustrine

impressions. . . .
—Nabokov, *Ada,* p. 553.

LAMBENT : *adj* flickering, licking

. . . gorging on long lambent kisses. . . .
—Davenport, "The Dawn in Erewhon,"
Tatlin!, p. 155.

LAMINA : *noun* a flake, scale, layer, or thin coating. LAMI-NAE, plural

. . . His pleasant sky-blue eyes no longer reflected the morning's shocked disbelief but were glazed with lami-nae of fear and submission.
—Aczel, *Illuminations,* p. 209.

LANUGO : *noun* down, as on new born animals. Compare FLUE, PLUMULACEOUS

. . . early spring mountains with young-elephant lanugo along their spines. . . .
—Nabokov, *Lolita,* p. 158.

LAODICEAN : *adj* and *noun* relating to the ancient city of Laodicea, the populace of which were renowned for lack of intensity towards religious and political issues; hence, apathetic, or lukewarm

The baths were mostly tiled showers, with an endless variety of spouting mechanisms, but with one definitely non-Laodicean characteristic in common, a propensity, while in use, to turn instantly beastly hot or blindingly cold upon you. . . .
—Nabokov, *Lolita,* p. 148.

. . . he is what we call a chipper, flirting with drugs but scared to go very far. A Laodicean of vice.
—Davies, *The Rebel Angels,* p. 288.

LAPIDATE : *verb* to throw rocks at

He already says that women who think should be lapidated by psychiatrists.
—Durrell, *Constance,* p. 291.

LATITUDINARIAN: *noun* someone tolerant, not strict in doctrine or beliefs

She got off to a bad start her first day at Blessed Sir Thomas More's School in Cadogan Square by asking a girl whether the policies of the school were "latitudinarian."
—W. Buckley, *Stained Glass,* p. 113.

LEA : *noun* uncultivated, open land

Nordhausen in the morning: the lea is a green salad, crisp with raindrops.
—Pynchon, *Gravity's Rainbow,* p. 289.

LEMNISCATE : *noun* closed curve in the shape of a figure eight: "a unicursal bicircular quartic" (Nabokov, *Pale Fire,* p. 136)

The miracle of a lemniscate left
Upon wet sand by nonchalantly deft
Bicycle tires.
—Nabokov, *Pale Fire,* p. 37

He remembered exploring those otherwordly curves from one degree to the next, lemniscate and folium,† progressing eventually to an ungraphable class of curve. . . .
—DeLillo, *Ratner's Star,* p. 63.

LENTICULAR : *adj* shaped like a lentil or a double convex lens. Compare MENISCUS

The carpet, a late Jugendstil pattern of compact circles in lenticular overply, rusty orange. . . .
—Davenport, "A Field of Snow on a Slope of the Rosenberg," *DaVinci's Bicycle,* p. 161.

LENTOR : *noun* slowness

> . . . she walked through dilating space with the lentor of one walking under water or in a flight dream.
> —Nabokov, *Lolita,* p. 122.

LEPORINE : *adj* concerned with hares or rabbits, rabbity

> The able psychiatrist who studies my case—and whom by now Dr. Humbert has plunged, I trust, into a state of leporine fascination. . . .
> —Nabokov, *Lolita,* p. 168.

LEPTORRHIN : *noun* someone with a long narrow nose, especially like a rabbit

> . . . those stouthearted leptorrhins with triple names and disposable incomes. . . .
> —Theroux, *Darconville's Cat,* p. 410.

LETHIFEROUS : *adj* deadly, death-bearing

> "A Lethiferous Letter"

> . . . I believe it my duty to resign—
> Thinking of Isabel, however, Darconville reconsidered and, running his great black pen over the words, registered a rainbow over the Universal Deluge.
> —Theroux, *Darconville's Cat,* pp. 77-78.

LEVIN : *noun* lightning

> The mutual frown with which the antagonists confronted each other was a kind of ocular thunder, while their eyes flashed levin enough.
> —Burgess, *Napoleon Sympathy,* p. 299.

LEVINER : *noun* a hound, a mongrel. See PATIBULARY

LEVIRATE : *adj* relating to a brother-in-law

> . . . in Taxila, at the mouth of the Khyber Pass, the widow of a childless man might contract a Levirate marriage with her brother-in-law.
> —Lowry, *Under the Volcano,* p. 307.

LIBANOPHOROUS : *adj* producing incense, scented

> He cradled her head to his neck, breathing her libanophorous hair. . . .
> —Theroux, *Darconville's Cat,* p. 374.

LICKERISH, LIQUORISH : *adj* originally, fond of good food; now, fond of fucking and other sexual acts. LIQUORISH-NESS, *noun.* Compare LUBRICITY, LUXURIOUS, RIGGISH

> She seems both whore and virgin. Something hot about her, something lickerish. And yet that heat *held.* Contained in a purity and stillness.
> —Nye, *Merlin,* p. 120.

> A self-possessed young person, clearly, and not impressed by Urky's noisy, lickerish gallantry.
> —Davies, *The Rebel Angels,* p. 50.

> (By the by, 'tis not quite so in France, where Women of Beauty and of Brains are not unknown, and oft' the greatest Courtesans have been renown'd for Learning as well as Liquorishness. But here in Merry England, where the Men, I fear, are all a little queer, 'Twill never wash!)
> —Jong, *Fanny,* pp. 176–177.

LIRIPOOP : *noun* the tail on the hood of an academic gown. See PATIBULARY

LIROPHTHALMY : *noun* "lewd-eyed (real Greek word, not a coinage)" (Davenport)

> Kaatje's lirophthalmy was scrupulously bawdy, bluff-

less, a practised lechery of eyes.
> —Davenport, "The Dawn in Erewhon,"
> *Tatlin!*, p. 257.

LIVID : *adj* blue, as in "black and blue"; obviously and noticeably blue-colored for a bad reason. See CREPUSCULAR

LIXIVIATE : *adj* leached from solids, alkaline

We're addicted to tit. . . . But this ain't a mother thing, we think, only obsessive thirst annihilating itself at the very wellhead of lixiviate, suffocate whelm.†
> —Elkin, *George Mills*, p. 343.

LLAREGUB and LLAREGYB : *nouns* See quotation

A less than tolerant view of how our little versions go astray is Dylan Thomas's juxtaposition of Llaregub and Llaregyb, which reverse into "Buggerall" and "Biggerall," in other words nothing and everything.
> —West, *Out of My Depths*, p. 98.

LOBDOTTEREL : *noun* a gullible klutz. See LOOBY

LOBLOGIC : *noun* clumsy reasoning, misdirected thought

> . When hot Aphrodite strikes,
> sanity shifts to loblogic.
> > —Gardner, *Jason and Medeia*, p. 102.

LOGODAEDALY : *noun* literally, "word-skill"; can also refer to the ability to coin new words. Compare BANAUSIC, DAEDALIAN

He was versed in logodaedaly and logomancy.†
> —Nabokov, *Lolita*, pp. 251-252.

LOGOMANCY : *noun* divination by the study of words. See LOGODAEDALY

LOGORRHEA, LOGORRHOEA : *noun* uncontrollable or uncontrolled and usually incomprehensible running off at the mouth

But, after those first painful stanzas, he found it hard to stop. He was led on ruthlessly, horrified by a growing facility, a veritable logorrhea.
> —Burgeses, *Enderby,* p. 40.

. . . handing round the cups and saucers to the assembled logorrhoea of ladies.
> —Fowles, *Daniel Martin,* p. 348.

LONGAMINOUS : *adj* suffering stolidly, patiently enduring

. . . Willard Lowe spoke also with the longaminous resignation of the sensible man of seventy who must find sad news about another person he has known for years no news.
> —Cozzens, *By Love Possessed,* p. 361.

LOOBY : *noun* from "lob," clumsy; a clod, a klutz

[Seventeenth-century English provided] . . . what rich neologisms! Slabberdegullion† druggels,† lubbardly louts, blockish grutnols,† doddipol† joltheads, lobdotterels,† codshead loobies, ninnyhammer† flycatchers, and other suchlike defamatory epithets!
> —Davies, *The Rebel Angels,* p. 50.

LOUCHE : *adj* unsavory, dishonest, perverse; indirect, coy

There were also two children, a boy and a girl, the girl somewhat charmingly louche.
> —Burgess, *The End of the World News,* p. 279.

. . . he was entranced. He'd never seen so many *louche* women. Had never sat beside couples who embraced and caressed each other in public.
> —Boyd, *An Ice Cream War,* p. 212.

. . . the doctor, in hinting something vaguely louche,

promiscuous, had once again been deliberately misleading him.

—Fowles, *Mantissa*, p. 32.

LOXODROMIC : *adj* tacking, oblique sailing

. . . a ship, as it were, straining at its moorings in a contrary current and arming for its sinuous and loxodromic voyage. . . .

—Fowles, *The French Lieutenant's Woman*, p. 433.

LUBRICITY : *noun* usually slipperiness, but also lewdness, lasciviousness, salaciousness. LUBRICIOUS, *adj*; LUBRICIOUSLY, *adv*. Compare LICKERISH, LUXURIOUS, RIGGISH

. . . a garage said in its sleep—genuflexion lubricity; and corrected itself to Gulflex Lubrication.

—Nabokov, *Lolita*, p. 284.

And Donnie, poor kid, had become for him the soul and vital symbol of all things lubricious and lewd, meretricious, debauched, profligate and goatish. . . .

—Gardner, *Mickelsson's Ghosts*, p. 338.

You have come here possessed by the devil knows what wickedness—inflamed with vicious and lubricious fantasies dreamed up in your bed at night. . . .

—Nye, *Merlin*, p. 32.

The Third Assistant Engineer was there, clacking his dentures lubriciously at the waitresses.

—C. Buckley, *Steaming to Bamboola*, p. 137.

LUCUBRATION : *noun* late night study by lamplight; hence, heavy serious consideration. LUCUBRATE, *verb*

I was just lost in the liana of my lucubrations as I unwound the *Times* leader. Rigorous, cleansing prose.

—Durrell, *Constance*, p. 129.

" . . . if they march into Germany, we'll dump on

Moscow: right down in the Kremlin courtyard—"
"And send John Hersey over a month later in a gas
mask to lucubrate on it all—"
—W. Buckley, *Stained Glass*, p. 81.

LUCULENT : *adj* bright, shining

. . . the luculent powers above us would doom us
willy-nilly,
whether we're wicked or virtuous, proud or not.
—Gardner, *Jason and Medeia*, p. 6.

LUCULLAN : *adj* referring to a Roman, Lucius Licinius
Lucullus, famous for his feasts. Compare TRENCHING

Mrs. Cullinane's Lucullan urges were an embarrassment
to herself. She blushed for being such a hog. . . .
—Theroux, *Three Wogs*, p. 12.

LUDIBUND : *adj* playful, frolicsome. See HETERONOMIC

LUPINE : *adj* having to do with wolves. Compare THOOID

For such flirtatious occasions my father had a smile
lupine rather than ursine,† a kind of engagingly slimy
grin. . . .
—DeVries, *Consenting Adults*, p. 10.

LURID : *adj* originally, pale-yellow, washed out; but now,
terrible, ominous, or ghastly

Late that afternoon it began to rain, a gray, smoky rain
that moved back and forth against the mountains like
curtains . . . A day like this—lurid gray sky, gray rain,
gray hills. . . .
—Gardner, *Mickelsson's Ghosts*, p. 154.

LUSORIOUS : *adj* playful

. . . Isabel, lusorious in a pew giggling and clicking her

tongue (always a colophon of her joy). . . .
—Theroux, *Darconville's Cat*, p. 182.

LUSTRATION : *noun* the act of brightening, a purification by cleansing. Compare ABLUTE

Enderby recognised that the coming occasion called for a bath. Lustration before the sacramental meal.
—Burgess, *Enderby*, p. 34.

It lasted a long time, this swim which seemed to have some of the qualities of an esoteric act of lustration.
—Durrell, *Monsieur*, p. 128.

LUXURIOUS : *adj* originally, "sumptuously enjoying" and often used in reference to sexual pleasures. LUXURY, *noun*. Compare LICKERISH, LUBRICITY, RIGGISH

But owing to inexperience he was not the best lover with whom the lady had performed the act of darkness (for she was much practiced in venery,† having inherited a luxurious nature from her mother.)
—Berger, *Arthur Rex*, p. 64.

Lear: Let copulation thrive . . .
         To't, luxury, pell-mell.
            —Shakespeare, *King Lear*, IV, vi, 116, 119.

M

MACHICOLATED : *adj* gap-toothed; furnished with holes, in the floor of a castle's ramparts, for the purpose of depositing unpleasant substances on besiegers. Compare CRENULATED

Machicolated walls grin with the gap-toothed, helot-dwarf expression of the louts in Breughel.
—Durrell, *Monsieur*, p. 232

MACKLE : *verb* to spot, to stain. See IANTHINE. Compare MACULATE, MENALD

MACQUEREAU : *noun* from French for "mackerel"; a pimp. Compare SCOMBROID

This fat one was out to seduce the girl, Victoria Wren, another tourist traveling with her tourist father. But was prevented by the lover, Bongo-Shaftsbury. The old one in tweed—Porpentine†—was the macquereau.
—Pynchon, *V.*, p. 64.

MACULATE : *verb* and *adj* to spot, to stain, to defile. Compare MACKLE, MENALD

Bruises like fermenting plums maculated her thighs.
—Boyle, *Water Music,* p. 194.

... though not a Catholic ... Paul saw the huge sky as
of our Lady's colour, maculate but elegant. ...
—Burgess, *Honey for the Bears,* p. 70.

MAELID : *noun* "apple nymph" (Davenport). Compare AR-
TEMID, DRYAD, MALIC, NAIAD, OREAD

... girls walking with poise of maelids. ...
—Davenport, "The Dawn in Erewhon," *Tatlin!,* p. 236.

MAENAD : *noun* from Greek for "raving"; an orgiastic
nymph

... well here come these cancan girls now, Folies-
Bergères maenads, moving in for the kill, big lipstick
smiles around blazing choppers. ...
—Pynchon, *Gravity's Rainbow,* p. 584.

MAFFICK : *verb* to celebrate a salvation, deliverance; in
reference to the relief of Mafeking, 17 May, 1900, and the
riotious celebrations in London. See TANTIVY

MALAPERT : *adj* saucy, insolent, impudent

... this malapert, threatening ignoramus of an eminence!
—Cozzens, *By Love Possessed,* p. 389.

MALAR : *adj* having to do with the cheek

Whose? *Les yeux morts d'Eurydice,* he says, but sus-
pects they beckon, they and that malar elegance. ...
—Davenport, "The Dawn in Erewhon,"
Tatlin!, p. 205.

MALEBOLGE : *noun* Italian for "evil hell-pit"; Dante's eighth
circle of hell. See also PRESCIND

Even when there are no wars think of the damage they
do. . . .I mean journalists, not goats. There's no punishment on earth fit for them. Only the Malebolge. . . .
                    —Lowry, *Under the Volcano*, p. 100.

MALEFIC : *adj* creating evil or evilly creative

. . . abandoned castles and keeps which still insist, by
their malefic silence and desuetude, that something
momentous and tragic came to pass. . . .
                    —Durrell, *Monsieur*, p. 245.

MALIC : *adj* having to do with apples. See GLANDES.
Compare MAELID

MALINS : *noun* See quotation

"You must never forget, Salim, that they are *malins*."
He used the French word, because the English words he
might have used—"wicked," "mischievous," "bad-
minded"—were not right. The people here were *malins*
the way a dog chasing a lizard was *malin,* or a cat
chasing a bird. The people were *malins* because they
lived with the knowledge of men as prey.
                    —Naipaul, *A Bend in the River,* pp. 55-56.

MALISON : *noun* a curse, a damnation, an anathema, a
malediction

. . . traduce† each day all pillars, pylons, fenceposts,
                                                    stocks
of trees, all shapes ophidian,† all tripod forms;
inveigh against all dangling things, hurl malisons
on winds not shrill, all shapes not bulbous, torous,†
                                                    paggled†
as the belly of a six-months' bride.
                    —Gardner, *Jason and Medeia,* p. 96.

MAMMETS : *noun* female breasts. Compare UNCHIES

Hotspur: I love thee not,
       I care not for thee, Kate: this is no world
       to play with mammets and to tilt with lips:
       —Shakespeare, *Henry IV, Part I,* II, iii, 93-95.

Therefore King Arthur gave to her his arm, onto which she put one hand and then the next, and finally her bosom. And the King was aroused once more, for he had not played at mammets since being a baby, and he had no memory of that time.
       —Berger, *Arthur Rex,* p. 51.

. . . there was a fig tree overshadowing Romulus and Remus, where they sucked on the mother wolf's mammets.
       —Nye, *Falstaff,* p. 6.

MAMMIFORM : *adj* in the form of human female breasts. See AUREATE

MAMMOCK : *verb* to shred, to tear apart. MAMMOCKED, *adj.*

I . . . mammocked a polecat of considerable heft.
       —Rooke, *Shakespeare's Dog,* p. 156.

. . . the shredded, mammocked tree. . . .
       —Gardner, *Jason and Medeia,* p. 69.

MANÈGE : *noun* French for the art of equitation, horsemanship

. . . I had the unfortunate idea of blustering a trifle— shaking her by the scruff of the neck and that sort of thing to cover my real manège. . . .
       —Nabokov, *Lolita,* p. 57.

. . . "Joanie" was in the saddle, ready with inherent female know-how, to sit her caught male with address. This manège had many devices.
       —Cozzens, *By Love Possessed,* pp. 292-293.

MANGOED : *adj* furnished with the fruit of that name or with something that has the same characteristics: pendulous, pulpy, ripe, juicy

She was small and pretty, lean and supple as a weasel through the waist, but mangoed above with breasts that swung provocatively when she bowed to take applause.
—Koster, *Mandragon,* p. 84.

MANTIC : *adj* divining, prophetic. Compare FATIDIC

... this very absence of definitive attitude, this shying away from the mantic or the vatic,† filled me with misgivings.
—Durrell, *Monsieur,* pp. 113-114.

Granted that her vocation as sacred prostitute and prophetess involved considerable orgiastic activity, characteristically cryptic speech, the use of laurel and other mantic drugs, and a certain abandon in costume and coiffure, I saw no good reason why she couldn't come off it a bit with an old friend. . . .
—Barth, *Chimera,* p. 267.

MANTISSA : *noun* See quotation. Compare EXIGUOUS, FILLIP, PARVIS

... to make them waste their vital intellectual aspirations and juices on mantissae.*
*Mantissa: "An addition of comparatively small importance, especially to a literary effort or discourse" *(Oxford English Dictionary).*
—Fowles, *Mantissa,* p. 188.

MARASMIC : *adj* withering, wasting away. Compare ANORECTIC, CACHECTIC, DYSCRASE, INANITION, MARCESCENCE, TABESCENT

... watch out for Northangerland's Cornish catamite, Iago Ink, the merest marasmic atomy of a mortal, a

shrimp, a grub, a monad, less than nothing is. . . .
—Nye, "The Story of Sdeath and Northangerland,"
Tales I Told My Mother, p. 31.

MARCESCENCE : *noun* a drooping, a withering without falling off. MARCESCENT, adj. Compare ANORECTIC, CACHECTIC, DYSCRASE, INANITION, MARASMIC, TABESCENT

. . . a whiff of fresh air, redolent with the marcescence of cones and pines. . . .
—Aczel, *Illuminations,* p. 238.

. . . granting that Mon Cul is a remarkable creature, that he is the elder statesman among monkeys, that his marcescent eyelids have opened upon sights and splendors about which the most romantic among us only dream. . . .
—Robbins, *Another Roadside Attraction,* p. 59-60.

MARGARIC, MARGARITE : *adj* pearly, having a pearly luster. See also EDENTULOUS

. . . a radiant smile . . . that . . . left that traditional after-image of a margaric effulgence†. . . .
—Burgess, *Napoleon Symphony,* p. 221.

MARGENT : *noun* a margin, a border, an edge

The dream had something to do with it: was it that I lingered yet in its sleepish margent?
—Barth, *Giles Goat-Boy,* p. 86.

MARTEL : *verb* to hammer; also, as noun, a brand name for brandy

Enderby had to stop, short of breath, his heart martelling away as though he had just downed a half-bottle of brandy. . . .
—Burgess, *Enderby,* p. 45.

MATTOID : *noun* a partly insane person

> Yunnum Fun all the while hissing like a mattoid. . . .
> —Theroux, *Three Wogs*, p. 26.

MAUGER, MAUGRE : *prep* despite, notwithstanding. See BLORE

MEACOCK : *noun* a cowardly, effeminate person. Compare DRUGGEL, FERBLET, NESH

> College presidents loved meacocks. So everyone tried to please President Greatracks in every way he could.
> —Theroux, *Darconville's Cat*, p. 191.

MELLEIRONIA : *noun* "the state of about to be, with overtones of about to be 20 years old (from somewhere in Plutarch)" (Davenport)

> The melleironia of his slyboots glance. . . .
> —Davenport, "The Dawn in Erewhon,"
> *Tatlin!*, p. 253.

MENALD : *adj* spotted, dappled, variegated. Compare MACKLE, MACULATE

> . . . in a nulliverse, in Rattner's 'menald world' where the only principle is random variation.
> —Nabokov, *Ada*, p. 416.

MENDICITY : *noun* begging

> But mendicity was a popular profession in those days and the competition was fierce. An army of amputees, lepers, pinheads, paralytics, gibberers, slaverers, and whiners lined the streets shoulder to shoulder.
> —Boyle, *Water Music*, p. 37.

MENISCUS : *noun* a crescent shape, a convex or concave lens. Compare LENTICULAR

There was a meniscus of snow on the black mountainside.
                    —Percy, *The Last Gentleman*, p. 338.

. . . finger that fine glass full of smoky grappa or sugary
Strega with a meniscus left by the dying sunlight on the
lagoon's horizon.
                    —Durrell, *Monsieur*, p. 186.

MEPHITIC : *adj* malodorous, stinking. See also AXILLA

. . . *Amanita virosa*, the Destroying Angel himself, described . . . as being one of the most furiously mephitic
members of its aristocratic clan. . . .
                    —Aczel, *Illuminations*, pp. 76-77.

MERDIVOROUS : *adj* French-Latin neologism for excre-
ment-eating. Compare COPROPHAGOUS, EXCREMEN-
TIVOROUSLY

People found a much greater fascination, you see, in
surfing, gamahuching† each other, and flashing through
those merdivorous TV weeklies. . . .
                    —Theroux, "Theroux Metaphrastes,"
                                  Three Wogs, p. 24.

MERKIN : *noun* "A sort of genital toupé, a plume for the
pussy worn by what Mencken almost called stripteuses [and
did call ecdysiasts], and, by the way, used as the [given
name] for the bumbleheaded President in *Dr. Strangelove*,
Merkin Muffley" (Koster). Compare COUN, COUNTRY
MATTERS, COYNTE, DELTA, ESCUTCHEON, FOTZE-
POLITIC, QUIM, QUIMTESSENCE

. . . horns blared dixieland and rumbas, and striptease
dancers flounced their feathered merkins.
                    —Koster, *The Dissertation*, p. 62.

Although I told myself I was looking merely for a
soothing presence, a glorified *pot-au-feu*, an animated

merkin. . . .
—Nabokov, *Lolita,* p. 27.

. . . he wears a false cunt and merkin of sable both handcrafted in Berlin by the notorious Mme. Ophir, the mock labia and bright purple clitoris molded of— Madame had been abject, pleading shortages—synthetic rubber and Mipolam, the new polyvinyl chloride. . . .
—Pynchon, *Gravity's Rainbow,* p. 95.

MESIAL : *adj* relating to the mid-line of the body

. . . a male midriff with navel and hairy mesial groove.
—Davenport. "The Dawn in Erewhon,"
Tatlin!, p. 226.

MESOPYGION : *noun* the crack of the ass

—Even if they have the mesopygion of Ganymedes . . . they steal your time, your rest, your attention. . . .
—Davenport, "Mesoroposthonippidon,"
Eclogues, p. 118.

MEW : *verb* to shut up in something, close in, confine

Having got word in advance from Medina, the Barra-condans have mewed themselves up in their huts and drawn all the water from their wells.
—Boyle, *Water Music,* p. 331.

MIASMA : *noun* odoriferous and gaseous by-product of organic decomposition

A miasma of evil suddenly enveloped Profane from behind; an arm fell like a sack of spuds across his shoulder and into his peripheral vision crept a beer glass surrounded by a large muff, fashioned ineptly from diseased baboon fur.
—Pynchon, *V.,* pp. 13-14.

MICTURATE : *verb* to urinate. MICTURATING, *adj*; MIC-
TURITION, *noun*

"You will now micturate," ordered Captain Salter. "Fall
out." They fell out; the duller men found out quickly
what that long word meant: the road was cosy with the
comfortable warm noise of hissing.
    —Burgess, *The Wanting Seed,* p. 251.

For sanitary reasons, and because it tends to bleach the
hair somewhat, the women prefer a rinse of camel's
urine, which is collected for the purpose (one can always
see a slave or two, cup in hand, pursuing a micturating
camel about the camp).
    —Boyle, *Water Music,* p. 55.

Cahill was an acne-scarred 18 yr. old, somewhat below
the median in intelligence, who presented an innocuous
and winning front, and who had been sentenced to life
imprisonment for sacrilege, public micturition and stealing woolen clothes from tenter grounds.
    —Boyle, *Water Music,* p. 314.

I broke laws regularly—purchasing and consuming con-
trolled substances, driving at a steady sixty-five on
freeways, fornicating in water beds and hot tubs, micturating in public, knowingly and willingly being in the
presence of persons who, etc., etc.
    —Boyle, *Budding Prospects,* p. 11.

MILLIHELEN, MILLIHERM : *nouns* "Erewhonian units of
beauty, feminine and masculine" (Davenport)

. . . the girl was deemed by a jury to be less than five
hundred millihelens. . . .
    —Davenport, "The Dawn in Erewhon,"
        Tatlin!, p. 171.

His penis, however, lacked but three minims of being a

stok in length, and was accorded the full complement of milliherms. . . .
>—Davenport, "The Dawn in Erewhon,"
>*Tatlin!,* p. 172.

MINATORY : *adj* threatening

. . . Miss Shirley Stickles, sharp of eye and pencil if not mind . . . his minatory and becorseted *derrière-garde.*
>—Barth, *Letters,* p. 9.

. . . he smoked dope, said it "mellowed" him out. In fact it did not mellow him out. When he smoked, his eyes narrowed to a minatory stare. . . .
>—C. Buckley, *Steaming to Bamboola,* p. 74.

MINIATE : *verb* literally, "to color red"; refers to illuminating manuscripts with cinnabar, red lead. Compare GULES, RUBESCENT

I trudged all night, through a labyrinth of moonlight, imagining the rustling of extinct animals. Dawn at last miniated my ancient map.
>—Nabokov, *Look at the Harlequins!,* p. 10.

MINIMUS : *noun* the little finger or toe

. . . let us imagine a gigantic hand with its thumb on one star and its minimus on another.
>—Nabokov, *Ada,* p. 544.

MISEMBODIED : *adj* put into the wrong body

. . . she declared herself misembodied: a heroical spirit trapped in a female frame.
>—Barth, *Chimera,* p. 180.

MISOGAMY : *noun* the hatred of marriage

—Philogyny?† I thought you said phylogeny.†
—I said, misogyny† recapitulates philogyny.

—Misogamy. . . .?
—Never mind.

—Gaddis, *The Recognitions*, p. 475.

MISOGYNY : *noun* the hatred of women. See MISOGAMY

MISONEISM : *noun* the hatred for anything new. Compare MISONEIST

" 'Stand still, act effectively?' Typical warning against change, I suppose."
"Highly typical of the misoneism of our age. . . ."

—Aldiss, *The Malacia Tapestry,* p. 16.

MISONEIST : *noun* one who hates anything new. Compare MISONEISM

Lovers of the future yearn really for nature, whereas, misoneists yearn for a pastoral idyll. . . .

—West, *Gala,* p. 47.

MOIL : *verb* to churn, to work woefully, to drudge with dread

. . . in this I put, or rather she put, my so-called virile member, not without difficulty, and I toiled and moiled until I discharged or gave up trying or was begged by her to stop.

—Beckett, *Molloy,* pp. 72-73.

MOLLESCENCE : *noun* a softening, a softness

Fully conversant with temporary mollescences. "George," she whispered lovingly, "George. Relax, baby, relax."

—Aczel, *Illuminations,* p. 59.

MOLLITUDE : *noun* softness

. . . the luxury and mollitude of my first Villa Venus. It was the difference between a den and an Eden.

—Nabokov, *Ada,* p. 353.

MOME : *noun* clown, fool, idiot; "a carping critic" (Samuel Johnson)

"Bate-breeder,† bed-swerver,† thou imperseverant† rancid mome!"
—Rooke, *Shakespeare's Dog,* p. 15.

MOPERY : *noun* loitering, vagrancy

The War must've been lean times for crowd control, murder and mopery was the best you could do, one suspect at a time.
—Pynchon, *Gravity's Rainbow,* p. 570.

MORMAL : *noun* an inflamed sore on the leg. See PATIBULARY

MORPH : *verb* to form, to shape

Scrub and jungle were morphed as by enchantment into lawn and asphalt.
—Koster, *The Dissertation,* p. 54.

MOTILITY : *noun* a condition of mentally sensing movement; feeling as opposed to seeing or hearing

Only in Plotsadika-Chotchki, whose inhabitants are blessed and cursed with a strange motility of mind, could someone stand fully clothed and be accused of nudity.
—Helprin, "Ellis Island," *Ellis Island and Other Stories,* p. 172.

MUCID : *adj* moldy, musty

Hardly down on the mattress, the mucid encompassment took place, he was invested by her.
—Cozzens, *By Love Possessed,* p. 412.

MUCILAGINOUS : *adj* gooey, gluey, viscous, slimy

He eats with his hands, chewing noisily, grunting and belching, sucking the mucilaginous glop from his fingers like a big henna lion lapping at its paws.
—Boyle, *Water Music,* p. 360.

Or perhaps I underestimate the clods? These are men, whatever else, who did not align themselves with the mucilaginous Head and his gang of homicides.
—Nye, *The Voyage of the Destiny,* p. 197.

MUCIN : *noun* proteins found in saliva and mucus

He zips in for a squinny,† mucin in his ringent† jaws, buzzing.
—Davenport, "Au Tombeau de Charles Fourier,"
Da Vinci's Bicycle, p. 80.

MULIEBRIA, MULIEBRITY : *noun* femininity, woman-hood. Compare GYNECIC, GYNECOMORPHOUS

Her soft members, that seemed all preternaturally rounded, achieved . . . effects of excessive muliebrity seldom seen outside Victorian paintings of the so-called Pre-Raphaelite school. . . .
—Cozzens, *By Love Possessed,* p. 380.

I see them dropping the coils of their hair, unfastening their brassieres, rubbing the makeup from their faces. They are soft, heavy, glowing with muliebrity.
—Boyle, "A Woman's Restaurant," *The Descent of Man,* p. 87.

. . . Delvaux's Cretan women half-dressed and richly pelted of muliebria. . . .
—Davenport, "The Dawn in Erewhon,"
Tatlin!, p. 236.

MUNDUNGUS : *noun* from Spanish for "entrails"; in English, the stench of tobacco

There was a faint odor of mundungus in the Sunday morning air, but the sun shone brightly.
—Theroux, *Darconville's Cat,* p. 284.

MUNG : *verb* to mix, to knead

Once when he had had his desktop open and was munging around inside for a book, she, passing down the aisle, had slapped the desktop down on his forearms with all her angry might.
—Gardner, *Mickelsson's Ghosts,* p. 206.

MUNGENCY : *noun* nose noise. Compare EMUNCTION

Ah is an undictionaried word implying joy, rich fatigue, accomplishment, fulfillment. How many such words are missing from the lexicon: the gasp after quenched thirst, the moo at finding food good, bleats and drones of sexual delirium, clucks, smacks, whistles, mungencies, whoops, burbles.
—Davenport, "The Death of Picasso," *Eclogues,* p. 18.

MURGEONING : *adj* contorting, writhing

All murgeoning dance when linked with mind and vehicular flesh. . . .
—Davenport, "The Dawn in Erewhon,"
Tatlin!, p. 252.

MURINE : *adj* concerning mice

Souris was not a murine man. He was very gross and he sweated what looked like crude oil.
—Burgess, *Enderby,* p. 320.

MURLED : *adj* crumbling, disintegrating

. . . various strigulous† pinks and muscadines in its murled heights.
—Davenport, "The Dawn in Erewhon,"
Tatlin!, p. 201.

MUSACEOUS :   *adj*   concerning the genus *Musa*, bananas or plantains

> . . . the fragile musaceous odor of Breakfast: flowery permeating, surprising, more than the color of winter sunlight taking over not so much through any brute pungency or volume as by the high intricacy to the weaving of its molecules, sharing the conjuror's secret by which—though it is not often, Death is told so clearly to fuck off. . . .
>
> —Pynchon, *Gravity's Rainbow,* p. 10.

MUSTH :   *noun*   from Urdu. See quotation

> . . . I entered the elephant lines, passing the stockades where the elephants in musth were kept. For three months in the year the male elephant goes mad and is extremely dangerous to handle.
>
> —Loyd-Jones, *Lord of the Dance,* p. 132.

MYTHOMANIAC :   *noun*   See quotation.

> "Do you know what a mythomaniac is?"
> The Ump threw me a look of wild alarm. "You mean I might be harboring a nut in the house?"
> "No, no," I said, suppressing a pang of my own at what had been another of Rose's words. "This is harmless fantasizing, they call it. People who tell fibs."
> "Oh," the Ump says with relief. "Liars."
> "Well, it's not that exactly. Less, and more. They weave this whole, like, tissue of stuff about themselves, that usually has a lot of wish fulfillment to it."
> "There's a lot of that going around," said the Ump.
>
> —DeVries, *Into Your Tent I'll Creep,* p. 183.

MYXOID :   *adj*   literally, "snot"; mucus. See HYDRANTH

N

NACREOUS : *adj* having to do with nacre, mother-of-pearl

... her unknown heart, her nacreous liver, the sea-grapes of her lungs, her comely twin kidneys.
—Nabokov, *Lolita,* p. 167.

She dreams often of the same journey: a passage by train, between two well-known cities, lit by that same nacreous wrinkling the films use to suggest rain out a window.
—Pynchon, *Gravity's Rainbow,* p. 471.

NAIAD : *noun* an aquatic nymph. Compare ARTEMID, DRYAD, OREAD, MAELID

... the record—*Le Sacre du Printemps*—caught in the groove with a gnashing squeal as if a stageful of naiads, dryads† and spandex satyrs had simultanously gone lame.
—Boyle, *Budding Prospects,* p. 4.

NATES : *noun* buttocks. Compare HURDIES, PRAT

... the swellings of her tense narrow nates clothed in black, and the seaside of her schoolgirl thighs.
—Nabokov, *Lolita,* p. 44.

NEAPNESS : *noun* the tidal condition of being at the lowest high-water level

All I sense is the current neapness! If Bellerophon might rebegin, unclogged, unsilted! Time and tide, however, et cetera.

—Barth, *Chimera,* p. 145.

NEB : *noun* nib, tip, bill. See PELLICULE

NECTAREOUSLY : *adv* excessively sweetly

Watching a nectareously obsequious or cretinously eye-rolling announcer on the television, the patrons were not regaled. . . .

—Exley, *A Fan's Notes,* p. 266.

NEMORAL : *adj* grove-dwelling

Its archaic handsomeness, nemoral and chthonic,† is the palustral† involution of the vagina folded out and distended, cave become tower. . . .

—Davenport, "The Dawn in Erewhon," *Tatlin!,* p. 155.

NEPOPHILE : *noun* lover of a nephew or niece

. . . my rival Phineus, who lusted after Andromeda . . . avuncular nepophile.

—Barth, *Chimera,* p. 65.

NEROTIC : *adj* characteristic of the Roman Emperor Nero; hence, sexually psychotic. Compare CALIGULAR

I had nothing at all to do but spin indolent daydreams of absolute authority—Nerotic, Caligular† authority of the sort that summons up officefuls of undergraduate girls, hot and submissive—leering professorial dreams

—Barth, *The End of the Road,* p. 89.

NESCIENCE : *noun* ignorance, of the cosmic, universal sort. Compare IGNAVIA, NIHILISCIENT

I have two really huge sturgeon—giants—brought live, in immense vats, now swimming in blissful nescience of their impending ah quietus.
—Burgess, *Napoleon Symphony,* p. 221.

At last with a groan she turned and tore away this veil of nescience, and made her yawning way to the lavatory. . . .
—Durrell, *Constance,* p. 280.

NESH : *adj* soft, delicate, prissy. Compare FERBLET, MEACOCK

. . . he saw nesh intellectuals and heard them giggling and bleating. That sort of café then.
—Burgess, *Napoleon Symphony,* p. 230.

NICTITATION : *noun* winking

. . . [a] blundering Cadillac half entered my driveway before retreating in a flurry of luminous nictitation.
—Nabokov, *Pale Fire,* p. 160.

NIHILISCIENT : *adj* See quotation. Compare IGNAVIA, NESCIENCE

". . . your supreme omnipotent nihiliscient majesty—"
"That word, what was that word?"
"A neologism. *Nichtswissend.* Nothingknowing."
—Burgess, *Napoleon Symphony,* p. 237.

NINNYHAMMER : *noun* a simple fool. See LOOBY

NOCTIVAGANT : *adj* night-wandering. Compare DIVAGATE

. . . noctivagant beings shackled to earth. . . .
—Gardner, *Jason and Medeia,* p. 58.

Unhappily, we lost the big fellow, Smirke, to noctiva-gant predators some days back. . . .
—Boyle, *Water Music,* p. 363.

NONSEQUITUR : *verb* (from noun) to say something that does not follow logically a previous statement

"... I am fed up with women taking over."
"What does that have to do with removing the Painted Bird?"
"Everything."
"Do you want to tell me more? Feel free to talk."
"Beebody has been good to me," the hard hat nonsequitured.
    —Eastlake, *Dancers in the Scalphouse,* p. 108.

NOUGHT, NAUGHT : *noun* 1) nothing; 2) see quotation

"Nought," I said, "your honor. An Elizabethan term meaning mistress or lover. Actually, nought being represented as a circle, it signifies the organ of ingress. It was in very common use."
    —Burgess, *Earthly Powers,* p. 490.

Snout: ... he is a very paramour for a sweet voice.
Flute: You must say "paragon"; a paramour is, God bless us, a thing of naught.
  —Shakespeare, *A Midsummer-Night's Dream,* IV, ii, 11-14

NOX : *noun* night. See PATIBULARY

NUCHAL : *adj* having to do with the nape of the neck

A nuchal kiss, daddled foreskin, tongue and whisper into an ear together.
    —Davenport, "On Some Lines of Virgil,"
                Eclogues, p. 233.

NUMEN : *noun* "divine power, deity" (Fowles). NUMINOUS, *adj*

"Never mind what it is. Look at it. Look into its eyes."
He was right. The little sunlit thing had some numen; or not so much divinity, as a having known divinity, in it;

of being ultimately certain.
>—Fowles, *The Magus*, p. 147.

Religion is increasingly confirmed as satisfying a numinous passion in all of us. . . .
>—Burgess, *The End of the World News*, p. 211.

Voluminous is next to numinous. Air has no memory, not of us, at least, any more than a deity needs a potato peeler.
>—West, *Out of My Depths*, p. 119.

. . . all those earlier Slothrops packing Bibles around the blue hilltops as part of their gear, memorizing chapter and verse the structures of Arks, Temples, Visionary Thrones— all the materials and dimensions. Data behind which always, nearer or farther, was the numinous certainty of God.
>—Pynchon, *Gravity's Rainbow*, pp. 241-242.

NUPSON : *noun* a fool, an idiot. Compare BOANTHROP, DODDIPOL, JOBBERNOWL

"What a nupson you can be, John Martin!"
>—Davenport, "John Charles Tapner,"
>*Da Vinci's Bicycle*, p. 50.

NUSUS : *noun* See quotation

"What," he gasped, "are the grounds?"
She smiled sweetly. . . . "The Muslims have a useful short word—*nusus*. It means the unwillingness of one of the marital partners to cohabit with the other."
>—Burgess, *The End of the World News*, p. 114.

NUTATIONAL : *adj* nodding. Compare DAVVEN

. . . Saturn's rings to whirl, moons their precessions, our own Earth its nutational wobble. . . .
>—Pynchon, *V.*, p. 239.

O

OBJURGATORY : *adj* rebuking, scolding. OBJURGA-
TIONS, *noun*

> . . . we heard objurgatory Tamil and metallic slaps. . . .
> —Burgess, *Earthly Powers*, p. 237.

> He used a lot of bad language under his breath, . . . but
> what the target of these objurgations was he could not
> say. . . .
> —Durrell, *Constance*, pp. 322-323.

OBLIQUITY : *noun* a going off at an angle, deviance, diver-
gence. Compare ABAXIAL, LOXODROMIC

> Adventure itself, bringing them through the random,
> compassless, ever swerving obliquity of tenuously joined
> place and across the stumbled, almost drunken vaulting
> of nameless . . . duchies and borders and diminishing
> jurisdictions. . . .
> —Elkin, *George Mills*, pp. 11-12.

> Father had a slight edge in the sly obliquities and
> ornately subtle ironies. . . .
> —DeVries, *Slouching Towards Kalamazoo*, p. 77.

169

OB-MANIPULATIONS : *noun* See quotation.

"I've remained absolutely true to you because those were only 'ob-manipulations' (sham, insignificant strokings by unremembered cold hands)."
—Nabokov, *Ada,* p. 195.

OCCAMY : *noun* an imitation silver

. . . the occamy spangles of once-proud concubines.
—Gardner, *Jason and Medeia,* p. 289.

OCCUPY : *verb* of a man, to copulate with a woman; considered extremely vulgar in the sixteenth century and subsequently fell into desuetude.

The healthy young Danes . . . with acrobatic aplomb, occupied forty-six times a minute 77.715 cubic inches of the same space, elastic and sussultatory.†
—Davenport, "The Dawn in Erewhon,"
Tatlin!, p. 202.

OCELLATE : *verb* to equip with spots that resemble eyes, as on an ocelot

The girl is no other than Ada Bredow, a first cousin of mine whom I flirted with disgracefully that very summer, the sun of which ocellates the garden table and her bare arms.
—Nabokov, *Look at the Harlequins!,* p. 169.

ODORIFEREN : *noun* a smell-producing or bearing thing

He smells like a foot, that over there. His whole body is like one large nonshapen foot in terms of odoriferens.
—DeLillo, *Ratner's Star,* p. 144.

OGDOAD : *noun* a group of eight. See PATIBULARY

OLEAGINOUS : *adj* oily, greasy; unctuously urbane

... the quality of the music—blurred, distorted in the tutti, too much (obligatory at the time) oleaginous saxophone.
—Burgess, *Earthly Powers,* p. 309.

"If you want a son so badly," Rebeca might say as they lay in the oleaginous post coital stifle of a dry season night ... "if your vanity demands a reproduction of yourself, please try your wife. There are sufficient bastards in this world already."
—Koster, *The Dissertation,* p. 32.

OLISBOS : *noun* a leather phallus used in the Dionysian Rites. See also BAUBON. Compare DILDO, DOLICHO-PHALLIC, HERMSPRONG, ITHYPHALLIC

I had blazed in her face an olisbos-like flashlight.
—Nabokov, *Lolita,* p. 96.

OLLA-PODRIDA : *noun* Spanish for "rotten pot"; a stew, a potpourri

... the usual olla-podrida of undergraduate worries and boasts. ...
—Theroux, *Darconville's Cat,* p. 406.

OMNIFUTUANT : *adj* all-fucking

He was probably an omnifutuant swine who could do it with anything.
—Burgess, *Earthly Powers,* p. 96.

ONEIRIC : *adj* dreamlike, dreaming

At night they watched the fireworks—fountains, spark-foaming rockets, yellow starbursts high over Poland. That oneiric season. ... There was no one in all the spas to read anything in the patterns the fires made.
—Pynchon, *Gravity's Rainbow,* p. 475.

ONEIROTIC : *adj* having to do with erotic dreams

. . . three young ladies, now suddenly divested of their clothes (a well-known oneirotic device). . . .
—Nabokov, *Ada*, p. 354.

Learning may be the enemy of thinking, and thinking, of learning. I have never known which I wanted and so am left with oneirotic circuses: fiction—the other barber in the mirror, shaving the other you.
—Theroux, *Darconville's Cat*, p. 333.

ONOMASTIC : *adj* having to do with names, especially their origins and forms

Courtland Willett: the sort of phony name an actor might take on. Willett . . . must have seen this onomastic scepticism in Val's eye. . . .
—Burgess, *The End of the World News*, p. 59.

OOIDAL : *adj* having to do with an egg or eggs

For the place was run by an ooidal-shaped sow with chin hairs, a venomous breath, and a grit-colored hair who always carried a ladle and trounced her girls.
—Theroux, *Darconville's Cat*, p. 143.

OOLOGY : *noun* the study of birds' eggs

"One cannot," he said with a triteness that surprised him only when it was too late to retreat from the locution, "make an omlette without breaking eggs. . . ." "We're concerned less with oology than herology, if there is such a term. And if there isn't," she said with a kind of young-miss bluntness, "there ought to be."
—Burgess, *Napoleon Symphony*, p. 342.

OPHIDIAN : *adj* serpentlike. See also MALISON. Compare COLUBRINE, HERPETINE

It was a hiss: faint, sibilant, saurian, nasty. . . . As I drew closer it became apparent that the hissing was not an expression of ophidian rage but rather the constant fulminating rush of burning gas.
—Boyle, *Budding Prospects,* p. 283.

OPSIMATH : *noun* someone who began to study late in life

. . . pathologically self-defensive opsimaths. . . .
—Theroux, *Darconville's Cat,* p. 71.

OPUNTIA : *noun* either a prickly pear or Indian fig. See PATIBULARY

ORCHIDACEOUS : *adj* from the Greek for "testicles"; having the characteristics of testicles or of orchids. Compare CULLION, DOUCET, STEREODIDYMOUS

. . . grandfather's balls. This was a sweet dish: cream enclosed in light pastry and plunged briefly into hot fat, little orchidaceous gobbets served with plum jam.
—Burgess, *Earthly Powers,* pp. 308-309.

ORCHIDEOUS : *adj* a portmanteau of the Greek for "testicle" and of "hideous." Compare TETRORCHID

Suddenly all dimples, she beamed sweetly at them, as she never did at my orchideous masculinity. . . .
—Nabokov, *Lolita,* p. 173.

OREAD : *noun* mountain nymph. See ARTEMID. Compare DRYAD, MAELID, NAIAD

OREXIS : *noun* desire, appetite. ORECTIC, *adj.* See also EUTRIPSIA

A sweet orexis rising in his cock. . . .
—Davenport, "The Dawn in Erewhon,"
Tatlin!, p. 238.

ORT : *noun* something left over, as from a meal: dinner scrap

Skip's Museum was a museum of mortal remains—of endoskeletons and exoskeletons—of shells, coral, bone, cartilage, and chiton—of dottles and orts and residua of souls long gone.
                    —Vonnegut, *The Sirens of Titan*, p. 24.

OUBLIATION : *noun* from French "oubliette" (oblivion), a well in a castle used to dispose of unwanted persons; thus the act, the process of being so disposed

And one thing I thought was that the creature comforts of the dungeon did nothing to mitigate the basic fact of oubliation.
                    —Vonnegut, *Cat's Cradle*, p. 214.

OUNCE : *noun* from French for a medium-sized feline, such as a lynx or a snow leopard. See DOUCET. Compare PARD

OUTASE : *noun* See quotation

"Outase," sez Enzian, which is one of many Herero words for shit, in this case a large, newly laid cow turd.
                    —Pynchon, *Gravity's Rainbow*, p. 325.

OXTER : *noun* British dialect for "armpit" from the Latin "axilla." Compare AXILLA, AXILLARY

. . . she held out gold blades of arms, gold foil gleaming in her oxters. And gold below on the mount.
                    —Burgess, *Enderby*, p. 399.

. . . we met this old-fashioned knight. . . .Helmed, armoured, encased in plate inches-thick. A dirty great lance under his oxter, couched at the ready. . .a chain-mail freak.
                    —Nye, *Faust*, p. 164.

OXYMORON : *noun* from Greek for "sharp-dull"; a paradoxical or ironic expression composed of two or more words that normally would not be used together

It was perfectly in key with all her other behavior, and to be described only by oxymoron; luring-receding, subtle-simple, proud-begging, defending-accusing.
— Fowles, *The French Lieutenant's Woman,* p. 351.

An oxymoron . . . Wisely Foolish.
— Lowry, *Under the Volcano,* p. 274.

EXAMPLES OF OXYMORONS

It seems to me that some people choose their vocations by a sort of inspired default, you know? A passionate lack of alternatives.
— Barth, *Chimera,* p. 186.

If out of my meager vocabulary only the term *unenthusiastic excitement* comes anywhere near describing the feeling with which all my thoughts were suffused, you must resolve my meaning from that term's dissonance.
— Barth, *The Floating Opera,* p. 205.

Prinz's peculiar, unaggressive forcefulness and inarticulate suasion. . . .
— Barth, *Letters,* p. 208.

. . . smirking in genial cruelty. . . .
— Berger, *Arthur Rex,* p. 202.

Probably even the tortoise
Moves with a sort of leisurely impetuosity. . . .
— Burgess, *The End of the World News,* p. 119.

One of the enchantments Hollier had for me was this quality of possessive indifference. He must know I worship him, but he never gives me a chance to prove it.
— Davies, *The Rebel Angels,* p. 81.

. . . one of those academic capons whom a lifetime of

unchallenged pontificating in the classroom has left with the conviction that they are also arresting outside it. The term "interesting bore" springs helpfully to mind.

—DeVries, *Slouching Towards Kalamazoo,* pp. 216-217.

Then I walk about the town at night with a sort of strenuous numbness, looking keenly about me, as if for a friend.

—Durrell, *Monsieur,* p. 290.

P

PAEAN, PAEN: *noun* a song or shout of praise

> . . . I suppose he and Mistress Stander whispered paeans to the absent monarch between couplings.
> —Cameron, *Our Jo,* p. 9.

PAGGLE : *verb* to bulge, to swell, to be pregnant. See MALISON

PALIMPSEST : *noun* paper or parchment from which previous writing has been erased

> Then I withdrew to escape her claws, which had already made my poor back and face a palimpsest of music paper that needed only the notes pricked out to sing "Woe, for my love lies bleeding" by.
> —Cameron, *Our Jo,* p. 52.

PALINDROME : *noun* 1) a sentence which reads the same backwards as forwards; 2) a bisexual; 3) someone who does things backwards as well as forwards; 4) someone who participates in mutual oral sex. PALINDROMIC, *adj.* See also ALDERMANIC

> —I am one to tell you, my lord, Stanley and a palin-

drome are making the beast with two backs†. . . .
    —Gaddis, *The Recognitions,* p. 477.

PALMERIN :   *noun*   a chivalric hero of sixteenth-century Spanish romances. See PATIBULARY

PALPEBRAL :   *adj*   having to do with eyelids. Compare SUBPALPEBRAL

The eyes had kept their voluptuous palpebral creases; the lashes, their semblance of jet-dust incrustation. . . .
    —Nabokov, *Ada,* p. 215.

PALUSTRAL :   *adj*   swampy, marshy

Here Ford and Hemingway corrected the palustral proofs of *The Making of Americans.*
    —Davenport, "Au Tombeau de Charles Fourier,"
      Da Vinci's Bicycle, p. 98.

PANDECT :   *noun*   a book of everything

. . . the old 45 records . . . each one a pandect of incontrovertible yammer and windsong. . . .
    —Theroux, *Three Wogs,* p. 63.

PANTICIVORE :   *noun*   See quotation. Compare PORCIPOPHAGIC

A certain gentleman—not one of those sausage-eating—or how might one neologize it—panticivore—Teuton beer-swillers. . . .
    —Burgess, *Napoleon Symphony,* p. 223.

PAPILLARY :   *adj*   having to do with buds or nipples. See also HYDRANTH

The Wartburg. That castle near Eisenach. Like a wart it is, too. A brown papillary excrescence on top of a hill.
    —Nye, *Faust,* p. 9.

PAPYROMANCY : *noun* See quotation

> ... Säure really turns out to be an adept at the difficult art of papyromancy, the ability to prophesy through contemplating the way people roll reefers.
> —Pynchon, *Gravity's Rainbow,* p. 442.

PARACHRONIC : *adj* anachronistic, out of correct historical time. See also FINNEGANSWAKE. Compare EXOLETE, PRETERIST

> Paul squinted at his wrist-watch, his only stitch of clothing (no matter how intense and parachronic the abandon, he never took it off.) ...
> —Burgess, *Honey for the Bears,* p. 25.

PARACLETE : *noun* supporter, comforter; sometimes the Holy Spirit. See PSITTACEOUSLY

PARANYMPH : *noun* bridesmaid or groomsman

> ... Lucette turned out to be, against all reason and will, the impeccable paranymph.
> —Nabokov, *Ada,* p. 337.

PARAPHIMOSIS : *noun* an irremediable retraction of the foreskin

> ... a kind of paraphimosis of the nose.
> —Theroux, *Three Wogs,* p. 174.

> ... same little abortive moustache, same little ferrety eyes, same paraphimosis of the nose, and a thin red mouth that looked as if it was raw from trying to shit its tongue.
> —Beckett, *Molloy,* p. 204.

PARD : *noun* archaic for leopard, panther. See EMPASM. Compare OUNCE

PARESIS : *noun* paralysis, general or slight. PARETIC, *adj*

And yet I feel that during three weeks of general paresis (if that is what it was) I have gained some experience.
—Nabokov, *Look at the Harlequins!*, p. 239.

. . . advertising, whose open chancres gaped everywhere, only a symptom of the great disease, this plague of newness, this febrile,† finally paretic seizure dictated by the beadledom of time monitored by clocks. . . .
—Gaddis, *The Recognitions*, p. 320.

PARLAMBLING : *noun* literally, "walking talk"; rambling speech

. . . Heidegger's parlamblings on "Nothing" and "Not" and "the Nothing that Nothings" were the last supposedly respectable gasp of classical philosophy. . . .
—Gardner, *Mickelsson's Ghosts*, p. 4.

PARLOUS : *adj* perilous

As if they possessed some tropism for grace which sifted them through danger and past all pitfalls' parlous, aleatory,† dicey circumstances. . . . .
—Elkin, *George Mills*, p. 5.

PARONOMASTIC : *adj* playing on the sound of words, punning

It wasn't the simple finality of death—which could have been a relief, even a truce between him and his paronomastic God. . . .
—Aczel, *Illuminations*, p. 234.

PARTHENIC : *adj* virginal, unfertilized. Compare AUTOFRUCTIFEROUS

Clarissa was fairly secure, un-get-at-able in her bright parthenic status of just Hendy. . . .
—Cozzens, *By Love Possessed*, p. 103.

PARVIS : *adj* 1) small; 2) often referring to a church porch or courtyard. Compare EXIGUOUS, FILLIP, MANTISSA

A professional photograph . . . including the common-place sweep of a bride's ectoplasmic† veil, partly blown by a parvis breeze athwart the groom's trousers. . . .
—Nabokov, *Ada,* p. 6.

PATIBULARY : *adj* "delicate in motion, graceful and muffled as in the quiet sound made by ballet slippers. Only to be used in winter and at night" (Helprin)

Mrs. Gamely's vocabulary was enormous. She knew words no one had ever heard of, and she used words every day that had been mainly dead or sleeping for hundreds of years. Virginia checked them in the Oxford dictionary, and found that (almost without exception) Mrs. Gamely's usage was flawlessly accurate. For instance, she spoke of certain kinds of dogs as Leviners.† She called the areas near Quebec march-lands. She referred to diclesiums,† liripoops,† rapparees,† dagswains,† bronstrops,† caroteels,† opuntias† and soughs. She might describe something as patibulary, fremescent,† pharisaic, Roxburghe,† or glockamoid,† and words like mormal,† jeropigia,† endosmic,† mage, palmerin,† thos,† vituline,† Turonian,† galingale,† comprodor,† nox,† gaskin,† secotine,† ogdoad,† and pintulary† fled from her lips in Pierian† saltarellos.†
—Helprin, *Winter's Tale,* p. 203.

PAUCIPLICATE : *adj* simple, uncomplicated, unsophisticated. Compare BANAUSIC, NINNYHAMMER

"Marriage is cannabalism! Pauciplicate vanity!"
—Theroux, *Darconville's Cat,* p. 437.

PAVID : *adj* frightened

. . . little pavid sandwichmen who gave their lives to religion. . . .
—Theroux, *Three Wogs*, p. 157.

PAVONINE : *adj* relating to peacocks

. . . the pavonine sun was all eyes on the gravel under the flowering trees. . . .
—Nabokov, *Lolita*, p. 165.

PAWK, PAWKERY : *noun* gadget; trick, stunt. See also FAITERY

Knowledge
was all, in the end; the pawks in the book he'd leave
to the future
if luck allowed its survival.
—Gardner, *Jason and Medeia*, p. 244.

PEDESTRIAN : *adj* 1) dull, undistinguished; 2) on foot, walking

Five minutes out on Route 17 he decided if he ever got back to the Trocadero unmaimed and alive to forget about Rachel and only be interested thenceforth in quiet, pedestrian girls. She drove like one of the damned on holiday.
—Pynchon, *V.*, p. 24.

PEDICATE : *verb* to bugger. See also ANDROCRAT

. . . Madame de Staël has gone so far in depravity that she is regularly pedicated by goats from the famous herd of the late Monsieur Voltaire.
—Burgess, *Napoleon Symphony*, p. 204.

PEDOMORPHIC : *adj* child-like

. . . much-admired Totenkopfverband, the Death's Head

Detachment— ... his pedomorphic playmates in the romper room of death. . . .
—Aczel, Illuminations, p. 217.

PEDOPHAGE : *noun* child-eating. Compare TEKNOPHAGY

Everbody was mad. . . .when I tried to close the bars he talked them into eating their babies. . . .I quite believed in order, measure, self-discipline, and was opposed on principle to indiscriminate house-wife orgy, not to mention pedophage.
—Barth, Chimera, p. 73.

PEENED : *adj* beaten thin with a hammer

... his face, through which shows the peened, the tenderized soul of a fighter who's not only taken dives, but also thought heavily about them all the way down.
—Pynchon, Gravity's Rainbow, p. 541.

PELAGIC : *adj* having to do with the wide, open, high seas

The stiffened corpses were dragged from their irons and tossed into the spume, where quick pelagic sharks fought over the remains.
—Boyle, Water Music, p. 186.

Out there on the plateaus of his loneliness he feels the freezing pelagic spray drying on his cheeks.
—Durrell, Monsieur, p. 239.

PELF : *noun* money, wealth; usually refers to ill-gotten gains

"You are a worthy knight," said Merlin. "One day you will know the value of your service and be well-rewarded."
But Sir Hector did frown. . . ."I do nothing for love of pelf," he said stoutly.
"Or love of self?" asked Merlin with his unique sense of

irony, quite foreign to the mortals of that straightfor-
ward time. . . .

—Berger, *Arthur Rex,* p. 18.

PELLICULE : *noun* literally, "small skin"; a thin membrane
such as that covering the clitoris

. . . her neb† of high-spirited flesh under its pellicule,
which when thrummed, wiggled, twitched, quivered,
licked, bobbled, joggled, launched her into a rapture.
—Davenport, "On Some Lines of Virgil,"
Eclogues, p. 180.

PENANNULAR : *adj* almost circular, like a ring with an
opening on its circumference. Compare SECOTINE

She brought it to her work-table in the penannular bow-
window. . . .
—Beckett, "Draff," *More Pricks than Kicks,* p. 177.

PENETRALIA : *noun* the inner sanctum, deepest recess.
Compare ABDITORY

The Aggregat is on route, nothing can be changed. No
one else here cares for the penetralia of the moment, or
last mysteries: There have been too many rational years.
—Pynchon, *Gravity's Rainbow,* p. 426.

Yet, paradoxically, if one wants to measure and compre-
hend the enormity of the beast, one must dissect it,
divide it into its component parts, enter into its penetralia, cut up its entrails.

—Aczel, *Illuminations,* p. 296.

Then you must be initiated to these *penetralia* and their
mysteries.

—Foxell, *Carnival,* p. 99.

PERCEPT : *noun* something taken, by way of something
else, one step beyond a concept; something perceived

To prefer just to *be* with somebody else, to engage of one's own free will in spiritual intimacy with another, that was true adultery.

It had been easy enough to accept this view of morality with one's brain, thought Edwin. It was when promiscuity changed from a concept to a percept that trouble began.

—Burgess, *The Doctor Is Sick,* pp. 13-14.

PERDURABLE : *adj* in ordinary terms, "everlasting," but short of eternal

"Everybody wants to get back to simplicity. Windmills, tidepower, little communes in Vermont. Nobody has the faintest understanding of, well, you know, the *awful* part, the perdurable evils." The catch came to his voice. Mickelsson squinted at him, thinking about the word *perdurable*.

—Gardner, *Mickelsson's Ghosts,* p. 107.

Not into a built-up and spent one like mine, but one enviably perdurable, spasm after spasm, until . . . convulsions set in. . . .

—Davenport, "On Some Lines of Virgil,"
Eclogues, p. 180.

PERFERVID : *adj* continuously feverish, ardently impassioned, zealous. Compare ECSTATIC, FEBRILE

. . . an old engraving—a beastly old Rembrandt exhaling the perfervid gloom of Protestantism and a diet of turnips.

—Durrell, *Monsieur,* p. 184.

PERFICIENTLY : *adv* decisively, effectively

His jeans were perficiently his by dint of pliant fit and accidence of bleachsores in seams and creases and in the

weathering wash of the scotched edging of fly and
pockets.
>　　　—Davenport, "On Some Lines of Virgil,"
>　　　　　　　　　　　*Eclogues,* p. 176.

PERICHORESIS : *noun* literally, "dancing around"; a theo-
logical term for God-in-Christ or Christ-in-God. Compare
THEANDRIC

. . . perichoresis. An isolation that was, at the same time,
begotten by an interpenetration.
>　　　—Lowry, *October Ferry to Gabriola,* p. 251.

PERIPETEIA : *noun* a change of fortune, a revolution

. . . Miss Gertie Girdle, whom he was to (and wished to)
marry in the very near future, in order to consummate
with her the act that was just a little intimidating to a
chaste young man, the strange act whose occult peripeteia transforms a young bint† from the virginal state
into the pregnant state.
>　　　—Queneau, *We Always Treat Women
>　　　　　　　　　　　Too Well,* p. 120.

PERIPTERAL : *adj* having columns on both sides

On the terrace of Larue, under the soiled statue of the
Madeleine's peripteral imposture. . . .
>　　　—Gaddis, *The Recognitions,* p. 74.

PERLUSTRATION : *noun* examination, scrutiny. Compare
SCRUTABLE

. . . a thorough perlustration of the loot that Andron
and Niagarushka had obtained. . . .
>　　　—Nabokov, *Pale Fire,* p. 255.

PERORATE : *verb* to speak longwindedly

Various machine-guns that the British must have cached

in the piles of wood began to perorate. Shrill bursts of
fire spattered the facade.

> —Queneau, *We Always Treat Women
> Too Well,* p. 102.

PESSARY : *noun* originally, a stone used as a suppository for
birth control; other materials are now used

Haiphong. For some reason the word had pharmaceuti-
cal sexual connotations for me and I never saw it
without thinking of a pessary.
"Insert your haiphong, darling, and let's fuck."

> —Exley, *Pages from a Cold Island,* p. 51.

PETRESCENCE, PETRIFACTION : *noun* becoming stone.
PETRIFACIENT, *adj*

"Sir, how does a man die when he's deprived of the
consolations of literature?"
"In one of two ways," he said, "petrescence of the heart
or atrophy of the nervous system."

> —Vonnegut, *Cat's Cradle,* p. 189.

... three Gorgons—snakehaired, swinetoothed, buz-
zardwinged, brassclawed—whereof ... only the middle
one, Medusa, was mortal, decapitable and petrifacient.

> —Barth, *Chimera,* p. 62.

PETROUS : *adj* rocky, stony

... he dashed their petrous visages with waves from
distinctly pagan tongues, voluptuous Italian, which flowed
over their northern souls like sunlit water over rocks.

> —Gaddis, *The Recognitions,* p. 24.

PHALANSTERY : *noun* from the Greek for "phalanx" or
"compact mass"; used by Charles Fourier for a "communal
building," a "socialistic monastery"

Wasps the meanwhile built several phalansteries in a china cabinet. . . .
> —Davenport, "The Invention of Photography in Toledo," *Da Vinci's Bicycle,* p. 126.

PHILOGYNY : *noun* the love of women or womanhood. See MISOGAMY

PHILONOETIC : *adj* intellectual. See DECUSSATED. Compare DIANOETIC

PHOCINE : *adj* having to do with seals or walruses

My darling . . . retreated to her mat near her phocine mamma.
> —Nabokov, *Lolita,* p. 44.

PHOTIC : *adj* having to do with light

A small patch of countryside kept floating before my eyes like some photic illusion. . . .
> —Nabokov, *Look at the Harlequins!,* p. 75.

Then sleep came—we were entering the countries of sadness, deep below the photic zone with its huge gogglefish, where in the darkness the real task outlines itself like a sort of flare-path, namely, how to make sense of oneself.
> —Durrell, *Monsieur,* p. 205.

PHRATRY : *noun* clan, brotherhood, fraternity

Clients must always be handled indirectly, through a specific phratry trained specifically *and* extensively in customer relations.
> —Aczel, *Illuminations,* p. 363.

PHTHISTIC : *adj* having to do with a lung disease

Säure has been calling him "Yankee Pig" all day now . . . often getting no further than "Yank__" before

collapsing into some horrible twanging phthistic wheeze of a laugh. . . .
—Pynchon, *Gravity's Rainbow*, p. 683.

PHYLOGENY : *noun*   the development or evolution of a group of living things. See MISOGAMY

PHYSIOCRAT : *noun*   a land-owner, and specifically, one who believes that all wealth derives from real estate

They were recruited from among the restless sons of provincial physiocrats, but for sometime failed to outnumber the society's symbols. . . .
—Koster, *The Prince*, p. 28.

PI : *verb*   1) the Greek letter "P"; 2) a printer's term for unsorting or discarding type; hence, to mix and jumble

As in a dream he watches Cockburn's men destroy the newspaper office, piing the type into Pennsylvania Avenue and wrecking the presses.
—Barth, *Letters*, p. 511.

PIACULAR : *adj*   appeasing, atoning, expiating, propitiating. See AUTOPTIC

PIERIAN : *adj*   referring to poetry and learning; from Piera, in ancient northern Thessaly, reputed home of the muses. See PATIBULARY

PILIGEROUS, PILIGINOUS : *adj*   bearing or wearing hair

It was cold, gray, half an hour before sunrise. Quick piliginous things flashed through the under-growth, birds nattered, a breath of stagnation soured the air.
—Boyle, *Water Music*, p. 182.

PINGUID : *adj*   full of fat, greasy

The rabble is shouting now, pink mouths like wounds in the dark pinguid faces.
>—Boyle, *Water Music,* p. 425.

PINTULARY : *adj* relating to penises, pins, or bolts. See PATIBULARY

PISTAREEN : *noun* a small colonial Spanish coin; hence, something trivial, picayune

... pistareen.... It is a debased coin, and as such the best symbol of the age in which we live, all of us together in the soup under the soupistareen.
>—Lowry, *October Ferry to Gabriola,* p. 171.

PIXILATED : *adj* literally, "possessed by pixies"; 1) pleasurably disturbed, bewitched, befuddled; 2) drunk

They bent over, unaware, the saucy darlings, of the fatal strips of white cotton knickers thus displayed, the undercurves of baby-fat little buttocks a blow to the Genital Brain, however pixilated.
>—Pynchon, *Gravity's Rainbow,* p. 13.

PLANGENT : *adj* loud, striking

Pink sneakers with white laces completed his plangent getup.
>—DeVries, *Slouching Towards Kalamazoo,* p. 151.

PLAT : *verb* to strike, smack, slap noisily; "used for the sound of the word more than the definition" (Koster)

... the small rain platting slow on the zinc roof.
>—Koster, *Mandragon,* p. 202.

PLATTED : *adj* laid out, arranged, planned as a city plan

... the back streets, which grow ever more mysterious and badly paved and more deeply platted. ...
>—Pynchon, *Gravity's Rainbow,* p. 239.

PLAUSIVE :   *adj*   ostensibly but not actually OK; specious

. . . rats of the castle, plausive adulterate beasts, villains, democrats. . . .
>—Nye, *Falstaff,* p. 54.

PLEACHED :   *adj*   pleated, folded over

. . . the roof, which was pleached of flattened oil tins.
>—Gaddis, *The Recognitions,* p. 728.

A path avenued with pleached lime trees led through the screen and flower beds. . . .
>—Boyd, *An Ice Cream War,* p. 55.

PLENILUNAR :   *adj*   full, abundant, like the light of the full moon

He had no idea of the time, but it was full night, with brilliant plenilunar light washing London.
>—Burgess, *The Doctor Is Sick,* p. 75.

PLEONASTICALLY :   *adv*   redundantly, superfluously

"Ice in the icebox," I said, pleonastically.
>—Burgess, *Earthly Powers,* p. 312.

PLOY :   *verb*   a military term for moving from a line abreast to a column; the opposite of "deploy" See GRIMP

PLUMBACEOUS :   *adj*   leaden, lead-colored

. . . this wan-looking though sun-colored little orphan *aux yeux battus* (and even those plumbaceous umbrae† under her eyes bore freckles). . . .
>—Nabokov, *Lolita,* p. 113.

PLUMULACEOUS :   *adj*   downy, covered with small feathers. Compare FLUE, LANUGO

. . . the occasional, slightly plumulaceous child. . . .
>—Theroux, *Darconville's Cat,* p. 304.

POGREBIN : *noun* from Russian for shaved head, jar-head.
Compare POLLSKEPPED

"Too many officers, too many criminals, too many
pogrebins, too many eggs." Then he popped an egg into
his mouth, swallowed it whole, and smiled.
—Helprin, *Refiner's Fire,* p. 312.

POLL : *verb* to cut off the horns of, usually, a cow

. . . 'twas in his rights to slay the twain of us, yet he had
no taste for bloodshed and loved his wife besides. The
horns were on his brow, he said, nor could his short-
sword poll him.
—Barth, *The Sot-Weed Factor,* p. 199.

POLLSKEPPED : *adj* basket-headed or bucket-headed. See
HATCHEL. Compare POGREBIN.

POOL-PAH : *noun* See quotation

"Sometimes the *pool-pah,*" Bokonon tells us, "exceeds
the power of humans to comment." Bokonon translates
pool-pah at one point in *The Books of Bokonon* as "shit
storm" and at another point as "wrath of God."
—Vonnegut, *Cat's Cradle,* p. 198.

POPLITEAL : *adj* relating to the back of the knee

Mrs. Proby breezed out the door, her popliteal fat
winking in several places just before she disappeared. . . .
—Theroux, *Three Wogs,* p. 33.

PORCIPOPHAGIC : *adj* pig-eating. Compare PANTICIVORE

In fact, as things turned out, the Queen didn't seem at
all indisposed by the presence of a porcipophagic albino
infidel in her lap—perhaps, in a strange way, she even
welcomed it.
—Boyle, *Water Music,* p. 51.

PORNERASTIC : *adj* having a penchant for prostitutes; horny

> So it is with all the Arts;
> so even Queen Theology turns a casual amusement
> for the pornerastic sky-and-earth-consumer. . . .
> —Gardner, *Jason and Medeia*, p. 290.

PORNOFORNOCACOPHAGOMANIACAL : *adj* insanely exotically erotic-in a furnace fornicating-shiteatingly

> . . . the hot pornofornocacophagomaniacal set of Bosch's unmusical hell. . . .
> —Theroux, *Darconville's Cat*, p. 67.

PORPENTINE : *noun* and *adj* Latin for "spiny pig," a porcupine

> *Ghost:* Thy knotty and combined locks to part and
> each particular hair to stand an end like
> quills upon the fretful porpentine.
> —Shakespeare, *Hamlet*, I, v, 18-20.

> Val felt his hair turning to a nest of porpentine bristles. . .
> —Burgess, *The End of the World News*, p. 217.

> Bongo-Shaftesbury turned to Porpentine. "Is it queer to favor the clean over the unpure?"
> "It may depend on one's employment," was Porpentine's rejoinder: "and employer."
> —Pynchon, *V.*, pp. 75-76.

PORTENTOUS : *adj* usually, foretelling; also, bizarre, extraordinary, monstrous, fantastic

> Those boys were unprecedented, portentous walkers. They thought nothing of walking twenty-five or thirty miles in a day.
> —Lowry, *Under the Volcano*, p. 18.

Novelist Nabokov ne'er conceived for his Lolita so

portentous a catalogue of motels as Ambrose and I have couched in. . . .

—Barth, *Letters*, p. 539.

POSTHION : *noun* foreskin. POSTHIA, *plural noun*. See and compare AKROPOSTHION, CARDIOID, STEGOCEPHALIC

PRAETERITIAL, PRETERITIAL: *adj* having to do with past events. See STERCORATION

PRASINE : *adj* green, as in stones or earth. Compare SMARAGDINE, VIRIDESCENT

He recalled . . . her prasine eyes as she turned toward him. . . .

—Nabokov, *Ada,* p. 367.

PRAT : *noun* the buttocks, the ass. Compare HURDIES, NATES

. . . those parched and juiceless prats with supercalendered† skin. . . .

—Theroux, *Darconville's Cat,* p. 344.

PREDORMIENT : *adj* before sleep

The length of the journey varied according to Van's predormient mood. . . .

—Nabokov, *Ada,* pp. 345-346.

PRELAPSARIAN: *adj* literally, "before the fall"; primitive, innocent

They were clearly in no hurry, and at times, briefly, their prelapsarian time-sense stirred his irritation.

—Gardner, *Mickelsson's Ghosts*, p. 42.

It was as if . . . the Juggler of Our Lady, miming the prelapsarian absence of ordinary gravity, had come true,

as everything was always coming true, the most current event incipient in the ancient, sleazy biologic sprawl.
—Elkin, *George Mills,* p. 67.

PRESBYOPIC : *noun* literally, "oldman's sight"; farsighted as opposed to nearsighted

He considered the presbyopic fussing, so full of what seemed uncertainty, with papers.
—Cozzens, *By Love Possessed,* p. 60.

PRESCIND : *verb* to cut off in front, preclude, nip in the bud

The Malebolge† was the barranca, the ravine which wound through the country, narrow here—but its momentousness successfully prescinded their minds from the goat.
—Lowry, *Under the Volcano,* p. 100.

PRETERIST : *noun* one who is overly fond of the past. See also quotation. Compare EXOLETE, PARACHRONIC

A preterist: one who collects cold nests.
—Nabokov, *Pale Fire,* p. 35.

PRETERITE : *adj* relating to those who have been "passed over" and who therefore are not among the Elect of God. PRETERITION, *noun*

. . . the preterite, the titless, and knee-dimpled Annette leading the other Mouseketeers into inquiring of the viewers their familiar and rhetorical *Why?*
—Exley, *Pages from a Cold Island,* p. 35.

He wrote a long tract about it presently, called *On Preterition.* It had to be published in England, and is among the first books to've been not only banned but also ceremonially burned in Boston. Nobody wanted to hear about all the Preterite, the many God passes over when he chooses a few for salvation.
—Pynchon, *Gravity's Rainbow,* p. 555.

PRITCHKEMP : *adj* standing erect and alert; armed and ready; locked and loaded. See COCKET

PROAIRESIS : *noun* See quotation

... I'm innocent, and in the respect that my role in those deaths was not an example of *proairesis* (by which will be meant a voluntary act preceded by deliberation). ...
—Barth, *Chimera,* p. 174.

PROBOSCIDATE : *adj* equipped with a long nose used for grasping; functioning or shaped like an elephant's trunk

... little Armande in her bath, pressing a proboscidate rubber toy to her shiny stomach. ...
—Nabokov, *Transparent Things,* p. 41.

PROCACIOUS : *adj* brash, saucy, impudent, precocious. Compare COCKET

Philosophy first became public when it proposed to teach character to this strapping lout with a procacious cock. ...
—Davenport, "The Dawn in Erewhon,"
Tatlin!, p. 149.

PROCUMBENT : *adj* lying face down, prostrate, prone. See also EXOLETE

... the procumbent Bel, collapsed cream dress, two pink-soled feet ... let's face it, one fancied her, one didn't know why but always had.
—Fowles, "The Cloud," *The Ebony Tower,* p. 296.

PROLEPTIC : *adj* preconceiving, expecting, or anticipating. PROLEPTICALLY, *adv*

Michel, grinning superbly, fondled his scrotum. I, proleptic, mirrored both grin and caress, adding a pendular

flip of my cock for punctuation.
> —Davenport, "On Some Lines of Virgil,"
> *Eclogues,* p. 226.

It doesn't sound like your father, God proleptically rest him and his finished lungs.
> —Burgess, *The End of the World News,* p. 116.

PRONOMINATE : *verb* to identify without specifying; a form of SYNECDOCHE

. . . they offered an up-yours finger to those they had pronominated The Citizens or The Sillies who cruised by and stared in audacious disgust or dismay at them.
> —Exley, *Pages from a Cold Island,* p. 14.

PROPAEDEUTIC : *adj* See quotation

. . . all this is propaedeutic, which means providing introductory instruction.
> —DeVries, *Consenting Adults,* p. 4.

PROREPTION : *noun* a creeping ahead. Compare SNOOVE

. . . the moral and physical advance of the citified man outruns the sly proreption of his smoking garbage
> dumps,

or the swifter havoc of his armies. . . .
> —Gardner, *Jason and Medeia,* p. 290.

PROSOPOEIC : *adj* imbued with human qualities

". . . I'm sure you'll agree that she has acquired a kind of apostrophic† and prosopoeic reality."
"Do get on with it. And I wish you'd try to stop talking like a dictionary."
> —Fowles, *Mantissa,* p. 91.

PROTREPTICOS : *noun* Greek for "admonishing"; persuasive instructions. Compare HORTATIVE

. . . a clattering windmill of cheerings up, pep tonics, across-the-fence chat, and general protrepticos. . . .
—Theroux, *Darconville's Cat,* p. 32.

PSITTACEOUSLY : *adv* like or of a parrot. PSITTACINE, *adj*

I shall not finish this inventory either, a little bird tells me so, the paraclete† perhaps, psittaceously named.
—Beckett, *Malone Dies,* pp. 341-342.

. . . gaudy psittacine colors.
—Burgess, *Earthly Powers,* p. 544.

PUDENCY, PUDEUR, PUDICITY : *noun* embarrassment, shame, shyness, modesty. PUDIBUND, *adj.* See also DELPHINET

That mannered pose, a goddess's modest quail of pudency, was quite uncalled-for.
—Cozzens, *By Love Possessed,* p. 382.

"It was spermatorrhea. Have you heard of that?"
Interest glowed faintly. "It sounds sexual," she said without pudeur.
—Burgess, *Tremor of Intent,* p. 111.

Consider the elephant. . . .Such is his pudicity . . . that he never covers the female as long as anyone comes into sight.
—Theroux, *Three Wogs,* p. 192.

During our children's kissing phase (a not particularly healthy fortnight of long messy embraces), some odd pudibund screen cut them off, so to speak, from each other's raging bodies.
—Nabokov, *Ada,* pp. 102-103.

PUDSY : *adj* plump. Compare FUBSY, PYKNIC

Some pudsy matron whom I'd never seen before came prancing up like a centauress and I found myself in her

arms, and her halo of perfume.
> —Foxell, *Carnival,* p. 44.

PUKKA : *adj* Anglo-Indian term for genuine, proper

> ... he turned up about a week ago in a distinctly unpukka outfit, looking like Hoot S. Hart in the Riders of the Purple Sage.
> > —Lowry, *Under the Volcano,* p. 60.

> You know what they mean in this outfit by celibacy? They mean the pure, true pukka gen.† ...They hang for wet dreams here. ...
> > —Elkin, *George Mills,* p. 380.

PULLULATE : *verb* to sprout, swarm, or teem. PULLULATING, *adj*

> ... the drooping forests pullulating with biting, stinging insects. ...
> > —Boyle, *Water Music,* p. 327.

> At the same time behind the heavily spotted fall-veil her plump face appeared to pullulate.
> > —Beckett, *Malone Dies,* p. 393.

PULPOUS : *adj* pulpy, filled with pulp

> In the muted light her skin seemed of the most incredibly golden texture, and her pulpous flesh, what I could see of it, looked the kind that, though infinitely soft, would in passion be as hard, hot, and animated as a stripper's pelvis.
> > —Exley, *A Fan's Notes,* p. 145.

> ... the pulpous pony-tailed girl student who served us and licked her pencil.
> > —Nabokov, *Pale Fire,* p. 21.

PYKNIC : *adj* and *noun* short, broad and muscular; one who has these qualities. Compare FUBSY, PUDSY

. . . the Duce. . .the pyknic atheist, as he termed him.
—Burgess, *Earthly Powers,* p. 306.

At a neat little racer with a giant faired-in radial engine
. . . she smiled as if recognizing a long-lost relative;
something silver-beefy, something pyknic-eager, got her
to caress the blebs†, the spats, and clamp in her fist the
tip of the two-bladed prop.
—West, *Gala,* p. 146.

The boy was a pyknic, like himself, with a round face
and shortish limbs and a tendency toward being over-
excited and overdepressed almost simultaneously.
—Aczel, *Illuminations,* p. 25.

PYRETIC : *adj* feverish. Compare FEBRILE

Already the broadleafed oaks of every coppice and hurst
had turned, pyretic, sealing their poisons away for the
time
of cold. . . .
—Gardner, *Jason and Medeia,* pp. 11-12.

PYTACORIAN : *adj* relating to questioning, trials

I always get drunk or go whoring the night before a big
trial. I find that wildness of that kind clears my mind
and makes it a tabula rasa, so to speak, able indeed to
accept the imprint of pytacorian energy.
—Helprin, *Winter's Tale,* p. 106.

Q

QUADRIROTAL : *adj* having four wheels

> . . . the stopped lines of impotent, quadrirotal man.
> —Fowles, *Daniel Martin,* p. 63.

QUAG : *noun* grass or turf over a mire or marsh

> There's the sink; there's the quag; there's the slough of
> my despond.
> —Barth, *Chimera,* p. 204.

QUAQUAVERSAL : *adj* going off in all directions

> . . . quaquaversal thoroughfares. . . .
> —Theroux, *Three Wogs,* p. 68.

QUEAN : *noun* a prostitute, whore, or harlot. See also
ANORECTIC

> . . . those tightly fleshed and loosely moraled queans.
> —Barth, *Giles Goat-Boy,* p. 402.

> For 'tis a rare queen these days can be told from a
> quean.
> —Berger, *Arthur Rex,* p. 198.

QUIDDITY : *noun* essence, whatever makes something what it is. See also ENTELECHY

... The feel of grass when he hunkered down, rolling a ball to Mark, had such quiddity, such authority, one might have imagined time had stopped, and the sacramental moment toward which everything tended had arrived.
—Gardner, *Mickelsson's Ghosts*, pp. 172-173.

... to draw the sword of quiddity from the scabbard of prevarication and come to the point, from whence do you return?
—Lloyd-Jones, *Lord of the Dance*, p. 45.

QUIDDLE : *verb* to fiddle or diddle idly

It made Victor, who was quiddling his foreskin while sipping his coffee, look at me cross-eyed. ...
—Davenport, "On Some Lines of Virgil,"
Eclogues, p. 161.

QUIDNUNC : *noun* Latin for "what now?"; a person overly occupied with trivial curiosity

... anti-intellectual rest homes which taught overadvantaged quidnuncs how to wear rep ties and smile. ...
—Theroux, *Darconville's Cat*, p. 38.

QUIM : *noun* cunt. See COYNTE. Compare COUN, COUNTRY MATTERS, DELTA, FOTZEPOLITIK, FURBELOW, MERKIN, QUIMTESSENCE

QUIMTESSENCE : *noun* the essence of womanhood, from a male perspective. See COYNTE. Compare COUN, COUNTRY MATTERS, DELTA, FOTZEPOLITIK, FURBELOW, MERKIN, QUIM

QUINCUNX : *noun* an arrangement of five things, with one at each corner of a square and one in the center, as the five on a die or playing card

Quatrefages knew the whereabouts of the orchard with its fabled quincunx of trees?
—Durrell, *Constance,* p. 178.

QUINQUANGLE : *noun* something with five corners, a pentagon

Surrounding the bed was a quinquangle of mirrored screens in which I saw myself reflected many times over.
—Lloyd-Jones, *Lord of the Dance,* p. 129.

QUISQUILIAE : *noun* Latin for "garbage"

... yahoos all ferreting and rummaging in the quisquiliae of time, making books out of a judicious mixture of other books, and carrying owls to Athens.
—Theroux, *Darconville's Cat,* p. 413.

QUISQUOUS : *adj* difficult to deal with or settle. Compare BATRACHOMYOMACHIA, FRATCH, TIRRIT

... quisquous, trifling matters better off forgotten. ...
—Gardner, *Jason and Medeia,* p. 133.

QUONDAM : *adj* former, once but no longer

... conversion to Rome appears to be the fashion. ...Quondam leading Reds or professional atheists. Uneasy Episcopalian ministers.
—Cozzens, *By Love Possessed,* p. 223.

The word quondam squats on the lilypad too, daring you to try to stare it out of countenance.
—DeVries, *Consenting Adults,* p. 52.

QUOPPING : *noun* a throbbing, a thumping

... the terrible quopping of her heart.
—Gardner, *Jason and Medeia,* p. 33.

QUOTIDIAN : *adj* daily

The word quotidian sits on the printed page and stares at you with those big awful frog's eyes, defying you to stare back.

—DeVries, *Consenting Adults,* p. 51.

R

RALLENTANDO : *noun* a gradual slowing down (music)

Interest from various numbered trusts was still turned, by family banks down in Boston every second or third generation, back into yet another trust, in long dying rallentando, in infinite series just perceptibly, term by term, dying . . . but never quite to zero.
—Pynchon, *Gravity's Rainbow,* p. 28.

RAMIFORM : *adj* branch-shaped, branching off

. . . a walrus-arsed microbiology professor with a face, spanned by a dirty ramiform mustache, that had the nasty whiteness of boiled veal.
—Theroux, *Darconville's Cat,* p. 70.

RANDONNY : *noun* travel, peregrination, wandering

. . . Lord Goal, Viceroy of France, when enjoying his randonnies all over Canady. . . .
—Nabokov, *Ada,* p. 329.

RAPPAREE : *noun* an irregular, a bandit, a robber. See **PATIBULARY**

RASCETA : *noun* creases on the inside of the wrist

He watched the thin wrist with its exaggerated rasceta
disappear. . . .
—Gaddis, *The Recognitions,* p. 630.

RASORIAL : *adj* referring to an animal or fowl which scratches
on the ground for food

. . . the paunchy guest of the evening moving . . . in an
unsteady rasorial attitude as though following a trail of
crumbs to the great world outside.
—Gaddis, *The Recognitions,* p. 620.

RAXED : *adj* stretched, as on awakening

Shoeless, he stood naked on his toes, his arms raxed
upward.
—Davenport, "The Dawn in Erewhon,"
Tatlin!, p. 192.

REAVE : *verb* to loot, pillage, plunder. See REBARBATIVE,
REFT

REBARBATIVE : *adj* repellent, unappealing as a week's growth
of beard

May the winged monsters be reaved† out of the infernal
pit to dwell therein and demons sit high forever in its
rebarbative trees to scourge it in satire and song!
—Theroux, *Darconville's Cat,* pp. 507-508.

REBOANT : *adv* loudly echoing. Compare REMUGIENT

. . . this scrolled silver rim of wash striking the shore
first in the distance, then spreading all along the curve
of the beach, its growing thunder and commotion . . .
now breaking reboant on our beach.
—Lowry, *Under the Volcano,* p. 37.

RECREANT : *noun* or *adj* a deserter, an apostate, a defector. Compare TERGIVERSATION

... comical bassoon solos over closeups of the old recreant guzzling some horrible fermented potato-mash lobotomy out of a jerrican, wiping her mouth on her sleeve, belching. . . .
—Pynchon, *Gravity's Rainbow,* p. 528.

Pistol: Puff; 'thy teeth, most recreant coward base!
—Shakespeare, *Henry IV, Part 2,* V, iii, 96.

RECRUDESCENCE : *noun* a reopening of an old wound

... the Shades dreaded a recrudescence of the polter-geist nuisance. . . .
—Nabokov, *Pale Fire,* p. 187.

REDOLENT : *adj* giving off something, as odor or emotion

The Widow Endicott was redolent in her white bed in the light of the seething coals.
—Helprin, *Winter's Tale,* p. 293.

... a proposal redolent of most unprofessional malice or else nescience† or even conceivably, since the British temperament is illogical enough to embrace totally incompatible elements, a combination of both.
—Burgess, *Napoleon Symphony,* pp. 324-325.

REFT : *adj* past participle of REAVE; robbed

... it might have been a library lifted bodily from an English country home and then reft of the books and furnishings.
—Faulkner, *A Fable,* p. 301.

REFULGENCY, REFULGOR : *noun* a shining by reflection. REFULGENT, *adj*

... the walls ... warm in a refulgency of afternoon sunlight. ...
> —Cozzens, *By Love Possessed,* p. 61.

Something glinting in the old man's hand: a knife? a gun? Was this it? was this what he'd been saved for? But suddenly he knew what that refulgent, light-gathering object was, knew why they were offering it to him, knew what he would do and how he would survive.
> —Boyle, *Water Music,* pp. 434-435.

There never was a nose that came near the nose of my man Bardolph. Not for brilliancy, refulgor, or resplendence.
> —Nye, *Falstaff,* p. 278.

RELUCT : *verb* to object to, to balk. Compare RENITENT

The truth was one that took getting used to. Discovering it, the heart relucted, had recourse to customary defenses, tried to add one more to the index of prohibited thoughts.
> —Cozzens, *By Love Possessed,* p. 113.

REMISE : *noun* originally an establishment that rented carriages; now, it suggests Hertz, Avis, and the like

A veritable Proteus of the highway, with bewildering ease he switched from one vehicle to another ... but I never could discover the remises he used.
> —Nabokov, *Lolita,* p. 229.

REMONTRANT : *adj* showing again, re-revealing, reappearing

... that remontrant goddess who annually clambered forth from the pool with her virginity renewed.
> —Gaddis, *The Recognitions,* pp. 14-15.

REMUGIENT : *adj* literally, "to bellow again"; resounding. Compare REBOANT

... remugient beasts stir up the undergrowth. ...
> —Boyle, *Water Music,* p. 96.

RENCOUNTER : *noun* a duel, a competition. Compare COLLUCTATION, DIGLADIATION

In the rencounter of minds, of sparring practice, he was offering to course a rabbit.
　　　　　　　—Cozzens, *By Love Possessed,* pp. 60-61.

RENITENT : *adj* recalcitrant, resistant, reluctant. Compare RELUCT

It was easy for Dr. Einstein: he could handle renitent equations single-handedly. Single-mindedly?
　　　　　　　—Aczel, *Illuminations,* p. 105.

RETICULATE : *verb* to form a network, to mesh like fish net. RETICULATED, *adj*; RETICULATION, *noun*. Compare TESSELLATE

The hammock, a comfortable oblong nest, reticulated his naked body ... under the weeping cedar that sprawled over one corner of the lawn.
　　　　　　　—Nabokov, *Ada,* p. 72.

In the train shed the reticulated vault was covered with half a century of soot. Leafy black patterns were engraved on the grated glass.
　　　　　　　—Helprin, *Refiner's Fire,* p. 93.

—*Light mush* the physicists call the inmost heart of the atom. The world is a reticulation of points of fire as furiously active as the sun.
　　　　　　　—Davenport, "The Dawn in Erewhon,"
　　　　　　　　　　　　　Tatlin!, p. 175.

REVENANT : *noun* a spook, a ghost, a returnee from the dead

... his mother stands, quite still, so still, so constantly, so irresolutely, so fleetingly still, *you would have thought she was a visitor from somewhere else*, a revenant, a

209

fugitive. . . .
———Nye, "Axel," *Tales I Told My Mother*, p. 35.

REVERBERATE : *verb* 1) to echo, to massively repeat; 2) to shine or glow by reflection

The sea stretched like a silk carpet across to the shadowy wall of mountains on the mainland to the west, a wall that reverberated away south, fifty or sixty miles to the horizon, under the vast bell of the empyrean†.
———Fowles, *The Magus*, p. 67.

Light of all frequencies will be shuffled, husbanded, harbored, held in reserve, magnified, reflected, reverberated, refracted, tuned, arranged, and focused so that it builds on its own strength.
———Helprin, *Winter's Tale*, p. 549.

RIGGISH : *adj* randy, horny, given over to sexual desire. "A great name for a porn magazine" (Koster). Compare LICKERISH, LUBRICITY, LUXURIOUS

"For vilest things
Become themselves in her, that the holy priests
Bless her when she is riggish."
———Shakespeare, *Anthony and Cleopatra*,
II, ii, 238-240

Full Moons had pranced pompom'd in vast stadiums, had pouted by the doors of jet planes, had preened her honey muff and custard bubbies across the double-fold of *Riggish*.
———Koster, *Mandragon*, p. 32.

Speaking the while however with a peculiar tenderness, as if slowly coming aware, maybe even as the yarn unlaid, that sex might be more of a mystery than he'd foreseen. . . .Which after forty-five years was nothing for any riggish Pappy Hod to be finding out.
———Pynchon, *V.*, p. 15.

There was a time, in my early days in London, in

company with the same riggish Mrs. Nightwork. . . .
—Nye, *Falstaff*, p. 201.

RINGENT : *adj* with mouth gaping open and teeth bared, a phenomenon often noticed in dogs and primates. See MU-CIN. Compare DEHISCENCE, GURN

RITORNELLE : *noun* a musical term for refrain or concluding passage

. . . for reasonable certainty is but the repercussion and ritornelle of belief.
—Coover, "Seven Exemplary Fictions,"
Pricksongs and Descants, p. 81.

ROACHORAMA : *noun* a roach's-eye view

. . . it's a good exercise to give that scene a rerun, scan it in upside-down roachorama from the ceiling. . . .
—Koster, *Mandragon*, p. 173.

ROGER : *verb* to copulate vigorously. ROGERING, RO-GUER, *noun*

. . . smut-crazed piratical Asians, roasting with satyriasis and ready with their poison juices to roger anything warm and horizontal. . . .
—Theroux, *Three Wogs*, p. 79.

We understood then that no woman on earth who wants a rogering will go unrogered, though she be sealed up in a tower of brass.
—Barth, *Chimera*, p. 44.

It was, besides, even less marvelous to consider that my esteemed visitor had glimpsed his spawn at roguer with my spouse, that he had no doubt watched close up and licked his chops.
—Koster, *The Dissertation*, p. 360.

ROILED : *adj* turbid, stirred up, disordered

... he knelt in the roiled grass glued to the sow's rump, clutching bristled flanks, deeply enswined.
—Koster, *Mandragon*, p. 221.

RORSCHACHED : *adj* splotched as the inkblots of the Rorschach psychological test

Chou is walking his bicycle. Chang, rorschached in mud and none too steady of foot himself, limps along beside him.
—Boyle, "The Second Swimming,"
Decent of Man, p. 71.

ROUNCY : *adj* fidgety, fussy

He worked absentmindedly during the day, rouncy and vague.
—Davenport, "The Dawn in Erewhon,"
Tatlin!, p. 164.

ROXBURGHE : *noun* a style of bookbinding with plain leather backs, gilt lettering, and paper sides. See PATIBULARY

RUBESCENT : *adj* blushing, turning red. Compare GULES, MINIATE

Ludicrously attired in a straw boater, a red suede vest making his stomach look like a rubescent mosquito's ripe for bursting. . . .
—Exley, *A Fan's Notes*, p. 315.

RUCKLE : *verb* to make a sound or a rattling in the throat; to coo, as a dove. Compare CURKLE

A ringdove ... the kind that chimes before a shower and ruckles afterwards.
—Davenport, "The Wooden Dove of Archytas,"
Da Vinci's Bicycle, p. 41.

S

SACCADE : *noun* a jerk or jerky motion

> . . . he . . . could feel in his skin each saccade of her olive, her amber, her coffee-colored eyes.
> —Pynchon, *Gravity's Rainbow,* p. 38.

SAGATIATE : *verb* "It's a nonsense word meaning nothing" (DeVries). SAGATIATING, *adj.* See EPIZOOTIC

SALAMANDRINE : *adj* referring to the fabular salamander, which was said to have been able to live in fire; hence, something which can live in flames, or fire that can be lived in by such a creature; fire-dwelling, or fiery dwelling

> Steel chambers, late the pyres
> Of her salamandrine fires,
> Cold currents thrid,† and turn to rhythmic tidal lyres.
> —Hardy, "The Convergence of the Twain," II, 4-6.

A lieutenant burst into the room. He surveyed the comfortable salamandrine flames, the cauldron of thousand eggs, the dancing shadows, the unfamiliar foreign faces.

> —Helprin, *Refiner's Fire,* p. 312.

SALTARELLO : *noun* a lively dance duet with much leaping and skipping. See PATIBULARY

SANGUINARY : *adj* bloody, bloodthirsty. See and compare antonym SANGUINE

SANGUINE : *noun* blood-colored; valiant; hopeful; amorously disposed; most commonly, confident, content. Compare antonym SANGUINARY

> . . . spare me thy physic. Nothing is sanguine now, when all is sanguinary.†
>
> —Berger, *Arthur Rex,* p. 493.

SAPOROUS : *adj* tasty, flavorful. Compare ESCULENT, INESCULENT

> It was really maddening . . . her attitude toward my saporous darling's letters!
>
> —Nabokov, *Lolita,* p. 83.

SAPROPHILE : *noun* rot-lover

> . . . a little saprophile of an anonymous politico-plough-boy. . . .the gimlet eyes of the saprophile probed his loins.
>
> —Beckett, "A Wet Night," *More Pricks than Kicks,* p. 51.

SCAPE : *noun* in architecture, the shaft of a column; in botany, a stem or stalk

> . . . some sixty yards away on the edge of the pines, a figure stood like a marble statue. With a new shock I realized that it was that of an absolutely naked man. He was just near enough for me to make out the black pubic hair, the pale scape of his penis; tall, well-built, well cast to be Apollo.
>
> —Fowles, *The Magus,* p. 181.

SCAPEAPE : *noun* King Kong, who may have died for our sins

... the legend of the black scapeape we cast down like Lucifer from the tallest erection in the world has come, in the fullness of time, to generate its own children. ...
—Pynchon, *Gravity's Rainbow,* p. 275.

SCHADENFREUDE : *noun* See quotation

"You ought to laugh more, Springer. It makes you look really cute."
"What *kind* of a discharge, Slothrop? *Honorable?* perhaps? Ah, ah-ha! Ha! Ha!"
Like Adolf Hitler, Springer is easily tickled by what the Germans call Schadenfreude, the feeling of joy at another's misfortune.
—Pynchon, *Gravity's Rainbow,* p. 526.

SCIENT : *noun* and *adj* literally, "knowing"; knowledgeable

"Scient," said Ada, writing it down.
"Oh, no!" objected Grace.
"Oh, yes! I'm sure it exists. He is a great scient. Dr. Entsic was scient in insects."
—Nabokov, *Ada,* p. 85.

SCOMBROID : *adj* having the physical shape of a mackerel and, perhaps, its predatory qualities as well. Compare MACQUEREAU

... the kindly scombroid face scanning Eventyr, quick as a fire-control dish antenna and even less mercy....
—Pynchon, *Gravity's Rainbow,* p. 217.

SCONCE : *verb* "Ensconce without the prefix. The reason is that *ensconce* is generally used in the passive voice. What we're after here is the action of lodging a candle in its sconce, partially suggested by the similarity in sound of *sconce* and [French] *enfoncer,* to thrust, and the candles in this little gem of Sade's (from *Justine*, I think), 'Mes bougies sont enfoncées dans leurs cons' " (Koster)

Sweeps left hand slowly through, wrist swaying, fingers fluting softly about Genghis's gilled truncheon. Flicks them up as Genghis sconces home.

—Koster, *Mandragon*, p. 220.

SCORIAC : *adj* relating to black basaltic lava

My single sip of her was a conflagration in the arteries, a Vesuvius to erupt and gush in scoriac torrents. . . .

—Foxell, *Carnival*, p. 91.

SCOTOMA : *noun* a blind spot. Compare AMAUROTIC, CECITY

Fort, an American, . . . the possessor, together with appalling insight, of all the scotomas and quirks of such dedicated powers.

—Lowry, *October Ferry to Gabriola*, p. 138.

SCROG : *verb* dysphemism for "fuck"; also, an obscure word meaning to "cut with a blade at the base of a bush." Compare FER, FIG, FIRK, DIGHT

Penelope: I do not wish to be scrogged—ever. I never heard that word, but when I heard it, I knew it was one thing I never wanted to have happen to me.
Harold: That's what you're *supposed* to say.
Penelope: This is not a coy deception. I do not want to be scrogged. I want love. I want tenderness.

—Vonnegut, *Happy Birthday, Wanda June*, p. 129.

SCROYLE : *noun* rapscallion, scoundrel, cad, cretin. See CACOCHYMICAL

SCRUMP : *verb* a portmanteau word from "scratch" and "rumple"

... she slipped her warm hand inside his pyjama jacket as she talked and scrumped softly at his chest hair and Tiresian tits.
—Durrell, *Constance,* p. 336.

SCRUTABLE : *adj* comprehensible through close concentration. Compare PERLUSTRATE

Coconut palms grow from the split coconuts, without (scrutable) design.
—Boyle, "Caye," *The Descent of Man,* p. 111.

SCUMBERED : *adj* fouled with dog dung

Rows of scumbered steps passed either side of a choked central gutter.
—Fowles, *The French Lieutenant's Woman,* p. 368.

SCUMBLE : *verb* 1) to unload; 2) to shit; 3) to spread paint thinly in order to blend colors together. Compare STERCORATION

... manure from a trio of prize Wessex Saddleback sows, ... dead leaves off many decorative trees transplanted to the roof by later tenants, and the odd unstomachable meal thrown or vomited there by this or that sensitive epicurean—all got scumbled together, eventually, by the knives of the seasons, to an impasto, feet thick, of unbelievable black topsoil in which anything could grow, not the least being bananas.
—Pynchon, *Gravity's Rainbow,* p. 5.

SEAGULL : *verb* to scavenge, to feed on cast-off remains. Compare VULTURED. "Seagulls follow liners to scavenge their garbage. I suppose they follow all sorts of ships. So here we have a hack scavenging themes that even *Cosmo* considers garbage" (Koster)

Whitbread, an overmuscled lacrosse player with a U.S. prime sirloin brain, possessed charms soothing to the

female breast. (He was, in fact, the model for the *jeune premier* of a film script and novel seagulled by his faculty adviser from themes dumped off the stern of *Cosmopolitan*).
— Koster, *The Dissertation*, p. 277.

SECOTINE : *noun* an organic compound; *adj* having a gap in a ring. Compare PENANNULAR, *adj*. See PATIBULARY

SEDULOUSLY : *adv* attentive; dutiful. Compare FIDIMPLI-CITARY, SEQUACIOUS

. . . my ardor exceeded his, and our physical connexion was sedulously procreative in intent if not in issue.
— Barth, *Letters,* p. 386.

SELENIAN : *adj* relating to the moon

. . . I passed a drive-in. In a selenian glow, truly mystical in its contrast with the moonless and massive night. . . .
— Nabokov, *Lolita,* p. 295.

SEMIDEMIGOD : *noun* See quotation. Compare GENETICODRAMATIC

". . . only gods sire heroes every time on mortal women. If a demigod's what you're after in the mother way, another demigod like myself has only a fifty-fifty chance of turning one out."
"I'll take the chance!" Anteia cried. "Let the kid be a *semi*goddamdemigod; who cares? Even a one-eighth god's better than nothing!" She pounded on the pallet. "Why can't men be raped by women? For pity's sake, *bang* me, Bellerophon!"
— Barth, *Chimera,* p. 181.

SEMINAR : *verb* to seed

All dally day it had snowed, it had seminared
snowflakes. . . .
—Nye, *Falstaff,* p. 333.

SENNIGHT : *noun* See quotation

There's also sennight, seven nights, for a week.
—Burgess, *Earthly Powers,* p. 334

SEPTENTRIONAL : *adj* Latin for "seven oxen," referring to
the Big Dipper; thus, northern. Compare TRAMONTANA,
BOREAL

. . . Well, no, we are all septentrional here, all a bit cool.
—Burgess, *Earthly Powers,* p. 159.

SEQUACIOUS : *adj* mindlessly adhering to the thoughts or
opinions of others. Compare FIDIMPLICITARY,
SEDULOUSLY

. . . the cowering, sequacious mob. . . .
—Gardner, *Jason and Medeia,* p. 65.

SESQUIPEDALIAN : *adj* Latin for "a foot and a half";
referring to excessively long words or speeches

. . . power plants . . . a collection of puffing samovars,
madly racing wheels, sesquipedalian drive rods in frantic
intercourse with capacious cylinders, boilers big enough
to cook the entire apricot crop of the Imperial Valley. . . .
—Helprin, *Winter's Tale,* p. 381.

SHODE : *noun* or *verb* a part in the hair or to part the hair.
See BENEPLACIT

SHOG : *verb* to shake, to rattle, but not to roll. See also
AGONAL

Pain shogged through Mickelsson, as if he himself had
become the burning rat. . . .
—Gardner, *Mickelsson's Ghosts,* p. 132.

SIBYLLINE : *adj* acting or speaking as one of the ancient prophetesses; occult, mysterious. See also ABREACTION, WHELM

She hesitated a moment, as if she knew she was being too cool and sibylline.
—Fowles, "The Ebony Tower,"
The Ebony Tower, p. 9

SILURID : *adj* having to do with catfish

When, after much purring and urging me on, she gave a silurid and lyric flip from haunch to heel, the hair crawled above my ears.
—Davenport, "On Some Lines of Virgil,"
Eclogues, p. 186.

SINISTRAL : *adj* 1) on the left side; 2) unlucky; 3) illegitimate; 4) wrong; 5) evil. SINISTRALITY, *noun*; SINISTRALLY, *adv.* Compare antonym DEASIL, synonym WIDDERSHINS

Sinistral but no wise sinister, long-haired and ascetic, Drew Mack looks to me less a hippie than a Massachusetts Minuteman in his denims, boots, and homespun shirt, his hair tied neatly back with a rubber band.
—Barth, *Letters,* pp. 87-88.

. . . the lady, holding the dagger sinistrally against a fold of skirt as with her dexter hand she followed the curve of the wall. . . .
—Berger, *Arthur Rex,* p. 51.

If the alternatives are side by side, choose the one on the left; if they're consecutive in time, choose the earlier. If neither of these applies, choose the alternative whose name begins with an earlier letter of the alphabet. These are the principles of Sinistrality, Antecedence, and Alphabetical Priority. . . .
—Barth, *The End of the Road,* pp. 79-80.

SIN-WAT : *noun* See quotation

"A *sin-wat*," she cried. "A man who wants all of somebody's love. That's very bad."
>—Vonnegut, *Cat's Cradle*, p. 170.

SIR-REVERENCE : *noun* an eighteenth-century euphemism for "shit"

The bullet caught him right through, and broke his neck. Sir-reverence, the bastard is dead.
>—Gaddis, *The Recognitions*, p. 878.

SLABBERDEGULLION, SLUBBERDEGULLION : *noun* a slobberer, a sloppy person. See DRUGGEL, LOOBY

SLENCH : *noun* a portmanteau of "sluice" and "drench"

The prow was lifted with force of rocketry. They hesitated at the summit, and heard the disheartening slench of water falling away from the hull.
>—Helprin, *Refiner's Fire*, pp. 216-217.

SLIDDER : *verb* a portmanteau of "to slither" and "to slide." SLIDDERY, *adj*. See CONSILIENT, SNOOVE

SMARAGDINE : *noun* an emerald

. . . here on Guernsey there are forty greens, viridities† of incredible brilliance, smaragdines, chartreuses, O leek and beryl and citrine.
>—Davenport, "John Charles Tapner,"
>*DaVinci's Bicycle*, p. 48.

SNEAKBUDGING : *adj* hostilely skulking. See HAMESUCKEN

SNEAPING : *adj* chilling severely, biting with cold

A sneaping frost crept over her heart.
>—Theroux, *The Great Wheadle Tragedy*, n.p.

SNOOVE : *verb* to glide, to move steadily foward. Compare
PROREPTION

When he snooved his hand to her crotch, she gently
took it away.
> —Davenport, "The Dawn in Erewhon,"
> *Tatlin!,* p. 165.

... I felt glans and intent shaft snoove richly into
slidderyt labia, a wellbeing like wine, like prancing
music swarming through me. . . .
> —Davenport, "On Some Lines of Virgil,"
> *Eclogues,* p. 180.

SNY : *noun* a curve upward as in the planking of a ship
toward the bow. See AKROPOSTHION. Compare EPINASTIC

SOFTOFF : *noun* the opposite of a hard-on

Slothrop's off the bed halfway across the room with a
softoff, one sock on the other in his teeth, head through
one armhole of his undershirt, fly zipper jammed,
yelling *shit.*
> —Pynchon, *Gravity's Rainbow,* p. 292.

SOLILOQUAL : *adj* talking to oneself

The group. *Our* crowd. And I as much their subject this
night as they mine. We were soliloqual. . . .
> —Elkin, *George Mills,* p. 345.

SOMNILOQUENT : *adj* sleep-talking

—She came to me there, Gwyon went on with somilo-
quent evenness. . . .
> —Gaddis, *The Recognitions,* p. 429.

... Vesta, normally a good solid Scots sleeper, had
decided to be restless and somniloquent.
> —Burgess, *Enderby,* pp. 175-176.

SORNER : *verb* to freeload, to sponge off others for food, and shelter

"What's he been up to?"
"Leeching and bumming and sornering."
—Davies, *Rebel Angels,* p. 98.

SORTILEGE : *noun* divination by lot-casting

. . . the sortilege of a local seer. . . .
—Gardner, *Jason and Medeia,* p. 112.

SOURDINE : *adj* muted, muffled

The streets had been considerably quieter in the sourdine Past.

—Nabokov, *Ada,* p. 554.

SPADGER : *noun* a sparrow, especially in the sense of something small and tasty, sparrows being a delicacy in Elizabethan times. See GUDDLE

SPANCEL : *verb* to hobble, to restrict movement by linking two legs with a rope

Michel unlatched his belt, slid his zipper down, and spancelled his thighs with his briefs. . . .
—Davenport, "On Some Lines of Virgil,"
Eclogues, p. 234.

SPATTLE : *verb* from Dutch for "spatula"; hence, to flip or turn something over

. . . tempt her with his leechy love and, once he had her wiggling, plaster-bandaged leg and all, spattle her over like a flapjack and pretend she was one of the poofs he had no money left to buy or the charm to con.
—Koster, *The Dissertation,* p. 23.

SPHINGINE : *adj* having to do with a sphinx; oracular, enigmatic, delphic

. . . that slightly sardonic, slightly disdainful look, and it seemed to me full of a certain enigmatic maturity. . . .The word I was looking for, I suppose, was "sphingine". . . .

—Durrell, *Monsieur,* p. 111.

SPICULED : *adj* spiked, as when raindrops hit the surface of water

A burnt-out Königstiger tank . . . its dead monster 88 angled down to point at the gray river, hissing and spiculed with the rain.

—Pynchon, *Gravity's Rainbow,* p. 433.

SPINTRY : *noun* a species of male prostitute

. . . zimmed† and clean-shaven spintries — shocking as parrots. . . .

—Gardner, *Jason and Medeia,* p. 91.

SPISSITUDE : *noun* thickness, density. Compare INSPISSATE

. . . he was Platonist to the ears, and hated Tom Hobbes as he hated the Devil, and was withal so fixed on things of the spirit—on *essential spissitude* and *indiscerptibility*† and *metaphysical extension* and the like, which were as real to him as rocks and cow-patties—that he scarce lived in this world at all.

—Barth, *The Sot-Weed Factor,* p. 20.

SPOUSEBREACH : *noun* adultery. Compare BED-SWERVER

"Everything is beautiful in its own way," must necessarily allow for the inclusion of killer viruses, wholesale spousebreach, sin.

—Theroux, "Theroux Metaphrastes,"
Three Wogs, p. 27.

SPRACKER : *adj* livelier, brisker, healthier. See GUDDLE

SPRAINTS : *noun* otter excrement. See CROTELS

SQUAB : *noun* "I can't defend this usage on linguistic grounds. What I want is the taste, not necessarily of squab, but of a dainty and costly delicacy. Everyone knows what physical part I'm referring to" (Koster)

On the sturdy table in the state dining room, with Angela's squab positioned at the edge of it and Mandragon standing to address it, crooking a slim leg in each brown elbow.

—Koster, *Mandragon,* p. 281.

SQUINNY : *noun* "a squinty look, a peering" (Davenport). See also MUCIN

I would get a good squinny at them as they trod past. . . .

—Davenport, "The Trees at Lystra," *Eclogues,* p. 4.

SQUIT : *noun* silly speech, idiotic talk

"Enough of this squit," says Vortigern. "What about *me*?"

"You," I say. "Find refuge if you can! But who may escape the shape of his own story?"

"What a load of verbal diarrhoea!" Vortigern sneers.

—Nye, *Merlin,* p. 107.

STAGIRITE : *noun* usually refers to Aristotle who was born in Stagira, a city in Macedonia

. . . Merlin, though he has no fiendish blood, he is long-lived through his lack of traffic with other humanity, for all men would live forever, if they were not, as the Stagirite hath said, social animals.

—Berger, *Arthur Rex,* p. 109.

STEATOPYGOUS : *adj* having a fat ass or bulging buttocks

> . . . if this body he held could become—just for twenty
> or thirty seconds—one of those harem dreams of his,
> pampered, pouting, perfumed, steatopygous. . . .
> —Burgess, *Enderby*, p. 154.

> . . . a steatopygous twelve-year-old in a striped shift.
> —Boyle, *Water Music*, p. 341.

STEGOCEPHALIC : *adj* having a covered head, capped.
Compare AKROPOSTHION, CARDIOID

> One munches an apple, one buzzes his lips like a hornet,
> the third twiddles the radical of his stegocephalic posthion.†
> —Davenport, "The Death of Picasso," *Eclogues*, p. 26.

STELLIFACTION : *noun* the act or process of star making

> . . . the cynical craft of stellifaction. . . .
> —Burgess, *Earthly Powers*, p. 322.

STELLIFEROUS : *adj* consisting of or containing stars

> What's stelliferous is beyond dog's howl, though up
> there is something ever pushing and turning it.
> —Rooke, *Shakespeare's Dog*, p. 37.

STENDAHL : *verb* from pseudonym of Marie Henri Beyle,
nineteenth-century French author of *Le Rouge et Le Noir*,
in which "Julien Sorel is put in the garden with Mme. de
Renal. Young man on the make socially steels up his courage
and forces himself to take her hand, the critical point in his
seduction of her. Stendahl does the whole thing blow by
blow—the hand inching over, etc." (Koster)

> There was a nurse assigned to midnight shifts . . . a
> greying Irish spinster. . . .By the third night she was
> prepared to give herself up to this kindness for a few
> minutes. Before long his attentions had traversed her
> pachydermic back and reached her hips, and she would

leave his room at once eased and excited. Then—But there is no need in a work like this to stendahl out a step-by-step account.
>   —Koster, *The Dissertation*, pp. 113-114.

STERCORATION : *noun* the act or process of spreading manure. Compare SCUMBLE

The past not only manures the future: it does an untidy job . . . praeteritial† stercoration. . . .
>   —Barth, *Letters*, p. 259.

STEREODIDYMOUS : *adj* having solid testicles. See EPI-DEICTIC. Compare CULLION, ORCHIDACEOUS

STERTILE : *adj* startling. STERTILITY, *noun.*

Stertile thunder tonitruated† terribly
>   —Burgess, *Earthly Powers*, p. 179.

"Stertility," he said with sober excitement.
>   —Burgess, *Earthly Powers*, p. 178.

STERTOROUS : *adj* snoring

Somewhere a bird cries out. But the guard sleeps on, stertorous, lips smacking and lids twitching.
>   —Boyle, *Water Music*, p. 26.

STICHOMYTHIA : *noun* dialogue or disputation with speakers alternating lines

". . . I think you're rather overdoing 'bleeding' in the stichomythia."
"And you know where you can bleedin' well stick that!"
>   —Fowles, *Mantissa*, p. 52.

STILLICIDE : *noun* column of raindrops falling successively from one point

>   . . . the svelte

Stilettos of a frozen stillicide—
> —Nabokov, *Pale Fire*, p. 34.

STRABISMUS : *noun* condition of being cross-eyed. STRA-BISMIC, *adj*. See also VENEREAN

... small strabismus, a half-squint—the sort of thing which would force one to become a sort of self-deprecating type of humorist.
> —Durrell, *Monsieur,* p. 290.

The dark-ringed eyes of her breasts ogled him, eyes capable of independent motion, like the eyes of some strabismic Mack Sennett comedian. . . .
> —Burgess, *Honey for the Bears,* p. 144.

STREEL : *verb* from Irish Gaelic for "to stroll"; to amble around aimlessly

I ration myself to one use of the verb 'streel' in each novel.
> —Koster, *The Dissertation,* p. 282.

He sang curses against his wife in the taproom and, roiling and hissing, streeled home drunk.
> —Theroux, *Darconville's Cat,* p. 142.

STREPITOUS : *adj* noisy

Cambridge now seemed small, dark, and strepitous.
> —Theroux, *Darconville's Cat,* p. 405.

STRIATE : *adj* grooved, furrowed, striped

At one end of the lawn a eucalypt cast its striate shade across the canvas of a lounge chair.
> —Nabokov, *Look at the Harlequins!,* p. 12.

STRIDULATE : *verb* literally, "to creak"; usually in refer-ence to crickets or grasshoppers. STRIDULATING, *adj*. Compare FRITINANCY

... the crickets were stridulating at an ominous speed in the black motionless foliage.

—Nabokov, *Ada,* p. 250.

... I found myself a nightly grasshopper ... at the abbey of Hulme. . . .I had to stridulate prayer all night long.

—Nye, *Falstaff*, p. 83.

STRIGULOUS : *adj* bristly or, in geology, furrowed. See MURLED

STRUMPET : *verb* to act like a whore, prostitute

Each night he sent for me I preened, strumpeted down the dark corridor. . . .

—Koster, *Mandragon,* p. 178.

STRUTHIOUS : *adj* having to do with ostriches

He could describe her dress only as struthious (if there existed copper-curled ostriches). . . .

—Nabokov, *Ada,* p. 486.

STYPTIC : *adj* contracting, pulling in together

Boyle turns to look over his shoulder, squinting into the styptic sun. . . .

—Boyle, *Water Music,* p. 328.

SUAGE : *verb* apheresis of "assuage"; to calm, soothe. "I want iambic rhythm, so I drop a syllable" (Koster)

... while I am unable to prove he never tossed her a hump in compassion, or suaged her passion in some other fashion, I tend to doubt it, there being metal more attractive strewn all about our happy little land, then as now.

—Koster, *The Dissertation,* p. 80.

SUBFUSC : *adj* dull, darkened tone or hue

It was like the inside of a well ... the scut-wake contrariety of the world. Not gay but murk, not glister but the subfusc verso of the year.
—Elkin, *George Mills*, p. 27.

SUBLUNAR : *adj* beneath the moon, terrestrial; inferior

Ellis was meat, after all, like the rest of them, a mere mess of gristle and ligaments and humours, a piece of sublunar anatomy. . . .
—Nye, "A Portugese Person," *Tales I Told My Mother*, p. 14.

SUBPALPEBRAL : *adj* under the eyelid. Compare PALPEBRAL

... I did glimpse off and on, through subpalpebral mirages, the shadow of a hand or the glint of an instrument.
—Nabokov, *Look at the Harlequins!*, p. 245.

SUBRUMINATIVE : *adj* digesting

... laze, all avuncular, subruminative, long Christmas dinner sloth. . . .
—Elkin, *George Mills*, p. 6.

SUB-VESTIMENTARY : *adj* referring to clothing worn beneath a robe or vestment

He could feel the straps of her brassiere under her armpits: this sub-vestimentary detail completed his confusion.
—Queneau, *We Always Treat Women Too Well*, p. 95.

SUCCEDANEUM : *noun* 1) a substitute or something that follows something else; 2) a remedy for ills. SUCCEDANEA, *plural*

Because it is only a dream, and as such no succedaneum

for life, I fight very well. . . .
—Exley, *A Fan's Notes,* p. 385.

. . . nothing to reflect the joy of living and succedanea, nothing for it but to try something else.
—Beckett, *The Unnamable,* p. 504.

SUCCUBUS : *noun* a female demon who copulates with sleeping men (the girl of your dreams); a male demon of the type is an INCUBUS

She visited him occasionally, as now, at night, like a succubus, coming in with snow. There was no way he knew to keep either out.
—Pynchon, *V.,* p. 30.

—What is a succubus? Esme asked. . . .
—It sounds like somebody that sucks, said Chaby.
—Gaddis, *The Recognitions,* p. 210.

SUCCUSIVE : *adj* throwing up from below, shaking. Compare SUSSULTATORY

The succussive, earthquake-like throwing-over of a counted-on years-old stable state of things had opened fissures.
—Cozzens, *By Love Possessed,* p. 404.

SUDORIFEROUS : *adj* sweat-producing, sweaty. Compare DIAPHORETIC

A few businessmen in sudoriferous shoes snuffled and snorted. . . .
—Theroux, *Darconville's Cat,* p. 193.

SUFFLAMINANDUS : *adj* Latin for braking, balking, obstructing

Mr. Livedog was a big funny fubsy† demiurge† who, *sufflaminandus* like Shakespeare, spawned unwanted life all over the earth.
—Burgess, *The Wanting Seed,* p. 12

SUFFLATED : *adj* inflated, blown-up, bloated

The idea of a harem. Or maybe you don't think it's barbaric, only wasteful. You Christers. To tell you the truth, if you want the opinion of one fatted, sufflated, darky gelding, it isn't. It isn't barbaric. If you're the Sultan himself it ain't even wasteful.
—Elkin, *George Mills*, p. 409.

SUILLINE : *adj* having to do with or sharing the characteristics of swine

. . . he . . . rooted and snuffled his way into her affections with a suilline avidity. . . .
—Beckett, "What a Misfortune,"
More Pricks than Kicks, p. 141.

SUPERCALENDER : *verb* to run through rollers in order to make smooth, emboss, or make thin. See PRAT

SUPEREROGATORY : *adj* beyond what is required, superfluous; extraordinary

. . . pages of very fair pornography, variations on the Laocoön theme though with more sexes, greater tortuosity, and no snake. A snake would have been supererogatory.
—Burgess, *Honey for the Bears*, pp. 174-175.

SUPERFOETATION : *noun* the production of successive ova, buds, blooms, etc.

"I thought maybe a bloom," said Harry.
"Superfoetation," said Sproule.
—Beckett, "What a Misfortune,"
More Pricks than Kicks, p. 130.

SUPERLUNAR : *adj* beyond the moon, heavenly, celestial, the opposite of SUBLUNAR. Compare SUPRAMUNDANE

. . . their train, braking late, ran into the rear of a stalled

work train. . . . there was a moment of superlunar calm.
—DeLillo, *Ratner's Star*, p. 5.

SUPERVENE : *verb* to interrupt unexpectedly and with opposing effect

. . . the tornado watch supervened and the Doctor issued his futile directives. . . .
—Barth, *Letters*, p. 476.

How close we had been before all this unhappiness supervened.
—Durrell, *Monsieur*, p. 16.

SUPPOSITITIOUS : *adj* imaginary, unreal, incorrectly theoretical, counterfeit

What you knew at fifty—that a hundred years far from being forever and ever, was not long; that all wonders, in time, will prove supposititious—left untouched the amazing thoughts you were at liberty to have at ten.
—Cozzens, *By Love Possessed*, p. 82.

SUPRALAPSARIAN : *adj* transcending the Fall of Man from the state of grace

—Ah, to dictate to the past what it has created is possible; but to impose one's will upon what it has destroyed takes a steady hand and rank presumption. . . .
—A supralapsarian criminal
—Gaddis, *The Recognitions*, pp. 358-359.

SUPRAMUNDANE : *adj* above the world, celestial, transcendent. Compare SUPERLUNAR

She had the power of making her own mistakes appear as the work of some supramundane agency, possibly one of those often vulgarly confused with fate. . . .
—Gaddis, *The Recognitions*, p. 78.

SURD : *noun* an insensitively stupid person

What Nietzsche had done to Christians, Mickelsson had done to the surds of Academia, and he'd reaped the same harvest: scorn and indignation.
—Gardner, *Mickelsson's Ghosts,* p. 76.

SURGER : *verb* to perform surgery. SURGERED, *adj*

Just before dawn on November 28, 1515, the helmsman heard him cry, "Jesus of the Great Power, free me from this darkness!" (Jesús del Gran Poder, líbradme destas tinieblas!"). Then Inchado jumped into the sea. His shark-surgered head was found washed up on a beach in what is now the Reservation.
—Koster, *The Prince,* p. 16.

SURSURRANT : *adj* murmuring, whispering

Her voice came back, pinched and sursurrant. "Ned, Ned—where are you, Ned?"
—Boyle, *Water Music,* p. 131.

SURVEIL : *verb* apheresis of surveillance, to survey

Since upper-class parents were too busy swiving† to surveil their daughters properly, an entire generation of the Tinieblan ruling class was married hastily and in July, 1937, the obstetricians of the city worked night and day delivering what everybody claimed were seven-month babies.
—Koster, *The Dissertation,* pp. 100-101.

SUSPIRANT : *adj* sighing, breathing

. . . Peterson sometimes insisted that we go up on deck where I might better practice the movement, the suspirant motion of the ship making everything even more difficult, much to the amusement of the sailors and the other passengers.

> Elkin, *George Mills*, p. 369.

SUSSULTATORY : *adj* heaving up and down. Compare SUCCUSSIVE. See OCCUPY

SWINK : *verb* to work hard, labor, toil and moil. SWINK-ING, *adj*. See COG

SWIVE, SWYVE : *verb* to copulate with a female. SWIV-ING, *noun* or *adj*

> . . . *swive* was a fine old verb whose desuetude in all but a few back-campus areas was much to be deplored, as it left the language with no term for *service* that was not obscene, clinical, legalistic, ironic, euphemistic, or periphrastic. . . .
>
> —Barth, *Giles Goat-Boy,* p. 235.

> "Think not we crave a swiving pure and simple at any time as do men always—'tis oft a pleasure with us, but rarely a passion."
>
> —Barth, *The Sot-Weed Factor,* p. 56.

> "I'll have his ugly head for that—after having swyved his beautiful wife.
>
> —Berger, *Arthur Rex,* p. 9.

> "Swives like a rattlesnake, so they tell me. Animal all right, and the brain isn't human.
>
> —Burgess, *Napoleon Symphony,* p. 73.

SYCOTIC : *adj* having an inflammation and encrustation of the roots of a beard

> —Scabs, he said. —I'm sycotic.
>
> —Gaddis, *The Recognitions,* p. 531.

SYLLEPSIS : *noun* a rhetorical device in which a word yokes two constructions—each with a different meaning

". . . —because I can't see through Adlai. Nor can most
Democrats. . . "
"You've 'committed,' as you put it, a zeugma†—or
more properly, a syllepsis."
—Buckley, *Stained Glass*, p. 30.

EXAMPLES OF SYLLEPSIS

My objectivity was peeled off with her chemise and
tossed unwanted into a corner.
—Barth, *The Floating Opera*, p. 121.

And I was too full of gin and Jane to do much besides
stare at the chicken breasts and hers.
—Barth, *The Floating Opera*, p. 25.

He has removed neither his cap nor thuggish sneer.
—Koster, *Mandragon*, p. 24.

SYNCHYSIS : *noun* a mingling, a confusion; the jumbling of
words in a sentence so as to be incomprehensible. Compare
GALLIMAUFREY

. . . the planets scatter in dismay, then quickly settle
on a new course, new synchysis. . . .
—Gardner, *Jason and Medeia*, p. 244.

SYNCOPE : *noun* a stopping of the heart beat, a faint, a
swoon

. . . as the real De Quincey (that mere drug fiend . . .)
imagined the murder of Duncan and the others insulated
self-withdrawn into a deep syncope and suspension of
earthly passion.
—Lowry, *Under the Volcano*, p. 136.

"Oh, they didn't go to *sleep, quelle idée,* they *swoon,*
it's a little syncope."
—Nabokov, *Ada*, p. 54.

SYNECDOCHE : *noun* a rhetorical device which uses a part of something for the whole thing or, vice versa, the whole for the part. SYNECDOCHIC, *adj.* Compare PRONOMINATE

To the now quite unashamedly suggestive synecdoches of her tongue were added quiverings and tremulous little borings in the surface beneath his hand.
—Fowles, *Mantissa,* pp. 31-32.

The moving people hustle, as it were, and once having hustled move on. (That this has been said of fingers is only a synecdoche proving quite the same point.)
—Theroux, *Three Wogs,* p. 61.

. . . the synecdoche of desire, he knew, waited crucially upon the larger understanding of love. . . .
—Theroux, *Darconville's Cat,* p. 144.

What he brought to the business was a knowledge of broken pieces, shard, some synecdochic, jigsaw sense of the whole.
—Elkin, *George Mills,* p. 108.

SYZYGY : *noun* " . . . when the moon lies in a straight line with sun and Earth. It's also a scansion term: two feet combined into a single metrical unit. Yoked animals [Greek meaning] at the root of all this" (West). Note that all of the quotations below, except Paul West's, seem to use the word in the Greek sense—"yoked together"—and not in the astronomical or poetical sense

The double sex was quite another thing, a syzygy of the male and female affect.
—Durrell, *Constance,* p. 298.

. . . a chinless, fat-legged whore . . . interested solely in that not uncommon syzygy of money and barbarities. . . .
—Theroux, *Three Wogs,* p. 24.

The result of this erotic frustration was, firstly, to make her eschew the experience entirely; secondly, to recom-

mend her itch for syzygy to more ideal measures, among which she found music and malt the most efficacious. . . .
—Beckett, "Love and Lethe,"
More Pricks than Kicks, p. 88.

I saw the three of us, expendable as shapes made from a child's building blocks, lined up in syzygy: a sun, a moon, an Earth. But who was which?
—West, *Gala,* p. 184.

T

TABESCENT : *adj* wasting away. Compare ANORECTIC, CACHECTIC, DYSCRASE, INANITION, MARASMIC, MARCESCENCE

The explorer lies there, racked with fever, riddled with worms, his stomach shrunken, sphincter wide open, barely able to raise his eyes. He is weakened and stinking, tabescent, at the far edge of hope.

—Boyle, *Water Music,* p. 42.

TALION : *noun* retaliation, retribution, or compensation following the rule of "an eye for an eye"

Simple talion may be fine for wartime, but politics between wars demand symmetry and a more elegant idea of justice, even to the point of masquerading, a bit decadently, as mercy.

—Pynchon, *Gravity's Rainbow,* p. 350.

TALIPED : *noun* club-footed; hence, awkward

He had appeared on all fours, though somewhat taliped because of the glass he maintained upright in one hand. . . .

—Gaddis, *The Recognitions,* p. 846.

TANLING : *noun* one tanned by the sun

> One of a wheen† of tanlings enrolled in the gymnasium. . . .
> —Davenport, "The Wooden Dove of Archytas,"
> *Da Vinci's Bicycle,* p. 38.

TANNHAUSERISM : *noun* a psychological state resembling that of Tannhauser, a thirteenth-century German poet. A sixteenth-century ballad tells the story of his descent into a cave, his affair with Venus in Venusberg, his attempt to reconcile himself with the church, and his final return to the depths. His story is also told in an opera by Wagner. See also quotation. Compare BATHYSIDERODROMOPHOBIA, CHTHONIC, TERRENITY

> There is that not-so-rare personality disorder known as Tannhauserism. Some of us love to be taken under mountains . . . the comfort of a closed place, where everyone is in complete agreement about death.
> —Pynchon, *Gravity's Rainbow,* p. 299.

TANTIVY : *noun* name which literally means "at full gallop" while on a horse, particularly while hunting

> The Ballad of Tantivy Mucker-Maffick†
> (*Refrain*): Oh—Tantivy's been drunk in many a place,
> From here to the Uttermost Isle,
> And if he should refuse any chance at the booze,
> May I die with an hoary-eyed smile!
> —Pynchon, *Gravity's Rainbow,* p. 191.

TARANTULOUS : *adj* "like large hairy spiders" (Davenport)

> A wart tarantulous and inauspicious sprouted from the flange of the old custus's† nose. . . .
> —Davenport, "C. Musonius Rufus,"
> *Da Vinci's Bicycle,* p. 20.

TARDIGRADE : *adj* and *noun* literally, "slow stepping"

> So it goes. The steady wash of the rain, the tardigrade

progress, the inexorable attrition. . . .
—Boyle, *Water Music*, p. 352.

. . . he moved forward, a headlong tardigrade, in a straight line.
—Beckett, *Watt*, p. 30.

TECTONIC : *adj* 1) relating to geologic changes in the earth's crust; 2) having to do with structure, architecture

Once again he clasped his hands on top of his head, moving them forward and back, enjoying the tectonic sensation.
—DeLillo, *Ratner's Star*, p. 340.

TEKNOPHAGY : *noun* child-eating. Compare PEDOPHAGE

. . . her sole anxiety was for her babies. . . . Whatever official fate waited in the capital, it would, surely, not stoop to teknophagy.
—Burgess, *The Wanting Seed*, p. 188.

TELESTICALLY : *adv* mystically, magically with the sense of spell-casting

. . . I side-swiped a parked car but said to myself telestically—and, telepathically (I hoped), to its gesticulating owner—that I would return later. . . .
—Nabokov, *Lolita*, p. 248.

TEMERARIOUS : *adj* reckless, bold

. . . the temerarious dead Siegfried.
—Cozzens, *By Love Possessed*, p. 339.

TEMULENT : *adj* intoxicating

In the afternoons I lay face up on a water mattress and watched the compact white clouds run down the sky; or face down looked into the blue-green water—chlorinated and temulent to the smell—of the mail-order,

children's swimming pool on which I floated.
—Exley, *A Fan's Notes*, p. 368.

TENDENTIOUS : *adj* biased, opinionated

"Tendentious," Maggie mused. . . .I get it mixed up with 'tenebrous.'† That means dark and gloomy. . . ."
—DeVries, *Slouching Towards Kalamazoo*, p. 214.

TENEBROUS : *adj* dark, obscure, murky, gloomy. Compare CALIGINOUS, THESTRAL

It [Avignon] had always waited for us, floating among its tenebrous monuments, the corpulence of its ragged bells, the putrescence of its square.
—Durrell, *Monsieur*, p. 11.

She floated on the tenebrous waves with childlike abandon.
—Aczel, *Illuminations*, p. 98.

TERGIVERSATION : *noun* literally, "the turning of one's back"; 1) desertion, apostasy; 2) evasion, equivocation. See EUPHUISTIC. Compare RECREANT

TERRAQUEOUS : *adj* having to do with both land and water, amphibious. See CONSUETUDE

TERRENITY : *noun* the state of belonging to the earth. See also quotation. Compare BATHYSIDERODROMOPHOBIA, CHTHONIC, TANNHAUSERISM

Trees creak in sorrow for the engineered wound through their terrain, their terrenity or earthhood.
—Pynchon, *Gravity's Rainbow*, p. 733.

TERSIVE : *adj* literally, "wiping"

In the cobwebbed corner of the toilet . . . a book of poems . . . most of the pages of which had been roughly

torn out for presumably a tersive purpose. . . .
—Burgess, *The End of the World News,* p. viii.

TESSELLATE : *verb* to make or form a mosaic. Compare RETICULATE

Overhead, lightning tesselates[sic] the sky until it glows like an illuminated map of some celestial river and its tributaries.
—Boyle, *Water Music,* p. 92.

TESSERA : *noun* mosaic tile. TESSERAE, *plural*

Fingal. . . .Its coast eaten away with creeks and marshes, tesserae of small fields. . . .
—Beckett, "Fingal," *More Pricks than Kicks,* p. 24.

TESSITURA : *noun* in music, the general range of a vocal part

A curious potency. Whatever it was the real visionaries were picking up out of the hard tessitura of those days and city streets, whatever Käthe Kollwitz saw that brought her lean Death down to hump Its women from behind, and they to love it so. . . .
—Pynchon, *Gravity's Rainbow,* p. 578.

TETRORCHID : *adj* having four testicles. Compare ORCHIDEOUS

"Being deflowered one afternoon. By a faun."
"They're not like ordinary men. They're tetrorchid, if you must know. They can do it again and again and again. And he did."
—Fowles, *Mantissa,* p. 82.

THALAMIC : *adj* 1) the inner, or bridal chamber; 2) relating to the interior of the brain, the pain perception center

. . . "dim-doom" visions: fatidic†-sign nightmare, tha-

lamic calamities, menacing riddles.
—Nabokov, *Ada*, p. 361.

THANATIZE : *verb* to process in a lethal manner

During his errantry and vagabondage he learned their cognate woes, error and vagueness; for having missed on three clean shots at what he thought would be oblivion, he set about to thanatize himself in messy increments of degradation.
—Koster, *The Dissertation*, p. 107.

THAUMATURGE : *noun* a wonder-worker, conjuror, magician. THAUMATURGICAL, *adj.*

. . . That Grouchy is a fucking thaumaturge. Would you not say that only a man of miracles could fail to do something decisive with only thirty-four thousand men and one hundred and eight fucking guns?
—Burgess, *Napoleon Symphony*, p. 277.

Chiefy kept repeating, "I'm *so fuckin'* happy." This was his way of letting the Captain know he was being insufficiently grateful for the heroic, if not thaumaturgical, efforts of the engine-room gang.
—C. Buckley, *Steaming to Bamboola*, p. 35.

THEANDRIC : *adj* embodying both god and man. Compare PERICHORESIS

We fall
in love with the image of a mythic, theandric father,
domineering
oakfirm tower of strength, and we find, as our
mothers found,
the tower is home to a mouse peeking groundward
with terrified eyes.
—Gardner, *Jason and Medeia*, p. 50.

THEOPHANY : *noun* the appearance or revelation of a god to a mortal person

Athene, cowled, came up, belted with the famous bridle, and seemed to move her lips. . . .My first theophany! I sprang up, dizzy at this evidence that I was on my way.
—Barth, *Chimera,* p. 173.

THEROID : *adj* beastly, wild, savage

The brief madhouse scene, the dumb byplay of the theroid idiots, the demented two sorrowers, . . . was no sooner begun than ended.
—Cozzens, *By Love Possessed,* p. 404.

THESTRAL : *adj* dark, dim. Compare CALIGINOUS, TENEBROUS

. . . the mightiest mortal who'd ever reached that
thestral shore. . . .
—Gardner, *Jason and Medeia,* p. 4.

THOOID : *adj* having to do with wolves, jackals, and/or hyenas. Compare LUPINE

Because of their skins, their wild beards, their thooid and mangy rawhide lacings . . . they seemed to be fit heirs for their peculiar forebears.
—Helprin, *Winter's Tale,* p. 625.

THOS : *noun* a dog-like beast of prey, usually a jackal. See PATIBULARY

THRASONICAL : *adj* from the character, Thraso, in Terence's *Eunuchus*; originally meant "bold, courageous," now means "bragging, boastful"

The news that my ensign was the son of a bastard Pope of the wrong sex did a lot to explain his bombastic and thrasonical manner of speaking.
—Nye, *Falstaff,* p. 358.

THRID : *verb* past participle of "to thread." See SAL-AMANDRINE

TIRADE : *noun* See quotation

> Funny what will stick in your mind. Know what I remember most about Racine? Your explanation about a *Tirade*. You know—*Teerahd*. These are long speeches every principal character gets at some point, to wrap up a whole lot of exposition about the story thus far and also give the audience a long hard look at him on his own. *It doesn't mean a chewing out.*
> —DeVries, *Into Your Tent I'll Creep*, p. 27.

TIRRIT : *noun* a tantrum, a fit. Compare ABREACTION, BATRACHOMYOMACHIA, FRATCH, QUISQUOUS

> It was a night full of 'tirrits and frights' (Nell's own words), Poins being scared out of his wits by the sight of her bird's nest. . . .
> —Nye, *Falstaff*, pp. 254-255.

TITUBATION : *noun* See quotation

> . . . I was failing to live up to potential in the moral sphere as well as the scholastic. "That is my titubation," I said
> " . . . What on earth is that?"
> "A halting, or stumbling in my progress toward what I should be."
> —DeVries, *Slouching Towards Kalamazoo*, p. 62.

TONITRUATE : *verb* to thunder. See STERTILE

TONTINE : *adj* or *noun* referring to any arrangement similar to one originally invented by Lorenzo Tonti in sixteenth-century France, whereby surviving subscribers received increased benefits as other subscribers died. Now, usually refers to the survivor taking all.

What holds them back is what comes next. The free-for-all, that winner-take-all frenzy of their terrible tontine arrangements. . . .They are sizing each other up. . . .
—Elkin, *George Mills,* p. 386.

TOROUS : *noun* and *adj* doughnut-shape. See MALISON

TORPID : *adj* numb, paralyzed; also, "compare Spanish—*torpe,* which can also mean clumsy" (Koster)

His supporters were fat and torpid from three years gobbling at the public trough.
—Koster, *The Prince,* pp. 161-162.

TORQUATED : *adj* marked with rings, usually referring to avian coloration. Compare ANNULATE

Torquated beauty, sublimated grouse.
—Nabokov, *Pale Fire,* p. 33.

TORTICOLLIS : *noun* a more or less permanently twisted neck

I kiss him first and his smile starts his head turning away in a long trembling torticollis.
—Percy, *The Moviegoer,* p. 137.

TORTUOSITY : *noun* the condition of being twisted, bent, sinuous, crooked

I have practiced the craft of fiction for many years, but I know less than I ever knew about the tortuosities of the human soul.
—Burgess, *Earthly Powers,* p. 145.

TOTTY : *noun* a higher-class prostitute. See FUBSY

TOXOPHILITE : *noun* and *adj* an aficionado of archery, a bow-and-arrow buff; relating to one who has this avocation

Now A.G.A. was a toxophilite humanist, well able, as Shakespeare says, to clap in the clout at twelve score, and carry a forehand shaft a fourteen and a fourteen and a half.
—Nye, "The Story of Sdeath and Northangerland," *Tales I told My Mother*, p. 30.

TRACASSERIE : *noun* a petty quarrel, a tempest in a teapot. Compare BATRACHOMYOMACHIA, FRATCH

. . . this very church . . . a hotbed of tracasseries and dissent . . .
—Theroux, *Darconville's Cat*, p. 20.

TRADUCE : *verb* to defame, to debase, to betray. See MALISON

TRAMONTANA : *noun* from Italian for "over the mountain"; the north wind; something northern. TRAMONTANE, *adj*

. . . it seemed more reasonable or seasonable to regard all this as some mere transitory tramontana, some boreal† thrust, yet it was most unfortunate for the poor dear roses.
—Burgess, *Napoleon Symphony*, p. 347.

TRANSANIMATING : *adj* transferring a soul from one body to another

Then blow me if she didn't startle the half-light with a transanimating smile.
—Foxell, *Carnival*, p. 61.

TRANSHUMANCE : *noun* the movement of animals and/or people according to the season, as from summer pasture to winter

. . . pausing and using her hands like some practiced lecturer, say Jacob Bronowski warming to the subject of transhumance, although without his semi-conspiratorial whisper, his oracular sigh.

—West, *Gala,* p. 132.

TRANSMOGRIFY : *verb* to change grotesquely and/or humorously

Third N. [Nut] or K. [Keeper]: Transmogrify common air into diamonds through Cataclysmic Carbon Dioxide Reducti-o-o-o-o-n-n-n. . . .
—Pynchon, *Gravity's Rainbow,* p. 260.

TRANSSECTITE : *noun* See quotation

. . . a transsectite, a Lutheran named Mausmacher who liked to dress up in Roman regalia.
—Pynchon, *Gravity's Rainbow,* p. 653.

TRASCINE : *verb* to rough up or to make rough. TRAS-CINED, *adj*

"I've always believed in free will," she said.
"And yet I seem, more than anyone I've ever known or heard of, to have been—well, drawn, tugged, trascined. Predestination."
—Burgess, *The End of the World News,* p. 368.

TRENCHING : *adj* feasting, stuffing one's face, pigging out. Compare LUCULLAN

Colonel Sanders was there, Arthur Treacher, Julia Child, James Beard, Ronald McDonald, Mamma Leone. It was the Trenching Event of the Century.
—Boyle, "The Champ," *The Descent of Man,* p. 20.

TRIBADISM : *noun* from Greek for "to rub"; Lesbianism. Compare EUTRIPSIA, FRICATIVE, FROTTAGE

Over in Tiryns I saw her bitter bullish like, Anteia, forcing docile girls into tribadism while Magapenthes

plotted coup d' état and double theta'd sodomocracy.
—Barth, *Chimera*, p. 302.

TRIPHTHONG : *noun* three vowels in one syllable

A hot thundery wind launched itself at them, spent itself, and somewhere a bell beat out wild triphthongs.
—Lowry, *Under the Volcano*, p. 280.

TRISKELES : *noun* a triad, something with three legs

"Mummy, let me go back to the beautiful brothel! Back to where those triskeles are strumming, the infinite trismus†. . . .
—Lowry, *Under the Volcano*, p. 313.

TRISMUS : *noun* a scream. See TRISKELES

TROGLE : *noun* a bunch of snakes

. . . blue-scaled snakes rolled coil on coil, their hatchet heads hovering, floating, the whole dark trogle alive with rattling and hissing. . . .
—Gardner, *Jason and Medeia*, p. 153.

TROGLODYTIC : *adj* cave- or hole-dwelling

He can picture them rifling his stores, breathing in his face, punching at his breastbone with their blunt cracked forefingers, all the while chattering away in some muddled troglodytic language that's like a barnyard flatulence, like pigs wheezing and kine† passing wind.
—Boyle, *Water Music*, p. 399.

TUCKET : *noun* a musical flourish, a trumpet call for cavalry

. . . you've smiled at bears who pompously, foolishly lord it over lesser bears but shake like mice at the tucket and boom of heaven. . . .

—Gardner, *Jason and Medeia,* p. 59.

TUMBRILITIS : *noun* the transportation of the condemned in a demeaning mode, such as by tumbril or boxcar; and by association, the tumult accompanying the disposing of a hated minority, a condition associated with but not limited to the Reign of Terror in France

Tumbrilitis has slopped over and reached the whole world now. To think that the first statue which was erected by the revolutionaries was one to the Goddess of Reason!

—Durrell, *Constance,* p. 320.

TUMESCENCE : *noun* the condition of being swollen. TUMESCENT or TUMID, *adj*

Tumescence had become as easy as filling a fountain pen.

—Burgess, *Honey for the Bears,* p. 19.

Already, with the first light, a fierce parching heat has set in and the tumescent air pours over the explorer as if it were slag.

—Boyle, *Water Music,* pp. 386-387.

Then, above that tumid silence, there came a nagging song like the song of a gnat. It was a siren approaching. . . .

—Vonnegut, *Cat's Cradle,* p. 117.

TUP : *verb* to copulate, specifically for a ram to do so with a ewe

Iago: Even now, now, very now, an old black ram is tupping your white ewe.

—Shakespeare, *Othello,* I, i, 88-89.

"I have me the peculiarity," said the King in this weak

voice, " with a woman I have long desired, to tup her so often with the tool of the mind that when it comes to close buttocks my actual meat will not stand."
—Berger, *Arthur Rex,* p. 6.

. . . I lay crippled on the reeking peat and saw my first love tupped by a brute Angora.
—Barth, *Giles Goat-Boy,* p. 5.

TURBO : *noun* Greek for "a top"; something that spins

Was I to spin forever, a *turbo* from which God himself had whipped the cord?
—Davenport, "C. Musonius Rufus,"
Da Vinci's Bicycle, p. 11.

TURONIAN : *adj* a subdivision of the (geologic) cretaceous† period. See PATIBULARY

TURPID : *adj* vile, foul, nasty

I was despicable and brutal and turpid. . . .
—Nabokov, *Lolita,* p. 286.

TURPILOQUENCE : *noun* foul speech. TURPILOCUTE, *verb.* Compare COPROLALIA, DYSPHEMISM

Did you know that it's a generally accepted fact about twins that we tend characteristically to regressiveness, one manifestation of which is a readier slipping into turpiloquence than is the case with other people . . . effing dirty language.
. . . Do I turpilocute?
—Barth, *Sabbatical,* p. 13.

TYROSEMIOPHILE : *noun* See quotation

. . . in attendance . . . an inventor celebrating his seventy-second rejection by the U.S. Patent Office, this time on a coin-operated whorehouse for bus and railway stations which he was explaining with blueprints and gestures to a small group of Tyrosemiophiles (collectors of labels on French cheese boxes) kidnapped by Iago from their annual convention.

—Pynchon, *V.*, p. 419.

U

UBEROUS : *adj* rich and plentiful, productive, bountiful

. . . an uberous flow of tea splashed down smoothly. . . .
—Theroux, *Three Wogs,* p. 131.

UGGR : *noun* fear, dread. See BLAEDSIAN

UMBRA : *noun* shade or shadow. UMBRAGEOUS, *adj.*
UMBRAE, *plural noun.* See also PLUMBACEOUS

Walls of tree trunks writhed in arm-thick creepers.
Lianas drooping snakily above. Flare of parrot feathers
against a monkeyed umbra of twined branches.
—Koster, *Mandragon,* p. 70.

Tilled fields jostling with deep umbrageous forests. . . .
—Boyle, *Water Music,* p. 336.

UNCHIES : *noun* a woman's breasts. Compare MAMMETS

The rat plummeted head first into the scoop neck of her
dress and lodged between her plump and heaving unchies, hind feet fluttering, tail swishing back and forth
like a runaway metronome across her screaming mouth.
—Koster, *Mandragon,* p. 109.

UNCONSTELLATED : *adj* 1) not considered as part of a constellation; 2) not under the influence of an astrological sign or house. See CONSTATATION

UNCTION : *noun* the act of anointing, smearing with oil

... but when your frantic member casts about for a rubbing-place, and the unction of a little mucous membrane. ...

—Beckett, *Molloy,* p. 74.

UNCTUOUS : *adj* oily, greasy. UNCTUOUSLY, *adv.* See also VELLEITY

Never, not even in the time of Dom Francisco, had Ouidah witnessed so unctuous a feast.
Pigs' heads were anointed with gumbos and ginger.
—Chatwin, *Viceroy of Ouidah,* p. 20.

Somewhere out of sight someone was being slowly, unctuously sick.

—Durrell, *Justine,* p. 56.

UNGULATE : *adj* referring to a hooved animal; hence, bovine. Compare BOANTHROP, VACCINE, VITULINE

But then, from the rear of the crowd, all the long way down the far end of the bar, came the low moan of ungulate distress. "Carrrrry, ohhhh baby, what have I done to you?"

—Boyle, "John Barleycorn,"
The Descent of Man, p. 208.

UNMOBLED : *adj* uncovered, unmuffled

First But who, Ah, woe! had seen the mobled
Player: queen. ...?
—Shakespeare, *Hamlet,* II, ii, 525.

It's Reg Prinz's played-out-prize perversely I would prong: the Bea you have become: unmobled quean† of bedroom, bar, B movie.

—Barth, *Letters,* p. 333.

UNPALTERINGLY : *adv.* without equivocation, without deception. See EXOLETE

UPANISHAD : *noun* Indian philosophical treatises dealing with universal questions; also, see quotation.

Upanishad of a worrier. "Upanishad" means "secret session."

—West, *Gala,* p. 136.

URSINE : *adj.* having to do with bears. See LUPINE.

URTICATION : *noun* flogging, whipping.

"The humility," murmured the janizary, "of a love too great for skivvying and too real to need the tonic of urtication."

—Beckett, "A Wet Night,"
More Pricks than Kicks, p. 57.

V

VACCINE : *adj* having to do with cattle. Compare BOAN-
THROP, UNGULATE, VITULINE

Here . . . is cow's milk. Milk, a lactic or lactal substance
obtained from the mammary glands of er vaccine
quadrupeds.
—Burgess, *Napoleon Symphony,* p. 323.

VAGITATE : *verb* to travel, to wander

To have vagitated and not be bloody well able to rattle.
—Beckett, *Malone Dies,* p. 341.

VASTATION : *noun* the opposite of "devastation"; a re-
newal, a cleansing of evil from something. See INCONCINNITY

VATIC : *adj* pertaining to prophets or poets. See also MAN-
TIC. Compare FATIDIC

Rawcliffe, out of the vatic residuum of a failed poet's
career, knew that he was going to be killed?
—Burgess, *Enderby,* p. 348.

. . . to fall from heaven into a thornbush, become a
blind lame vatic figure, float upon the marshy tide,

reciting my history aloud, in my own voice.
—Barth, *Chimera*, p. 139.

VATICIDE :   *noun*   a killing of a prophet; according to Samuel
Johnson, killing a poet

. . . Morgan, a rationalist but nowise a quietist, is
indignant to the point of seriously contemplating vaticide (if that term may be extended to cover fictionists as
well as poets). . . .
—Barth, *Letters*, p. 364.

"The man who disvalues words is always a vaticide."
—Theroux, "Theroux Metaphrastes,"
Three Wogs, p. 9.

VELLEITY :   *noun*   a state of desiring wishfully but making
no effort to fulfill the desire. VELLEITARY, *adj*. Compare
antonym CONATION

Can he have loved her for nearly a decade? It's incredible. This connoisseuse of "splendid weakness," run not
by any lust or even velleity but by vacuum: by the
absence of human hope. She is frightening.
—Pynchon, *Gravity's Rainbow*, p. 149.

. . . life itself, had not been a velleity, but a genuine
impulse, of which he still even could feel the sickening
and desperate volition.
—Lowry, *October Ferry to Gabriola*, p. 301

Wignall's themes . . . occasionally exhibited perverse
velleities of a fetishistic order. . . .
—Burgess, *Earthly Powers*, p. 20.

So that each kiss was in reality two kisses, first Watt's
kiss, velleitary, anxious, and then Mrs. Gorman's, unc-
tious† [*sic*] and urbane.
—Beckett, *Watt*, p. 140.

VELLICATION :   *noun*   twitches, tickling, irritation, the feeling of being "picked on." VELLICATIVE, *adj*. See also

EUTRIPSIA. Compare FLOCCILLATE

At sight of how ready he was for her, she started to tremble. At his advance, a patent fury, a torment, of inner vellications that would not admit of delay made her encounter him instantly.
> —Cozzens, *By Love Possessed*, p. 412.

VELUTINOUS : *adj* velvety, smooth and soft

> . . . a huge mug of soft, white, sweet, milk-warm *café au lait*, a pleasant, mild, consoling, velutinous tonic. . . .
> —Aczel, *Illuminations*, p. 321.

VENDITATE : *verb* to advertise flagrantly, to display ostentatiously. Compare EPIDICTIC

> Perhaps he deems it enough to merely—'venditate'—not plink out his thoughts in words.
> —Gardner, *Jason and Medeia*, p. 10.

VENEREAN : *adj* having to do with Venus, with sexual desire. See also ACROAMATICAL

> She had a slight venerean strabismus† and a strong straight French nose.
> —Burgess, *Earthly Powers*, p. 64.

VENERY : *noun* 1) the sport of hunting game animals; 2) the pursuit of sexual pleasure. See also LUXURIOUS

> . . . V. ambiguously a beast of venery, chased like the hart, hind or hare, chased like an obsolete, or bizarre or forbidden form of sexual delight.
> —Pynchon, *V.*, p. 61.

> . . . for whilst Joy uplifts our Hearts, it doth not always stir us to Venery; but Grief, by low'ring our Spirits, causes Humours to rise from the lower Part of the Human Corpus, which must be vented somewhere, and the Bed, dear Belinda, oft' proves the most convenient

place.
—Jong, Fanny, p. 108.

VENTER : *noun* womb, uterus

. . . her spouse, by that frail venter, was to have three children.
—Cozzens, By Love Possessed, p. 126.

VENTRIPOTENT : *adj* big-bellied. Compare GORBEL-LIED, GOTCH-GUT

. . . the stately Embassy kavasses waited in their regal uniforms like great ventripotent pashas. . . .
—Durrell, Monsieur, p. 159.

VERIDICAL : *adj* truthful

. . . one slim eyebrow crooking into a perfect caret in his no-nonsense, veridical way. . . .
—Theroux, Three Wogs, p. 51.

VERMICULAR : *adj* undulating, wavy, wormish

Skipper never failed to bellow "Montezuma's revenge!" at her retreating back, and then collapse in a vermicular spasm, as if this comment were the culmination of thirty centuries of Western wit.
—Boyle, "Quetzalcoatl Lite,"
Descent of Man, p. 174.

VERMICULATED : *adj* covered with raised lines like wormtracks

. . . he stared at her thighs from behind, as a collector stares at the fine patina glazed over the courses of worms, for those vast vermiculated surfaces were furrowed so.
—Gaddis, The Recognitions, p. 329.

VERMIFUGE : *noun* something which gets rid of worms. See DIABOLIFUGE

VESPERTINE : *adj* having to do with twilight. Compare COCKSHUT, CREPUSCULAR

Everything else was aquamarine, a sunken meadow, fresh vespertine breezes, sounds he'd never heard before. . . .
—DeLillo, *Ratner's Star,* p. 156.

VIATIC : *adj* literally, "of the road"; traveling

. . . Hitchhiking Man, *Homo pollex* of science, with all its many sub-species and forms: the modest soldier, spic and span, quietly conscious of khaki's viatic appeal. . . .
—Nabokov, *Lolita,* p. 161.

What are dreams? A random sequence of scenes, trivial or tragic, viatic or static, fantastic or familiar featuring more or less plausible events patched up with grotesque details. . . .
—Nabokov, *Ada,* p. 359.

VIATICUM : *noun* 1) travelling money; 2) the holy eucharist for someone dying or in mortal danger

In his right hand he carried a small Gladstone bag, containing, no doubt, the entire viaticum of a life spent badly. . . .
—Exley, *A Fan's Notes,* p. 116.

Mrs. Cullinane . . . watched the sacrament and took her cup and saucer as the last word in the way of viaticum.
—Theroux, *Three Wogs,* p. 11-12.

VILIPENDING : *noun* a disvaluing, a rendering valueless

. . . the daily weary weight of the not-often-expressed, yet seldom absent, vilipending of hostility or contempt in almost all his fellow men. . . .
—Cozzens, *By Love Possessed,* p. 454.

VIN-DIT : *noun* See quotation.

> . . . *vin-dit,* a Bokononist word meaning a sudden, very personal shove in the direction of Bokononism, in the direction of believing that God Almighty knew all about me, after all, that God Almighty had some pretty elaborate plans for me.
> —Vonnegut, *Cat's Cradle,* p. 64.

VIRIDESCENT : *adj* growing green, greening. VIRIDITY, *noun*

> Here it [the early crop] is suddenly, a conspiracy of water, chlorophyll and cellulose standing erect and viridescent in the sun. . . .
> —Boyle, *Water Music,* p. 329.

> . . . from the woods . . . slow currents of air moved; wafted with them was viridity, a smell of coolness, of shadowed tree trunks, of shady leaves, of ferns, and not-quite-dry moss. . . .
> —Cozzens, *By Love Possessed,* p. 79.

VISCID : *adj* from Latin for "bird-droppings"; sticky, wetted, gooey. VISCIDITY, *noun*

> . . . the spurt shot fluent and high, parabolas of viscid lace that rained down on his chest and tummy, spattering her face and hands.
> —Davenport, "The Dawn in Erewhon,"
> *Tatlin!,* p. 166.

> Quite suddenly there is blood, but it seems almost of a different color and viscidity than that which flows from the wounds of punctured men.
> —Elkin, *George Mills,* p. 386.

VISTULA : *noun* "Cross between 'vista' and 'fistula.' Also river in Russia" (Helprin).

I would appreciate an answer to rectify the vistula in my

yesterday's transcrible. And could you also tell us about rattlesnakes?
—Helprin, *Refiner's Fire,* p. 160.

VITULINE : *adj* referring to calves, veal. See FREMES-CENT. Compare BOANTHROP, UNGULATE, VACCINE

VOLITATION : *noun* a flight of some sort, usually figurative.

Flight from physical self . . . was futile. Volitations of that kind were, for the expedition's rank and file at least, neither afforded nor countenanced.
—Cozzens, *By Love Possessed,* p. 397.

VOLUTED : *adj* spiraled, scrolled

Then his heart jumped as he saw two figures disappear beyond a wavelike hill of roseate voluted sand.
—Helprin, "Martin Bayer," *Ellis Island
& Other Stories,* p. 56.

VULTURED : *adj* watched over with a measuring, anticipatory aspect.

In the very dorm waiting room . . . a barren veldt of frayed carpet vultured with an oil portrait of the foundress. . . .
—Koster, *The Dissertation,* p. 277.

W

WAGGYING : *noun* excrement of a fox. See CROTELS

WAMPETER : *noun* See quotation

> ... the pivot of a *karass*†.... Anything can be a *wampeter:* a tree, a rock, an animal, an idea, a book, a melody, the Holy Grail. Whatever it is, the members of its *karass* revolve about it in the majestic chaos of a spiral nebula.
>
> —Vonnegut, *Cat's Cradle,* pp. 50-51.

WATCHET : *adj* light blue

> Short denim cycling pants faded watchet....
> —Davenport, "The Dawn in Erewhon,"
> *Tatlin!,* p. 215.

WATCHLAR : *noun* "A *lar* [Roman household godlet] that watches, coined on the model of watchdog" (Davenport)

> Or the djinn of love and architecture, a slender ephebic† winged watchlar who cycles souls, whelms† bodies with

lust, and presides over the sense of home and enclosed space. . . .
>—Davenport, "The Dawn in Erewhon,"
>*Tatlin!*, p. 219.

WEASAND, WEZAND: *noun* throat, gullet

Not the hope that some sane man will slit the rotten old Catmit's wezand from ear to ear. . . .
>—Davenport, "C. Musonius Rufus,"
>*Da Vinci's Bicycle*, p. 24.

WEETING : *noun* knowing, knowledge

. . . their loathsome business. To burn Moll Braxton for her weeting (a Latin phrasing), as I gauged it.
>—Rooke, *Shakespeare's Dog*, p. 103.

WELKIN : *noun* See quotation. Compare EMPYREAN

"My father reads things to us. He's a great one for that family tradition, reading aloud. He takes all the parts and makes the welkin ring."
"The what?"
"Welkin. The vault of heaven."
>—DeVries, *Slouching Towards Kalamazoo*, p. 8.

WERDEROBE : *noun* excrement of a badger. See CROTELS.

WHEEN : *noun* 1) a few; 2) a reasonable number. See TANLING

WHELK : *noun* pustule or welt. See BUBUKLE

WHELM : *verb* to turn up, to engulf, to cover over

And in a strangely, he could only think of it as *sibyl-*

line,† tone she said, "*Our* evening is over us, *our* night whelms, whelms and will end us." [from Gerard Manley Hopkins, "Spelt from Sibyl's Leaves"]
—Burgess, *Napoleon Symphony,* p. 345.

Because I'm in pain. . . . Because the griefs ain't leaking no more, they're *whelming.* There's flash-flood griefs, man overboard.
—Elkin, *George Mills,* p. 451.

WHELM : *noun*   the act or cor.dition of being engulfed, capsized

. . . engulfed in a whelm of embarrassment. . . .
—Theroux, *Three Wogs,* p. 95.

WHID : *noun*   1) a lie, falsehood; 2) a word

Ev'n ministers, they ha'e been kenn'd,
In holy rapture,
A rousing whid at times to vend,
And nail't wi' Scripture.
—Robert Burns, "Death and Dr. Hornbook," ll. 3-6.

In your teeth, hypocrite! Just *stow your whids,* or I'll commit some more honeyseed!
—Nye, *Falstaff,* p. 162.

WHILOM : *adj*   former, once but no longer. See CONSTA-TATION, CONSUETUDE

WIDDERSHINS : *adj*   to the left, counter-clockwise; also, inauspiciously. See also and compare antonym DEASIL. Compare synonym SINISTRAL

. . . the Nazi arts. . . .everywhere swastikas seemed to spin widdershins.
—Burgess, *Earthly Powers,* p. 343.

It dances in a slow and complicated, a concentrated, circle, deasil† and widdershins, tracing and retracing its shuffling steps.
>—Nye, *Merlin*, p. 5.

Indeed, for Dilip, there *was* no place—to re-emphasize, and run the adage widdershins—like home.
>—Theroux, *Three Wogs*, p. 100.

WINZE : *noun* a shaft or passage between two levels in a mine

The shop, adjacent to the Palace, but divided from it by the breadth of a steep narrow street desperate as a winze, was opening early.
>—Lowry, *Under the Volcano*, p. 54.

WITTOL : *noun* a man who is aware that his wife is unfaithful but who does not mind or who acquiesces

None save the wittol know he is no cuckold.
>—Barth, *The Sot-Weed Factor*, p. 199.

. . . "wittol"—creatures who wrapped their cracked and heavy hearts in the disguise of jests and tiny poems?
>—Theroux, *Darconville's Cat*, p. 217.

WLAT : *noun* old English for nausea

Whatness translated into wlatness.
>—Theroux, *Darconville's Cat*, p. 359.

WOMPSTER : *noun* someone who thumps or pounds something, usually a bible or other sacred text. See BURKE.

WRANG-WRANG : *noun* See quotation

. . . according to Bokonon, is a person who steers people away from a line of speculation by reducing that line, with the example of the *wrang-wrang's* own life, to an absurdity.
>—Vonnegut, *Cat's Cradle*, p. 71.

Z

ZEPPELINICALLY : *adv* swollen in the sense of being filled with gas like the dirigible airships of the early twentieth century named for the Graf von Zeppelin

General Isidro Bodega's Dutch Finance Minister, who would have confiscated the island for his personal estate, was, for example, visited with the Curse of the Tides, and his belly alternately swelled zeppelinically and shrivelled to his spine—the tides run twenty feet in Mituco Bay—until he gave the project up.
—Koster, *The Dissertation*, p. 9.

ZEUGMA : *noun* the use of a word in relationship to two other words in such a way that it is not grammatically correct with one of the pair. For example: "He divorced his wife and children." See SYLLEPSIS

ZIM : *verb* according to the OED, a spurious word for "gem" or "jewel." ZIMMED, therefore, would mean bedecked with jewels. See SPINTRY

ZINZULATION : *noun* echoic for the sound of power saws

. . . zinzulations of shingle-mills. . . .
—Lowry, *October Ferry to Gabriola*, p. 160.

ZOOMORPHIC : *adj* taking the shape of an animal. See CENAL

ZOOPHILIAC : *adj* animal-loving or copulating with animals

These Otukungurua are prophets of masturbating, specialists in abortion and sterilization, pitchmen for acts oral and anal, pedal and digital, sodomistical and zoophiliac—their approach and their game is pleasure. . . .
                    —Pynchon, *Gravity's Rainbow,* p. 318.

APPENDICES

AUTHORS' RESPONSES

from Tamas Aczel:
I could, paraphrasing Descartes, say that *I choose words, therefore I am*—a novelist, that is. For some, it may sound like the exaggerated enthusiasm of the writer tipsy by words—by the possibilities words offer—but it isn't. Simply, it is a neatly disguised statement of fact which should tell the reader how I feel about words—the language in general—that not only justify my existence, but also define it. The choice of words is as much crucial to me as the choice of idea or plot or character, especially since English isn't my native tongue (Hungarian is) and my appreciation and admiration for my adopted language is boundless. I agree with Samuel Beckett who switched from English to French that it might be a good idea for a writer to leave his mother-tongue behind (at least for a while) so that he could learn to see the world through the filter of a different language and become, in his choice of words, more precise, more accurate, closer to the realities and unrealities of life, simply because unfamiliar words force one to be more careful even with familiar ideas.

But, of course, there are other considerations. One's choice of words is also determined by a host of factors other than linguistic. In *Illuminations* it was influenced by the novel's basic idea and by the central character I have chosen to carry and express that idea in his particular way. From the very beginning, I felt that I had to work out, for my protagonist, a special style—a special way with words—that would uniquely create his world and himself therein. I wasn't deliberately chasing after arcane or obsolete or difficult words—although I must admit I truly enjoyed picking them—but I wanted to use them as characterization to show both the stupidity and the intelligence of my protagonist, the narrowness of his snobbery, for instance, and the wideness of his insights. It may well have been a mistake, for critics and readers alike pointed to the difficulties of reading the novel, but surely it was fun, and truly it was a memorable experience. In my next novel I may use different linguistic "tactics," but, as long as I write, language will be as important for me as existence as a novelist. Being bilingual has its moral obligations, too.

from William F. Buckley, Jr.:
I am not . . . in a position to say why I used a particular word, any more than many musicians are able to say why they use a particular chord.

from Guy Davenport:
Each of my ravings has its own range of diction (I like to think). I like a texture suitable to my subject. In "The Dawn in Erewhon," as elsewhere, I had to solve the problem of describing things and events for which the received concepts and words were unacceptable to me. Obviously I ran the risk of being "precious," but then I don't consider myself a writer. I don't expect to be remembered as one, but as an experimenter who searched out some alternatives in style and subject matter.

Diction is color range, texture, technique. In my new book, for example, *Apples and Pears,* I assigned a range of diction to first violin, another to second violin, another to viola, and another to bass viol, for the sense of quartet. I don't expect anybody to see this: it was a device that kept me knowing what *kind* of word I had to have at any one place, and what kind of music I was making with my imaginary string quartet. (It is also a text—it's part of Adriaan van Hovendaal's *Erewhonisch Schetsboek* mentioned up front in *Tatlin!* as a source for "The Dawn in Erewhon"—written in English by a highly literate Dutch-speaker, so that an English word with a Dutch cognate is always chosen over the better-known English word, and words for which van Hovendaal doesn't know the idiomatic English are in Dutch.)

from Peter DeVries:
I'm glad you found so many words of interest to your own purpose in the two books from which you've culled examples. You'll find some in the opening chapter of *Consenting Adults,* I think. They're there for much the same reason the big or obscure words are present in *Slouching Towards Kalamazoo.* They fit the character.

from Frederick Exley:
I have no explanation other than sheer pain-in-the-ass pretentiousness and a fat thesaurus.

from John Fowles:
My own general feeling is that we must try to keep the language as rich as possible. So I do usually try to use a few unusual words; but of course this can be extremely irritating if done too often.

from William Gaddis:
... [I] can't offhand comment on reasons for their selection except in some cases (as Eliot) plain homage.

from Mark Helprin:
As to why I coin words, well, any boomatooq knows that the brain generates words continually, and that a certain granile discipline is needed not to spring them. The dirty little bastards occur to me contrumptuously ... and choke my days and nights. I only let them out on occasion, for relief, or because of lapsis. Unfortunately, I "know" half a dozen languages, and can read half a dozen more by pattern sympolisis and anagolisis. This gets quite confusing, as originate forms also perofulate. And not only that, but they sound nice and sometimes it's good not to be understood, since one is seldom properly understood anyway, even when writing orthodontically.

from R.M. Koster:
A good writer does what's necessary to get the right word.

from Robert Nye:
In general, the only comment I would make is that I love and respect the English language and have always sought to use it as

carefully as possible. If this sometimes causes me to use an unusual word then I like to think that it is because the unusual word more exactly expresses what it is that I am trying to say. Of course there have also been occasions when I have used words *playfully,* and you should allow for that. . . .In general, again, with each of my novels I suppose I try to give the reader a high old time linguistically as part of the business of soaking him in the story and the story's time. But I would like to drop you the hint that there is no sense in which I am really an "historical" novelist. In fact, it occurs to me that my stuff is the work of some sort of dangerous "modernist" playing games with history, myth, language, and the lucky or unlucky reader.

from Alexander Theroux:
. . . people mistakenly believe, through stupidity and sloth, that the "big" word is used by writers in pretentious excuse for showing-off, when the fact is, for anyone who takes his work seriously, such words are used not to obfuscate but to *clarify.* A given word is neither pompous nor plain when you come right down to it, but a person is either educated or un-. As far as neologisms, it is no different than a painter mixing a new and better color in order to express something or other more accurately.

from Paul West:
Although I now seem to go for simple, thewy words, I confess to more often than not reading etymologically, as much aware of my ancestors as of what someone has meant to say.

SOURCES

Aczel, Tamas. *Illuminations*. New York: Pantheon, 1981.

Aldiss, Bryan. *The Malacia Tapestry*. New York: Harper & Row, 1977.

Barth, John. *Chimera*. New York: Random House, 1972.

—. *The End of the Road*. Garden City: Doubleday, 1967.

—. *The Floating Opera*. Garden City: Doubleday, 1967.

—. *Giles Goat-Boy*. Garden City: Doubleday, 1966.

—. *Letters*. New York: Putnam, 1979.

—. *Sabbatical*. New York: Putnam, 1982.

—. *The Sot-Weed Factor*. Garden City: Doubleday, 1967.

Beckett, Samuel. *Malone Dies*. New York: Grove, 1956.

—. *Molloy*. New York: Grove, 1958.

—. *More Pricks than Kicks*. New York: Grove, 1972.

—. *Murphy*. New York: Grove, 1957.

—. *The Unnamable*. —. New York: Grove, 1958.

—. *Watt*. New York: Grove, 1959.

Berger, Thomas. *Arthur Rex*. New York: Delacorte, 1978.

Boyd, William. *An Ice Cream War*. New York: Morrow, 1983.

Boyle, T.C. *Budding Prospects*. New York: Viking, 1984.

—. *The Descent of Man*. Boston: Little, Brown, 1979.

—. *Water Music*. Boston: Little, Brown, 1981.

Buckley, Christopher. *Steaming to Bamboola*. New York: Congdon & Weed, 1982.

Buckley, William F., Jr. *Stained Glass*. Garden City: Doubleday, 1978.

Bunting, Josiah, III. *The Advent of Frederick Giles*. Boston: Little, Brown, 1974.

Burgess, Anthony. *The Doctor Is Sick*. London: Heinemann, 1960.

—. *Earthly Powers*. New York: Simon & Schuster, 1980.

—. *Enderby*. New York: Norton, 1968.

—. *The End of the World News*. New York: McGraw-Hill, 1983.

—. *Honey for the Bears*. London: Heinemann, 1963.

—. *Napoleon Symphony*. New York: Knopf, 1974.

—. *Tremor of Intent*. London: Heinemann, 1966.

—. *The Wanting Seed*. London: Heinemann, 1962.

Caine, Jeffrey. *Heathcliffe*. New York: Knopf, 1978.

Cameron, Kenneth M. *Our Jo*. New York: Macmillan, 1974.

SOURCES

Chatwin, Bruce. *The Viceroy of Ouidah*. New York: Summit Books, 1980.

Coover, Robert. *Pricksongs and Descants*. New York: Dutton, 1969.

Cozzens, James Gould. *By Love Possessed*. New York: Harcourt, Brace, 1957.

Davenport, Guy. *DaVinci's Bicycle*. Baltimore: Johns Hopkins University Press, 1979.

—. *Eclogues*. San Francisco: North Point Press, 1981.

—. *Tatlin!* New York: Scribner's, 1974.

Davies, Robertson. *The Rebel Angels*. New York: Viking, 1982.

DeLillo, Don. *Ratner's Star*. New York: Knopf, 1976.

DeVries, Peter. *Consenting Adults*. Boston: Little, Brown, 1980.

—. *Into Your Tent I'll Creep*. Boston: Little, Brown, 1971.

—. *Slouching Towards Kalamazoo*. Boston: Little, Brown, 1983.

Durrell, Lawrence. *Constance*. New York: Viking, 1982.

—. *Justine*. New York: Dutton, 1957.

—. *Monsieur*. New York: Viking, 1975.

Eastlake, William. *Dancers in the Scalp House*. New York: Viking, 1975.

Eco, Umberto. *The Name of the Rose*. San Diego & New York: Harcourt Brace Jovanovich, 1983.

Elkin, Stanley. *George Mills*. New York: Dutton, 1982.

Exley, Frederick. *A Fan's Notes*. New York: Harper & Row, 1968.

—. *Pages from a Cold Island*. New York: Random House, 1975.

Faulkner, William. *A Fable*. New York: Random House, 1954.

Fowles, John. *Daniel Martin*. Boston: Little, Brown, 1977.

—. *The Ebony Tower*. Boston: Little, Brown, 1974.

—. *The French Lieutenant's Woman*. Boston: Little, Brown, 1969.

—. *The Magus*. Boston: Little, Brown, 1977.

—. *Mantissa*. Boston: Little, Brown, 1982.

Foxell, Nigel. *Carnival*. Ottawa: Oberon Press, 1968.

Gaddis, William. *The Recognitions*. New York: Harcourt, Brace, 1955.

Gardner, John. *Jason and Medeia*. New York: Knopf, 1973.

—. *Mickelsson's Ghosts*. New York: Knopf, 1982.

—. *The Wreckage of Agathon*. New York: Harper & Row, 1970.

Helprin, Mark. *Ellis Island and Other Stories*. New York: Delacorte, 1981.

—. *Refiner's Fire*. New York: Knopf, 1977.

—. *Winter's Tale*. San Diego & New York: Harcourt Brace Jovanovich, 1983.

Jong, Erica. *Fanny*. New York: New American Library, 1980.

—. *Fear of Flying*. New York: Holt, Rinehart & Winston, 1973.

Koster, R.M. *The Dissertation*. New York: Harper's Magazine Press, 1975.

—. *Mandragon*. New York: Morrow, 1979.

—. *The Prince*. New York: Morrow, 1972.

Lloyd-Jones, Robin. *The Lord of the Dance*. Boston: Little, Brown, 1983.

Lowry, Malcolm. *Hear us O Lord from heaven thy dwelling place*. Philadelphia: Lippincott, 1961.

—. *October Ferry to Gabriola*. New York: World Publishing, 1970.

—. *Under the Volcano*. Philadelphia: Lippincott, 1947.

SOURCES

Masters, John. *Bugles and a Tiger.* New York: Viking, 1956.

—. *Coromandel.* New York: Viking, 1955.

Nabokov, Vladimir. *Ada.* New York: McGraw-Hill, 1969.

—. *Lolita.* New York. Putnam, 1958.

—. *Look at the Harlequins!* New York: McGraw-Hill, 1974.

—. *Pale Fire.* New York: Putnam, 1962.

—. *Transparent Things.* New York: McGraw-Hill, 1972.

Naipaul, V.S. *A Bend in the River.* New York: Knopf, 1979.

Nye, Robert. *Falstaff.* Boston: Little, Brown, 1976.

—. *Faust.* New York: Putnam, 1981.

—. *Merlin.* New York: Putnam, 1979.

—. *Tales I Told My Mother.* New York: Hill & Wang, 1969.

—. *The Voyage of the Destiny.* New York: Putnam, 1982.

Percy, Walker. *The Last Gentleman.* New York: Farrar, Straus & Giroux, 1966.

—. *The Message in the Bottle.* New York: Farrar, Straus & Giroux, 1975.

—. *The Moviegoer.* New York: Knopf, 1961.

Pynchon, Thomas. *Gravity's Rainbow.* New York: Viking, 1973.

—. *V.* Philadelphia: Lippincott, 1963.

Queneau, Raymond. *We Always Treat Women Too Well.* New York: New Directions, 1981.

Rooke, Leon. *Shakespeare's Dog.* New York: Knopf, 1983.

Theroux, Alexander. *Darconville's Cat.* Garden City: Doubleday, 1981.

—. *The Great Wheadle Tragedy.* Boston: Godine, 1975.

—. *Three Wogs.* Boston: Godine, 1975.

Vonnegut, Kurt, Jr. *Cat's Cradle.* New York: Holt, Rinehart & Winston, 1963.

—. *Happy Birthday, Wanda June.* New York: Delacorte, 1971.

—. *The Sirens of Titan.* New York: Dell, 1959.

Waugh, Evelyn. *The Loved One.* Boston: Little, Brown, 1948.

West, Paul. *Gala.* New York: Harper & Row, 1976.

—. *Out of My Depths.* Garden City: Doubleday, 1983.

Wolfe, Tom. *From Bauhaus to Our House.* New York: Farrar, Straus & Giroux, 1981.

—. *The Pump House Gang.* New York: Farrar, Straus & Giroux, 1968.

These are words found since the publication of the *Oxter English Dictionary* and *The Penguin Dictionary of Curious and Interesting Words*.

ABSEIL : *verb* German rock climbing term, literally "off-rope," a technique for moving on vertical surfaces. Compare GRIMPEN in main text

> The mountain had been covered with snow when they were coming down. They had abseiled down the ridge.
>
> —Salter, *Solo Faces*, p. 209.

ABYSM : *noun* the bottomless pit, hell. An old form of "abyss," still seen in the adjective "abysmal" which has more unpleasant connotations than "abyssal" which now has oceanographic denotation

> This world of imagination is a universe wherein quality leaps to cohere with quality across the abysms of classification that divide and categorize the universe of intellectual apprehension. Its true citizens are few and far between; they are the masters of metaphor, and the authentic messages they bring from that near yet distant country perplex our brains and comfort our souls with the half-assurance that the things that are may be otherwise than we know them.
>
> —Murray, John Middleton, "Metaphor," In:
> Shibles, *Essays on Metaphor*, p. 37.

AGELAST : *noun* Greek. See quotation

> . . . The West Virginia State Home for Agelasts . . .
> Agelasts? They are according to the Oxford English
> Dictionary, people who never laugh, but I think in
> the main I would call them unfortunates without
> any option but to look on the universe realistically.
> —Grubb, *Ancient Lights*, p. 34.

AIRT : *noun* or *verb* from Scottish. See quotation

> "What [words] do you go for?"
> "Old or Middle English ones. Grit. Moil. Bast. All
> the four-letter monosyllables aren't obscene. Cull.
> Airt."
> "Nice. What's it mean—airt?"
> "As a noun—a height or direction. One-quarter of
> the compass. As a verb –'to guide.' "
> —Calisher, *On Keeping Women*, p. 98.

AMERCED : *verb* to punish with a fine, to exact.
AMERCEMENT, AMERCIEAMENT : *noun* fines levied
arbitrarily by a judge as punishment.

> . . . the sheer tax-manoeuvring his wife's behavior
> had now got him into! his own cursing yeoman
> forebears hadn't been amerced with a blacker set of
> reliefs and merchets†, church-scott† and plough-
> alms and smoke-farthings and hearthpenny on Holy
> Thursday, and nowadays who could he tallage† in
> return?
> —Spackman, *An Armful of Warm Girl*, p. 34.

AMERCIEAMENT : *continued*

> . . . the said Falstaff has been vexed. . . in great
> oppressions, grievous and outrageous amercie-
> aments and many great horrible extortions. . . .
> —Nye, *Falstaff*, p. 412.

ANACOLUTHIA : *noun* a lack of grammatical sequence, a non sequitur. See MOLIMINOUS

ANTABUSE : *noun.* See quotation

> . . . The redemption of alcoholics by the adminis-
> tration of a drug, with the above trade name, which
> associates the consumption of alcohol with the most
> unpleasant consequences.
> —Bowler, Peter, *The Superior Person's Book of
> Words*, p. 7.

> "I drink for my brother," he said later. "I'm his
> antibuse [sic]."
> —Calisher, *On Keeping Women*, p. 164.

ANTANACLASIS : *noun* a pun in which a word is repeated with a different meaning or sense

> He and Melony were doomed to become a kind of
> **couple** because there was no one else for them to
> **couple** with.
> —Irving, *Cider House Rules*, p. 119.

> ". . . On good authority I have it that you and Mrs.
> McKee **couldn't be happier. You couldn't be, so
> you haven't been, happier.**"
> —Morris, *Ceremony in Lone Tree*, p. 181.

ANTANACLASIS : continued

He let the curtain drop and the terrible light that had **played** on his features went off to **play** somewhere more healthy.
—Adams, *The Restaurant at the End of the Universe*,
p. 100.

Gertrude was a **spoiled** one, and knew it, and knew that the world soon stops **spoiling** children, except in the other sense of the word.
—Jarrell, *Pictures from an Institution*, p. 179.

"Most magnificent example of the pre-Vedic art that I've ever seen!" . . . Blight sprang with the speed and finesse of a master thief. (Who doubts it?) With a thin, Oslo-forged blade, he pried the plaque from the wall and pushed it into Katy's hands.
"What. . . ?"
"Quick! Hide it under your skirt!" He whipped out his belt and, never hesitating, strapped the treasure twixt her legs and flat against her abdomen. The whole affair, from **snatch to snatch**, had not taken fifteen seconds.
—Schneck, *The Nightclerk*, p. 105.

ANTHIMERIA : *noun* a rhetorical device in which one part of speech is used as another: noun as a verb, verb as a noun, etc. The technical expression is "functional shift" which is woefully uneuphonious. See BURGLARIOUS, MANGOED, SURGER, VULTURED in the main text

I slid a hand down her back, slipped the fingers inside the edge of the costume, **appled** a curved cheek. . . .
— Fowles, *The Magus*, p. 351.

Probably she is thinking about the birds. No, not those crows that just **haiku-ed** by. . . .
— Robbins, *Even Cowgirls Get the Blues*, p. 3.

A cutworm moth **Icarused** into her beer. . . .
— Nichols, *The Magic Journey*, p. 427.

. . . a splenetic grudge which ripened into a bouncing **loath**. . . .
— Theroux, Alexander, "Childe Roland," *Three Wogs*, p. 79.

She and Bart shared a fairly good rapport, as any fool kid my age could see. They squeezed and jostled and poked and prodded each other a lot, told dirty jokes, squealed with laughter, and, in general, **friendlied** up a storm.
— Nichols, *A Ghost in the Music*, p. 23.

ANTIMETABOLE : *noun* a figure of speech in which the order of repeated words is reversed. If the words are re-used in different or contrasting senses it is a form of ANTANACLASIS

> All his life he'd been a man of mystery, who never **did** what he **said** or **said** what he **did**.
> —Koster, *Mandragon*, p. 250.

> Nothing distinguishes us more clearly from the Americans, nothing characterizes better the very different ways we use our shared language––the way they use it as a **tool**, even when they are being **poetic**, and the way we treat it as a **poem**, even when we are using it as a **tool**.
> . . . and it is the same with the enormous semantic subtleties of middle-class English intonation and the poverty of nuance in even the most intellectually sophisticated American equivalent.
> —Fowles, *Daniel Martin*, p. 72.

> He had that formidable easygoingness of the landed farmer; half out of knowledge of his social position, perhaps, but also half out of his familiarity with natural processes. It was a **virtue** of **privilege** that became a **privilege** of **virtue** of a kind.
> —Fowles, *Daniel Martin*, p. 304.

ANTONOMASIA : *noun* a figure of speech, a trope and a form of METONYMY in which an epithet, a nickname, is substituted for the proper name or vice versa

> As the fire burned, its resinous pine and bone-dry hickory became a **Waterloo** of advancing red lines and tiny gunshots.
> —Helprin, *Winter's Tale*, p. 577.

> Victor England's London home is in a newly whitened, newly heightened, newly brightened terrace facing a royal park. Victor feels a proud uneasiness as he approaches this flat-faced Parthenon with its grin of pillars, forever open wide, in a **Nashing*** of plaster teeth.

> *John Nash, English architect
> —Raphael, *California Time*, p. 19.

> [Ambrose Bierce] scathed religion and dealt **Swift*** blows against corrupt politicians.

> * Jonathan Swift, Anglo-Irish satirist, author of *Gulliver's Travels*. This example is also equivocation, a pun.
> —Brophy, *The Adventures of God in his Search for the Black Girl*, p. 20.

ASSORT : *verb* to keep company (with someone)

> I had no knowledge then of Carlo's taste for comedy.
> Even when I got to know him well, I must say I
> continued to think his low talent for foolery assorted
> ill with his political agility and subtle grasp of
> situations.
> —Friedman, *Hermaphrodeity*, p. 269.

ATTERCOP : *noun* English dialect literally, "poison
head," a spider. Originally "natter," the "N" dropped off and
later the "T" changed to "D" becoming "adder"

> [18th century description of a UFO]. . . thy flying
> mawk† and its attercop legs. . . .
> —Fowles, *A Maggot*, p. 361.

AUDASTIC : *adj* an insolent incompetent variant on
"audacious" perhaps a portmanteau word combining
"audacious" with "spastic". See Nichols, BDELYGMIA

AUTOLOG : *noun* a word (such as "autolog"), phrase,
sentence or passage that refers to itself

> He **flolloped** around in astonishment and alarm.
> He almost **lurgled** in fear. . . He listened, but there
> was no sound on the wind beyond the now familiar
> sound of **half-crazed etymologists calling to each
> other** across the sullen mire.
> —Adams, *Life, the Universe and Everything*, p. 59.

BARTON : *noun* an English term for a farm yard

> ... the green pond of Devon voices, his Devon and
> England, quick and tortuous ancestral voices ... A
> language so local, so phonetically condensed and
> permissive of slur that it is inseparable in his mind,
> and will always remain so, from its peculiar
> landscape; its combes† and bartons, leats† and
> linhays†.
>
> —Fowles, *Daniel Martin*, p. 6.

BDELYGMIA : *noun* Greek "loathing, disgust"
expression of loathing, disgust, insult, invective, cursing.
Pronounced *bdel IG mia* think of Porky Pig's *bduh-bduh-
that's all folks.* Examples:

> You were born a companion to spiders, to scutter
> through a sputum-lobbied world trailing a slime of
> fear. Your sewer universe is narrow, low, and dark,
> a haven for roaches lighted only where the deepest
> drift of mine plummets to graze it.
>
> —Koster, *The Prince*, p. 305.

> "... I only wonder why the fuck you don't just finish
> with your silly fictions and accept the fact that
> you're selfish, and thoughtless and cynical ... And a
> goddam kazoo of self-pity."
>
> —Theroux, Alexander, *An Adultery*, p. 220.

> ... Jerry Payne, of all the cross-eyed square-toed
> pink-phalanged five-uddered knuckle-brained clap-
> congested audastic† atavistic Bavarian Yeti sons of
> cabbage-headed hogbody bigluvulating bastards,
> YOU TAKE THE ROYAL CAKE!
>
> —Nichols, *The Sterile Cuckoo*, p. 40.

BDELYGMIA : continued

"God, you stink," Angel said, kicking him onto the floor. "You're just a worthless collection of molecules . . . Garbage wrapped in skin, right?"
—Kimball, *Firewater Pond*, p. 43.

"I must remind you that you are an entirely chance and very transient biological eventlet and that—"
"A what?"
"You heard. A microscopic nothing, an amoebic drone, a lost bluebottle flying through the hall of eternity."
—Fowles, *Mantissa*, p. 140.

BUDDLE : *verb* a mining term for washing ore in a shallow container, sluicing. In this usage, washed out, cleared

I thought they must come near their journey's end, and I must ride no more sir. That if I did they might hear or see me from their better vantage. So I took me my horse to a thicket and tied him, the best I could hide in so buddled a place.
—Fowles, *A Maggot*, p. 213.

APPENDIX

CADASTRAL : *adj* from French "cadastre" a polltax; pertaining to valuation for tax purposes. A Cadastral Survey is a large scale tax map

> . . . man in a word from his own well-fed well-brought-up decent dying generation, to whom by god there was still a residual meaning in Domesday Book's ancient cadastral *quantum silvae quantum prati** (but now co-parceners† of what moss-hung and abandoned avenues, what crumbling porticoes).
> . . .

> * Latin: how much woodland, how much meadow
> —Spackman, *An Armful of Warm Girl*, p. 128.

CATOBLEPAS : *noun* from Greek "to look downward;" a genus of quadrupeds including the gnu whose eyes are oriented downward and a mythical beast whose eyes kill anyone looking at them.

> "Is Señora Gutusso that kind of catoblepas who spends her time talking to Gekrepten?"
> "Yes, it's her turn to be friends this week. You'll see in a few days, that's how things go in this neighborhood."
> —Cortázar, *Hopscotch*, p. 229.

CHIASMUS : *noun* a figure of speech in which contrasted terms are reversed in order in successive phrases. Often confused with ANTIMETABOLE which is a reversal of order of repeated words

> The left of the brain, where intuitions leap like lightning, controls the dextrous right hand, logic, speech, our sense of space. The right of the brain, where reason stands alert, controls the awkward left hand, suspicion, primal fear, our sense of time. . . the animal man is a chiasmus of complementary and contradictory functions.
>
> —Davenport, "A Field of Snow on a Slope of the Rosenberg," *DaVinci's Bicycle*, p. 151.

CHOWER : *verb* English dialect to grumble, to scold;
CHOWRING : grumbling, scolding

> The two gentlemen studiously avoided the watching eyes; and a sterness and gravity in their demeanor forbade greeting or enquiry [sic], if not chowring comment.
>
> —Fowles, *A Maggot*, p. 13.

CHURCH-SCOT : *noun* old English tax on crops for the support of the clergy. See AMERCED

CLUNALLY : *adv* behaving in the manner of a Cluniac monk from the monastery at Cluny or Clugny near Mâcon, France who chose to live cloistered lives locked away from the vexations of the outside world

> Esau became a babbling prison buff, clunally manic. He plotted how he could commit the most grievous crimes within the venue of those prisons populated by the most violent men and somehow win a preposterously long sentence.
> —Condon, *The Vertical Smile*, p. 182.

COMBE : *noun* a small valley or hollow in the south of England; see BARTON

CONCESSIVE : *adj* yielding, willing to give in, up, or out

> "I see what you mean," he says at last. He makes little humorous concessive noises in his throat, to admit his mistake.
> —Frayn, *Sweet Dreams*, p. 125.

CONGRUOUS : *adj* agreeable, harmonious, suitable

> She was given a drink. Everyone was friendly. They laughed, they talked softly, they were the most congruous people she had ever seen, they accepted her.
> —Salter, *Light Years*, pp. 232-233.

CONSTERNED : *adj* amazed, dismayed, terrorized

> Without consideration, she lumped her way past the consterned guard, scattered the indoor footmen, heaved herself up the grand staircase, burst into her suite and flung herself at her glass.
> —Brophy, "The Singularly Ugly Princess," *The Adventures of God in Search for the Black Girl*, p.11.

CO-PARCENER : *noun* a person who shares equally with others in an inheritance. See CADASTRAL

CORACOID : *adj* shaped like a crow's beak

> . . . his shoulder blades jutted behind, coracoid through the white-on-white shirt.
> —Bellow, *Herzog*, p. 83.

CUNEAL : *adj* wedge-shaped

> Her robe was open—he had untied it—her eyes concealed in shadow. The black print of her navel, the even blacker cuneal hair shone up at him like dark stones at the bottom of a pond.
> —Salter, *Light Years*, p. 284.

DETRIMENTAL : *adj* capable of causing damage, inflicting loss

> "Did they have guns?"
> "No self-respecting robot could be fully detrimental without one," said Trinity.
> —Wright, *M 31*, p. 53.

DIABLERIE : *noun* French for malice and roguishness.

> He'd always been a pretty well-groomed killer. I guess cleanliness is next to diablerie, or something like that.
> —Zelazny, *This Immortal*, p. 147.

DIDASCALIC : *adj* from Greek for "teacher," didactic, moralistic

> But Berthe Trépat was lost in didascalic convolutions and had begun to tell with enthusiasm of her meeting with Germaine Tailleferre . . . .
> —Cortázar, *Hopscotch*, p. 115.

DISSEVER : *verb* to separate one thing from another, divide into parts

> They are just below—the nearest ones can't be seen. The talk, only a bit dissevered, rises up as if to include him.
> —Salter, *A Sport and a Pastime*, p. 128.

DRISK : *noun* a drizzly mist

> Rather pathetically, they envied Parisian Catholic groups for the seasoned subtleties that Russian mysticism so obviously lacked. Dostoevskian drisk could not compete with neo-Thomist thought; but were there not other ways?
> —Nabokov, *Speak, Memory*, p. 284.

DUFFIL : *verb* to be left behind

> I wanted to see the town, but I was afraid of being duffilled. . . there would not be another train for three days.
> —Theroux, Paul, *The Old Patagonian Express*,
> p. 336.

DUPPY : *noun* See quotation

> ". . . they is ghosts."
> "Of dead people," Father said.
> "Of alive people."
> "I see."
> "Everyone got a Duppy. They is the same as yourself. But they is you other self. They got bodies of they own."
> —Theroux, Paul, *The Mosquito Coast*, p. 147.

ELEATIC : *adj* referring to the school of philosophy of Elea and the idea that the immutable (unchangeable) is the only knowable reality and change is the subject of mere opinion

> Those shadows in the cornice; the room has lungs, it palpitates. Yes, electricity is eleatic, it has turned our shadows to stone . . . Now they are part of the furniture and the faces.
> —Cortázar, *Hopscotch*, p. 42.

ENUCLEATION : *noun* from Latin the removal of a kernel from something; clarification, nutshelling, explanation or the removal of something without cutting, such as shelling peanuts or popping out eyeballs

> Here however his lawyer worked his weighty way through the uproar and started holding these dockets up against the cabin wall for him to sign one after another, affably bawling his full-phrased enucleation of each in turn into his ear....
> —Spackman, *An Armful of Warm Girl*, p. 127.

EDULCORATED : *verb* to soften or sweeten or purify or all three.

> I would say I wanted to fight simultaneously on two fronts, challenging the Resistance's detractors and at the same time, those high priests of hagiographic and edulcorated Resistance
> —Calvino, *The Path to the Nest of Spiders*, p. *xiii*.

EPIGONE : *noun* from Greek *epigonos* (singular) *epigonoi* (plural) "born after" referring to the sons of the Seven against Thebes, who imitated their fathers; thus a second rate imitator

> On the one hand the period of adventure which characterized the New England of Colonial and Federal times had exhausted itself in a generation of epigonoi.
> —Wiener, *The Human Use of Human Beings*, p. 29.

EPOPT : *noun* from Greek   a beholder, an initiate of Eleusinian mysteries

> . . . and now the horselaughs come shrieking out across Sixth Avenue to where all the obedient epopts of old-sample sentiment are bunched in front of Kaiser's. That was a good hit! Twenty or thirty of them, free squares of New York, bunched together and all conned! gulled! faked out! put on! had! by the Voices of Village Square.
>> —Wolfe, *The Kandy-Kolored-Tangerine-Flake-Streamlined Baby*, p. 313.

EQUIVOCATION : *noun* as a figure of speech, a pun in which two meanings can be understood in the use of one word. As Samuel Johnson referred to a one word pun—"two words for one." You read it once, notice something odd about it, then reread it to catch what you saw out of the corner of your mind's eye.

Examples:

> ". . . You're [screen-writers] locked up in the untenable dream , we're [philosophers] condemned to the tenable proposition . The word as game. The word as tool. Just as long as the one doesn't pretend to be the other."
> "You never **play** with your tools?"
> "Oh, I couldn't deny that we have self-abuse in common."
>> —Fowles, *Daniel Martin*, p. 182.

> Morality, to him, was making a good impression on everybody, **selling** himself (that accurately ambiguous phrase) to everybody.
>> —Jarrell, *Pictures from an Institution*, pp. 72-73.

EQUIVOCATION : continued

Jumping to conclusions was the only exercise they ever got. They got offended when others talked while they were interrupting.
> —Theroux, Alexander, *An Adultery*, p. 69.

"Of course I had to sit through the whole thing," he related, licking his thin, ascetic lips. "You can imagine what it was like, all alone, there in the dark. **I felt a perfect ass.**"
"Like the man fishing for the pearls that slipped down the back of the lady's gown," I said from the edge of the group.
> —DeVries, *The Glory of the Hummingbird*, p. 78.

". . . And what Mummy always quotes he said to her when he first met her? That he liked to play with his mental **blocks**, he had so many of them?"
> —Calisher, *On Keeping Women*, p. 217.

"You are my India," Magog said, **partitioning** Hadassah's thighs with his right hand.
> —Sinclair, *Magog*, p. 32.

"Trade Follows the Flag"
"I'm afraid we shall have to make a small **charge**," said the cavalry commander.
> —Brophy, *The Adventures of God in his search for the Black Girl*, p. 37.

EQUIVOCATION : continued

Oh, man, she thought, any minute I'm gonna crash, but not in public, pleeze dear God, or these yokels may discover I'm a runaway nun from Campeche who's exchanged one **habit** for another.

—Fraser, *The Pyrates*, p. 242.

"And don't be too hard on animals... There's a lot of **good** in animals, especially when they're killed and cooked."

—Burgess, *The Eve of Saint Venus*, p. 131.

Talent was always the best insurance. Someone would always want you again for what you had done before. To get him for less than they had promised struck them as a victory. Let it be so: being somebody's trophy meant you always had a **case**.

—Raphael, *California Time*, p. 206.

ESURIENT : *adj* from Latin hungry

I couldn't have kept up with Sebastian at the most esurient moment of my hollow-bellied adolescence. I had no taste for the succession of dishes that arrived on the trolley, which never stayed long at rest. . . .

—Berger, *Nowhere*, p. 59.

EXCIPIENT : *noun* an inert substance such as gum, syrup, or starch used to make a medicine stick together to be used in pill or tablet form

> . . . Morelli had been suspicious of the demoniacal nature of all re-creative writing (and what literature wasn't like that, even if it was something like the excipient that would make a person swallow a gnosis, a praxis, or an ethos out of all the ones that were wandering around or that could be invented?).
>
> —Cortázar, *Hopscotch*, p. 534.

EXIMIOUSLY : *adv* exceptionally, singularly, excellently

> You say his Lordship must conceal, he must dissemble his true allegiance, to wit that he is, or was, of the spirit of the Redeemer. How, is this, mistress? Is it so Our Lord conducted himself—did He not most eximiously hold truth above all else?
>
> —Fowles, *A Maggot*, p. 418.

EXTRAVAGATE : *verb* to wander away, or to exceed acceptable bounds

> "Four months since in the county of Devon you passed as Brown. Do you dare deny it?"
> The actor looks abruptly away.
> "You extravagate, sir. I take my leave.
>
> —Fowles, *A Maggot*, p. 109.

FASTIGIUM : *noun* Latin "top, summit." See quotation

> . . . isn't it a lot like the fastigium, the most critical and serious moment of an illness."
> . . . "Fastigium is a very pretty word," Talita said. "Too bad it means what it does."
> —Cortázar, *Hopscotch*, p. 252.

FELDHERRENHÜGEL : *noun* German. See quotation

> . . . the mound upon which the commanding generals stood to direct the battle.
> —Deighton, *Funeral in Berlin*, p. 47.

FOSSICK : *verb* Australian to mine gold in a minor manner

> But he would contrive to fossick in desperation through his memories of all evil dreams.
> —White, *Voss*, p. 178.

FOUDROYANT : *adj* French "thundering," terrifying, overwhelming. See DeLillo, SCESISONOMATION

FRASS : *noun* insect excrement. Compare CROTELS in the main text

> In a sweating glass jar, several spiny caterpillars were feeding on nettle leaves (and ejecting interesting, barrel-shaped pellets of olive-green frass).
> —Nabokov, *Speak, Memory*, p. 80.

GARDYLOO : *verb* Scottish warning to passersby when a container is being emptied from an upper story out onto the street. Probably from French *regardez-vous*, "Watch-out"

> O you strange town! Your every stone holds as many old memories as there are motes of dust . . . the king's horses struck sparks from you, and the dandies in brown and the poets in black repaired to the coffee houses while you dripped with slops to the merry echoes of gardyloo.
> —Nabokov, *Bend Sinister*, p. 33.

GELTUNGSBEDÜRFNIS : *noun* German. See quotation.

> "Can anyone tell me," he inquired without lifting his head, "how I translate *Geltungsbedürfnis?*"
> "A need to assert oneself," de Lisle suggested. . . .
> —Le Carré, *A Small Town in Germany*, p. 12.

GERENT : *noun* Latin a manager, overseer. See ULLAGE

GOPAK; *noun* Ukrainian hopping folk dance with much heel tapping.

> Dawlish began to move items off the top of his desk like he was going to climb on it and do a gopak. It was a sign of deep emotion.
> —Deighton, *Funeral in Berlin*, p.144.

HAUST : *verb* from Latin to suck in, drink up, drain

> He grabbed a bottle of bourbon, filled Darconville's glass, and tapping a toast hausted right from the bottle in one long suck.
> —Theroux, Alexander, *Darconville's Cat*, p. 194.

HELMENSIVE : *adj* from Greek for "intestinal worms." See quotation

> Given to worming in where unwanted. (She's always injecting herself into the society, confidences and affairs of others through devious and insidious means.).
> —Burr, *BISBA*, p. 354.

HONORIFICABILITUDINITATIBUS : *noun* sesquipedalian† coinage for honorableness as found in:

> "Thou are not so long by the head as honorificabilitudinitatibus.
> —Shakespeare, *Love's Labour Lost*, V, i.

> ". . . I marvel thy master hath not eaten thee for a word, for thou art not so long by the head as hon—hon—honorif-"
> "Honorificabilitudinitatibus."
> —Burgess, *Nothing Like the Sun*, p. 111.

HRÖNIR (plural) : *noun.* See quotation

> In the most ancient regions of Tlön, the duplication of lost objects is not infrequent. Two persons look for a pencil; the first finds it and says nothing; the second finds a second pencil, no less real, but closer to his expectations. These secondary objects are called hrönir and are, though awkward in form, somewhat longer. . . Stranger and more pure than any *hrön* is, at times, the *ur:* the object produced through suggestion, educed by hope.
> —Borges, "The Zahir," *Labyrinths*, pp. 13-14;
> translated by J.E. Irby.

HYPAETHRAL : *adj* fromGreek "under the sky" roofless, open at the top

> I looked toward the earth again and watched the line of first clouds which, very low, clove the city in two. Slowly we gained it, flowing through smooth, hypaethral air.
> —Salter, *The Arm of Flesh*, p. 135.

HYPALLAGE : *noun* using an adjective that normally would not be considered appropriate with the noun it modifies. Many slang expressions fall under this usage and get squashed flat into commonplace roadkill. A form of METONYMY, also known as "transferred epithet.". If the adjective is contradictory to the sense of the noun the phrase is an OXYMORON.

> A youngish-looking man came up to him, an aggressive-looking type with a hook mouth, a lantern nose and small **beady little cheekbones**.
> —Adams,, *Life, the Universe and Everything*, p. 153.

> A monocle dangled on his chest, making a little **anxious dot** of light.
> —Nye, "A Portuguese Person," *Tales I Told My Mother*, p. 23.

> I suddenly understand better the frightening gesture of Masaccio's Adam. He covers his face to protect his vision, what had been his; he preserves in that small **manual night** the last landscape of his paradise.
> —Cortázar, *Hopscotch*, p. 511.

ILORIDAA ENJEKAT : *noun.* See quotation

> [The Masai] "Referred to us, jocularly, as iloridaa
> enjekat, I'm afraid. Sounds lovely if you don't know
> what it means.
> " 'those who confine their farts.' Has to do with the
> kinds of breeches we wear."
>> —Bishop, *No Enemy But Time*, p. 318.

IMPRECATION : *noun* calling evil down on someone, a
curse. See SCOLOPENDRINE

INFANTINE : *adj* infantile

> I looked back into the infantine slack-jawed face,
> thinking: Mooncalf you are just a lucky child.
>> —Styron, *The Confessions of Nat Turner*, p. 9.

INNOMINATE : *adj* without a name, unnamed

> "What is it?" their friends asked Catherine.
> It was innominate.
> "We don't know," she would say.
>> —Salter, *Light Years*, p. 250.

INSTAR : *verb* to make something (or one) a star, or to
adorn with stars. Compare STELLIFACTION in main text

> He tried to teach me to find the geometrical
> coordinations between the slender twigs of a leafless
> boulevard tree, a system of visual give-and-takes,
> requiring a precision of linear expression, which I
> failed to achieve in my youth, but applied gratefully,
> in my adult instar, not only to the drawing of
> butterfly genitalia....
>> —Nabokov, *Speak, Memory*, p. 92.

KADAVERGEHORSAM : *noun* German. See quotation

> I thought about my code name—Kadaver—and about *Kadavergehorsam*, which is the sort of discipline which makes a corpse jump up and salute.
> —Deighton, *Funeral in Berlin*, p. 51.

KWAZINKA : *noun.* See quotation

> . . . he was accused of having peeped through the kwazinka (a slit between the folding parts of a screen).
> —Nabokov, *Bend Sinister*, p. 125.

LEATS : *noun* an artificial waterway, small canal, sluice. See BARTON

LILAS : *noun.* See quotation

> To him all that was not the great meeting was what the Buddhists call lilas—the futile pursuit of triviality.
> —Fowles, *The Magus*, 306.

LINHAY : *noun* three-sided farm shed, lean-to. See BARTON

LOPE : *verb* to run with a long stride, but in this usage it obviously has an altered sense

> They caught Tompkins in the head comparing his reflection in the mirror to the pen-and-ink drawing of a sallow, riddled face atop an orange tract against self-abuse which Skeens had given him.
> "Grow hair in your palm, big boy," Al had razzed him.
> "Strike you blind," Gorilla warned.
> "Hair on his thumb," Jack amended. Tompkins had such a peeny pecker he'd of had to lope it with forefinger and thumb.
> —Thompson, *Tattoo*, p. 244.

LUSTRAL : *adj* purifying ceremonially or pertaining to a five year period. Compare ABLUTE, LUSTRATION in main text

> "Let's sit down by the fountain, the trickle of water has a lustral air about it that will do us good."
> "It smells like naphtha," Traveler said, "Really lustral, as a matter of fact."
> —Cortázar, *Hopscotch*, p. 304.

LUSTRUM : *noun* Latin Roman purification ceremony performed after the census was taken every five years; thus a period of 5 years, sometimes four years

> Q.   Now, sir, if you would be so kind as to guess upon his age.
> A   Forty-five years are certain. I would guess a lustrum more.
> —Fowles, *A Maggot*, p. 93.

LYROPHOROUS : *adj* lyre-bearing, song-making

> . . . he recited from memory the well-aimed prayer of our father and celestial lyrophorous master who keepeth afloat airplanes in the heavens and liners on the seas.
>> —García Márquez, *The Autumn of the Patriarch*.
>>> p. 265.

LYSTEN : *noun*. See quotation. Compare LUXURIOUS in main text

> . . . not lust exactly, in the current meaning, but lust rather in the Old English sense of *lysten*, to please or take delight. Because lust is a craving and *lysten* is a taking and giving of delight.
>> —Percy, *Lost in the Cosmos*, p. 235.

MANKY : *adj* 1920's Cockney slang for "rotten, inferior." See quotation

> "Christ, you look manky," he said. It was a word the groundcrew used for anything made foul by neglect.
>> —Robinson, *Piece of Cake*, p. 369.

MAWK : *noun* English dialect for a maggot, fly larva. See ATTERCOP

MARIOLATRY : *noun* worship of the Virgin Mary

> "Mariolatry" he says, savoring it. He likes the longer words; they reach for him like pairs of hands, out of the mists of the philosophical systems he's been reading in. . . .
>> —Calisher, *On Keeping Women*, p. 237.

MEINIE : *noun* a household, family, retinue, herd, or collection of game pieces but especially see quotation

> The "meinie that be risen" is our Reggie's sly way of getting in a dig at Glendower's supporters. (*Meinie* in this context being an old word for *crew*, or *set*, or generally unsavory *party*.)
>
> —Nye, *Falstaff*, p. 160.

MELANCHROID : *noun, adj* from Greek   black-haired. Compare ATRAMENTAL and ATROCIFY in main text

> Young Tyge Brahe appeared then, leaning down from on high into the carriage window, a pale moist melanchroid, lean of limb, limp of paw, with a sly eye.
>
> —Banville, *Kepler*, p. 3.

MELISMATIC : *adj* ornately, floweryly melodious

> . . . the song of Christ, Computer, shifted into an Alleluia, composed in B flat with all of Pope Mellon's melismatic flourishes; the sort of unification which had been brought to the chant under Pepin and Charlemagne but which had been refurbished to meet the needs of the New Feast.
>
> —Condon, *The Vertical Smile*, p. 162.

MENSTRUUM *noun* Latin   a month's provisions or a month's term of office

> The fish linger, aligned with the flow. A few drift across the pale flats where the water is clear, pass to a deep menstruum, vanish.
>
> —Salter, *A Sport and a Pastime*, p. 147.

MERCHET : *noun* fee paid by a tenant or bondsman to his overlord for the privilege of marrying off his daughter. See AMERCED

METHEGLINS : *noun* Welsh for spiced or medicated mead

> I shall ignore his self-interruptions on the usual themes—of fornications, and taverns, and sack, and wine, and metheglins, and drinkings, and swearings.
>
> —Nye, *Falstaff*, p. 422.

METONYMY : *noun* a figure of speech in which a cause is subsituted for its effect, vice versa, possessor for the possessed, etc. includes nicknames, epithets, BDELYGMIA, SYNECDOCHE, and ANTONOMASIA
METONYM : *noun* the object or concept that is substituted for another

> . . . her mother even considered her to be a snob for placing herself above the neighbors. Neighbors? asked Isabel with fire, metonym of war, in her eyes. *Neighbors?*
>
> —Theroux, Alexander, *Darconville's Cat*, p. 173.

> His Royal Highness the Prince of Wales saw fit graciously to observe that I was a globe of sinful continents.
> I put away my **Africa**.
>
> —Nye, *Falstaff*, p. 310.

> Virgil slouched in, a sheaf of **problems** under one arm.
>
> —Nichols, *The Magic Journey*, p. 427.

METONYMY : continued

> . . . see the grocery's shelves full of trimmed and weighed **slaughter**.
>> —Dillard, *The First Man on the Sun*, p. 103.

> He laughed and coughed up a few cubic centimeters of **trench warfare** and spit it in his spitcan alongside the bed. It's a good thing he got his emphysema in the war and not just from his homeland air.
> [result of exposure to chemical weapons such as mustard, chlorine, or phosgene gas as used in World War I and more recently in the Gulf War]
>> —Davis, *Vision Quest*, p. 71.

> . . . it was everyday in the park, with the **dogs walking their owners** and **tracksuits sweating** out the early runners and the **geese honking the bread** from the hands of those who loved to feed living things and had no families.
>> —Sinclair, *Magog*, p. 149.

MOCKSHADE, MOGSHADE : *noun*   twilight of some particular type. Compare COCKSHUT, CREPUSCULAR, VESPERTINE in main text

> Q. It was not yet dark?
> A. Near, Sir, the mogshade full upon us.
>> —Fowles, *A Maggot*, p. 240.

MOLIMINOUS : *adj* from Latin for "effort," painstaking, laborious

> . . . we may say in such matters that fire is as an anacoluthia† in grammar. All natural logick of expression in the elements is made thereby interrupted and most obscure, howe'er so skilled and moliminous the adeptist.
> —Fowles, *A Maggot*, p.282.

MORMOPE, MORMOOP : *noun* a bat of the genus *Mormops*, which is Greek for a particularly unattractive she-monster

> They burred off down Wigmore Street and into Oxford Street with a hook movement, [Reverend] Which fulminating at the wheel and his mother hanging onto the bar at the passenger's side like a dark silk mormoop.
> —Theroux, Alexander, "The Wife of God," *Three Wogs*, p. 150.

MUCKLING : *verb* hitting with a heavy hammer, especially when killing cod. Compare MARTEL in main text

> "I cannot drive much faster," said Dr. Alexander steadily looking ahead, "because the wrestle-cap of the lower slammer is what they call muckling."
> —Nabokov, *Bend Sinister*, p. 32.

OPHRYON : *noun* space between the eyebrows on a line with top of the eye sockets

> Bending from my warm seat, I liked to press the middle of my brow, its ophryon to be precise, against the smooth comfortable edge of the door. . . .
> —Nabokov, *Speak, Memory*, p. 85.

NAPERY : *noun* household linen, towels, sheets, etc.

> What do these Americans want? They come over here and everyone installs them in the best hotels with lavish napery, but still, complaints of every kind.
> —Barthelme, *Guilty Pleasures*, p. 11.

NIGRESCENT : *adj* turning black, blackened. Compare ATRAMENTAL, ATROCIFY in main text

> At a side chapel was the Virgin of Chiquiniquira, a black madonna with an ebony face. Black Guatemalans. . . had prostrated themselves before the nigrescent Virgin.
> —Theroux, Paul, *The Old Patagonian Express*,
> p. 107.

OBLECTATION : *noun* from Latin delight, pleasure, enjoyment. Compare LYSTEN

> . . . Theresa Neumann of Konnersreuth had taken no solid food from 1923 to her death in 1962 and had lived in the wildest sort of oblectation. . . .
> —Condon, *The Vertical Smile*, p. 67.

ONIRIC : *adj* from Greek having to do with dreams. See ONEIRIC, ONEIROTIC in main text

> "When one thinks of the Egyptians, of the men of the renaissance who could dream of obelisks, of learned geometries, of mathematical proportions which enabled them to carry over into a waking state the application of subtle problems of architectural aesthetics which their oniric life had solved, the lack of rigour of the dreams of our contemporaries is a scandal, and their oniric episodes are barely distinguished from the wretched vaudevilles of their pitiful daily lives!"
>
> —Dali, *Hidden Faces*, p. 134.

OPPORTUNANT : *noun* a person who presents an opportunity to someone seeking one

> Taking a shower with the first opportunant (if there was such a word) was put at the absolute top of his erotic agenda, the very next of the rosebuds to be gathered while he might.
>
> —DeVries, *Peckham's Marbles*, p. 56.

OXYMORON : *noun* a condensed paradox, usually an adjective and noun or adverb and adjective that would not normally be used together. See main text for other examples

> A **listlessly aggressive** junkie, his hapless days unraveled in a tense banality.
>
> —Nichols, *The Magic Journey*, p. 266.

OXYMORON : continued

[1960's] the mood of that decade in Africa, of engaging oneself and being available for the purpose of national development. . . is over; what was engagement is now detachment, a prevailing spirit of **passionate disregard**.
—Theroux, Paul, "The Killing of Hastings Banda,"
Sunrise with Seamonsters, p. 71.

He had stood **staunchly irresolute** in the face of capricious and adverse fate.
—Kennedy, *Ironweed*, p. 75.

"It is not oxymoronic to say that your role has been **massively petty**," Washburn asseverated, "yet essential, because the same could be said of a shoelace."
—Berger, *Who is Teddy Villanova?*, p. 170.

He felt a sort of **hateful tenderness**, something so contradictory that it must have been truth itself. "We ought to invent the sweet slap, the bee-kick."
—Cortázar, *Hopscotch*, p. 37.

Her director, plump with plums and **modest** with **megalomania**, comes back from America and announces, in the spirit of **generous malice** with which God granted free will to Man, that he has no immediate plans for her.
—Raphael, *California Time*, p. 82.

PADOGRAPH : *noun*. See quotation

> ... a portable affair looking like a typewriter made to reproduce with repellent perfection the hand of its owner.
>
> —Nabokov, *Bend Sinister*, p. 60.

PALETOTED : *adj* clothed with a loose garment, such as a cloak, mu-mu, bedsheet (KKK or toga party)

> A man he knew, a former Member of Parliament, a mild bore who used to take out his two polite paletoted dachshunds at nightfall, had been removed a couple of days before from number fifty in a motor truck already crammed with other prisoners.
>
> —Nabokov, *Bend Sinister*, p. 30.

PALMIPED : *noun* from Latin "palm-foot" more familiarly "duck-footed"

> "Do you have any reason to reproach me," she asked, as if she were talking to the palmiped.
>
> —Cortázar, *Hopscotch*, p. 270.

PANOPTICON : *noun* Jeremy Bentham's contribution to modern (1791) penology; from the Greek for something fully visible. He proposed a circular prison with a central well for the warders so that guards could maintain total observation on the prisoners. Big Brother would have approved. See RHYPAROGRAPHIC

PARAVISIONS : *noun.* See quotation

> It's very simple, every exaltation or depression pushes me towards a state suitable for
> > I will call them paravisions
> An instantaneous aptitude for going out, so that suddenly I can grasp myself from outside, or from inside but on a different plane.
> As if I were somebody who was looking at me.
> (better still--because in reality I cannot see myself—like someone who is living me).
> > —Cortázar, *Hopscotch*, p. 405.

PARONOMASIA : *noun* a pun substituting a word similar in sound to another. If unintentional, such a pun is a Malapropism. The first quote from Nabokov is a good example of the pot, with tongue firmly placed in cheek, calling the kettle black

> Paronomasia is a kind of verbal plague, a contagious sickness in the world of words. . . .
> > —Nabokov, *Bend Sinister*, p. *ix*.

> "The General give [sic] you more **leaves** now," she said, gesturing toward his lapels.
> "Yes," Holly replied, amused by the pun she wouldn't understand. "I may have to apply for another **branch**."
> > —Wright, *Meditations in Green*, p. 135.

PARONOMASIA : continued

. . . 'Mademoiselle Condor*.' Best Franco-English pun I've ever heard. . . .

* French : *con d'or* = gold cunt. Also SOERESMUS
—Nabokov, *Ada*, p. 481.

They grin yellow, their teeth have been planted in their gums by surgery, but the gums are giving out, and increasing softness has given them precarious grins (pun).
—Durrell, *Monsieur*, p. 253.

You are **illegible** bachelor. So do **write** and never wrong. In forty ways does a Woming Object accost a man; bewife none and wise up.
—Theroux, Alexander, "Mrs. Proby Gets Hers,"
Three Wogs, p. 23.

They seldom even meet each other, yet what outsider can doubt that those who live **chic-to-chic** in such a place are implicated in some common plot.
—Raphael, *California Time*, p. 19.

Phallocentric†, someone once said of Freud. He thought the **sun** revolved around the penis. And the daughter, too.
—Jong, *Fear of Flying*, p. 27.

PARONOMASIA : continued

> I am not a criminal sexual psychopath taking indecent liberties with a child. **The rapist** was Charlie Holmes; I am the **therapist**—a matter of nice spacing in the way of distinction.
>
> —Nabokov, *Lolita*, p. 152.

> "She's actually a genteel young lady of a fine old family of Queens."
> He chortled coarsely. "Queans*†, jades, wenches!"
>
> * See main text. Both are pronounced "kween"
> —Berger, *Who is Teddy Villanova?*, p. 209.

PATHIC : *noun* from Greek "suffering" one subjected to sodomy, the buggeree

> Clermont (known to his friends as Cordelia) was a nancy, a pathic, a male varlet, a masculine whore.
> —Nye, *Falstaff*, p. 418.

PAUCILOQUENCE : *noun* from Latin less speech, the faculty of using few words, laconic speech

> I wanted to be sitting with him on the porch beside the river, hearing the measured slow pauciloquence of his words. . . .
> —Salamanca, *Southern Light*, p. 520.

PENDEJO : *noun* Spanish for pubic hair or coward, also see quotation

> Bailey rose jerkily from a bed of anguish and plot. Sitting up, he looked through the window of his pajama crotch, saw his pubes growing wild, plucked a few, held one. the Puerto Ricans had a word for it : pendejo. A pube. A jerk.
> —Kennedy, *The Ink Truck*, p. 5.

PENICULAS : *noun* from Latin peniculus, a small penis

> His finger floats away, her calyx hand guides his peniculas in, and the three-month-long orgasm begins at the meeting of thrust and hunch, a suffusion of light through honey, spreading like music along every course and nest of nerves.
> —Davenport, *Apples and Pears*, p. 96.

PERILEPSIS : *noun* Greek seizing, embracing or comprehension, understanding

> . . . the old nemoral† godling Pothos, the uncivilized Eros, charge of the archaic Hermes, of Priapos, the Satyrs, of ballockproud bullocks and longhung asses, smelling of beebalm and allium*, adept at perilepsis.

> * genus of plants including garlic, onions and leeks
> —Davenport, *Apples and Pears*, p. 282.

PERIPATOTTERING : *verb* portmanteau word combining "peripatating" and "tottering"

> But no Master Woodford was on his feet, peripatottering in drunken discourse....
> —Burgess, *Nothing Like the Sun*, p. 50.

PERVIVACIOUS : *adj* from Latin "headstrong" obstinately maintaining ones opinion.

> Nicholas instantly resumed, demanding of Mrs. Barclay with amazed innocence other women other women [sic] must she like a pervivacious angel think that because he loved her with every beat of his heart....
> —Spackman, *An Armful of Warm Girl*, p. 37.

PETECHIA : *noun* New Latin from Italian for "skinspot" or English "grog-blossom", tiny hemorrahges on the skin or mucous membranes. **PETECHIAL** : *adj*

> The light in the corridor revealed Colonel Wallace Donaldson to be tall, a dapper man of about fifty, with the high petechial complexion of a spirits-lover.
> —McCullough, *An Indecent Obsession*, p. 41.

PHALLOCENTRIC ; *adj* centered on the penis. See Jong, PARONOMASIA

PIGNOCHER; *verb.* See quotation

> The French have a lovely word—*pignocher*. It has
> two meanings: one, to pick at one's food, and the
> other—O, lovely language!—to paint with tiny
> strokes. That was how Puddintame looked to
> me—*pignochée*—picked out in bird's-peck tints on
> the tiniest of canvases.
>> —Grubb, *Ancient Lights*, p. 476.

POLYPTOTON : *noun* figure of speech, a scheme of
repetition of a word root with different prefixes and/or
suffixes. May be ANTANACLASIS, when the whole word is
repeated and the meaning changes

> And Catherine lies, **compos**ing and de**compos**ed,
> **writ**ing and **writt**en, here and tomorrow, in the
> deep grass of the other hidden place she has found.
>> —Fowles, "The Cloud," *The Ebony Tower*, p. 299.

PREVENIENT GRACE : *adj* the grace of God which
precedes any human action, such as repentance or conversion, thus leading the recipient to God. In a secular sense,
that state of well-being preceding any physical manifestation
of love.

> ... [They] never passed a minute when that sublime
> and prevenient grace arresting their young hearts to
> love didn't assure them that to watch the morning
> star one's eyes must always be a little brighter,
> neither did it fail to whisper low that once upon a
> time never comes again.
>> —Theroux, Alexander, *Darconville's Cat*, p. 347.

PROTANDRY & PROTOGYNY : *nouns.* See quotation

> . . . a general phenomenon in nature. Sex change might go either way (or both) during growth, from male to female or from female to male. Both phenomena occur, but *Crepidula*'s [species of limpet] pattern of male first and female later, called *protandry* (or male first) is by far the more common. (Creatures that are first female and then male are *protogynous*, or female first). Protandry seems to represent the prevalent path of changing sex, with protogyny as a rarer phenomenon evolved under special (but not particularly uncommon) circumstances.
>
> —Gould, "Sex and Size," *The Flamingo's Smile*, pp.58-59.

QUOTIDIAN : *adj* from Latin by way of French everyday, mundane.

> The decade of the eighties [1680's], which had begun so promisingly, petered out in the unimpeachable dullness of the quotidian.
>
> —Boyle, *World's End*, p. 376.

RADABARBÁRA : *noun* from Russian? a "delightful Barbara" See quotation.

> Almost extravagantly healthy, a regular radabarbára (full-blown handsome woman): those wide radiant eyes, that flaming cheek to which she would press the cool back of her hand, that shining white forehead with a whiter scar. . . .
>
> —Nabokov, *Bend Sinister*, p. 27.

RACKLING, RACKILING : *adj* Scottish and Northern English dialect for brute strength, vigorous.

> . . . little Doit and I once filled a barrel with stones, and sent it rolling down Gracechurch Street to London Bridge, making such a rackiling racket as it went that the people thought Glendower had arrived in person, complete with horns.
>
> —Nye, *Falstaff*, p. 161.

RELIEF : *noun* under Scottish law, reimbursement of expenses incurred by an obligation. See AMERCED.

RHYPAROGRAPHIC : *adj* from Greek description, depiction of filth. A painting of corrupt, foul, repulsive things. Compare BEBELOGLYPIC in main text

> He had a vision of the world as the Ultimate Panopticon†, the perfect prison so designed by a rhyparographic God that He could, just for His Own amusement, send His minions to distress and thrash away from men even the least of their paraplegic opinions, their most harmless and unspoken dreams.
>
> —Theroux, Alexander, "The Wife of God," *Three Wogs,* pp. 212-213.

SANGUISUGENT : *adj* from Latin blood-sucking. Compare SANGUINARY, SANGUINE in main text

> They halted, when they reached higher ground, to burn off leeches with their cigarettes. A Cama-guayan sergeant named Raoul helped Jones, who could not bear to see the little sanguisugent lumps on his inner thighs.
>
> —Mano, *War is Heaven!*, p. 31.

SCESISONOMATON : *noun* Greek *skeh sis oh NO mah ton* a scheme of rhetorical arrangement, a collection of nouns, each with an adjective or modifying phrase.

> "Elvis pelvis," Softly said. "Unscrupulously seductive mouth. Belly a bowl of fruit. Labyrinthine navel. Resilient milky thighs. Cute pudendum, hee hee. Lickable armpits. Predatory eyes. Surging breasts. Hair rare. Smile terribly foudroyant†. Backside a-twinkle."
>
> —DeLillo, *Ratner's Star*, p. 312.

> [Captain] Blood read in the intrepid set of his chin, the hard calm of his clear grey eyes, the stern purpose of his clear brow, the resolute tension of his knees, and the implacable poise of his armpits, a grim determination which was awesome.
>
> —Fraser, *The Pyrates*, p. 109.

> He walked across the top of Islington Green, where winos get beaten up, past the site of the old Collins Music Hall which got burned down, and through Camden Passage where American tourists get ripped off.
>
> —Adams, *Dirk Gently's Holistic Detective Agency*,
> p. 112.

SCREOD : *noun.* See quotation

> . . . he taught her the time-bending Druid sneeze
> called the Screod. It is to be used on occasions of
> great personal peril only. It is a sneeze which rends
> clouds and splits oaks with its violence. It splits
> Time, too. It casts the sorcerer—or sneezer—into a
> pellmell past or future, he knows not which.
> —Grubb, *Ancient Lights*, p. 131.

SCOLOPENDRINE : *adj* having to do with centipedes

> . . . a scolopendrine beggar scuttled forward and
> opened his mouth at them through the carriage
> window in speechless imprecation†.
> —Banville, *Kepler*, p. 79.

SHCHEKOTIKI : *noun* Russian *sheh cheh koh Tee kee*
ticklishness

> . . . a feeling of shchekotiki (as we used to say in our
> childhood) half-tingle, half-tickle, when you are
> trying to remember something or understand some-
> thing or find something, and probably your bladder
> is full, and your nerves are on edge, but the com-
> bination is on the whole not unpleasant (if not
> protracted) and produces a minor orgasm or *'petit
> éternuement intérieur'** when at last you find the
> picture-puzzle piece which exactly fits the gap.

> * French "small interior sneeze"
> —Nabokov, *Bend Sinister*, p. 140.

SIALOGOGUE : *noun* from Greek something that makes the mouth water. Compare ESCULENT in main text

> And in the Polyphemian dungeon the crewmen had built Esolog-9 [an android] into a fat man. He was not an ordinary fat man. . . a sialogogue that tantalized the men, that set up such a flow of juice in them all that they almost drowned in their own slaver. They'd have stuck a fork in him if they had one.
> —Lafferty, *Space Chantey*, p. 86.

SLAUNCHWISE : *adj* Naval expression, to hang down loosely

> . . . thin black coolie pants. . . so loose at the waist that the extra material had to be folded and lapped. . . The seats always sagged slaunchwise and the sailors laughed and called them "droopy drawers."
> —McKenna, *The Sand Pebbles,* p. 13.

SNORFEL : *verb* portmanteau word of snort and snuffle

> Fifty years from now . . . she could see him in whatever they had for a kitchen, snorfeling through his nose because his mouth was full, dipping his cereal spoon into the sugar. . . .
> —Morris, *Ceremony in Lone Tree*, p. 67.

SOERESMUS : *noun* the use of foreign words and phrases mixed with your own language's text. Also called "macaronics" and "mingle mangle" which is often a more apt phrase

> "**Dieu caillou les corbeaux!**" he cried aghast. "**Regardez sa chevelure!** She 'as flipped 'er wig! What do I see, me? Un moment, **ma belle brun**, le next une bébé peroxide! **C'est trop fort!***
>
> * fractured French for : *God stone the crows, Look at her hair, my beautiful brunette, It's too much.*
> —Fraser, *The Pyrates*, p. 238.

> The **mierda**, as the saying in bastardized local lingo went, had really hit the **abanico**.
> —Nichols, *The Magic Journey*, p. 56.

SULL : *verb* to be sullen, the action of being uncommunicative and unpleasant. Compare FAROUCHE in main text

> . . . all Frenchman's Bend knew Houston: sulking and sulling in his house all alone by himself since the stallion killed his wife four years ago.
> —Faulkner, *The Mansion*, p. 10.

SUPTION : *noun* the body, the essence, the flavor of something

> ". . . the judge—is going to give you another trial."
> "What for?" he said. "I done already had one that I never got much suption out of."
> —Faulkner, *The Mansion*, p. 46.

SYLLEPSIS : *noun* a figure of speech (pun, EQUIVO-CATION) in which one word (usually a verb) can be understood in two different ways, usually, one in a literal sense and the other figurative. See examples below and others in main text

> So she **closed** Magog's mouth and fears with her own.
>
> —Sinclair, *Magog*, p. 274.

> A change of environment is the traditional fallacy upon which **doomed** loves, and lungs, rely.
>
> —Nabokov, *Lolita*, p. 241.

> . . . the daughter had grown into a teen-ager, in this very house, here, **dribbling** jam on the floor, pee in the bowl and dreams on the pillows. . . .
>
> —Robbins, *Even Cowgirls Get the Blues*, p. 278.

> She sat beside me and ate my lunch with one hand and squeezed my prick with the other. I wanted to get away, but I couldn't move. I had a hard-on that big. 'Please signora, that isn't necessary.' She wouldn't stop. That hard gypsy hand was all over me. Well, it happened. I'm a man—jerk me and I come. She **finished** me and my lunch at the same time.
>
> —Elkin, Stanley, *Boswell*, p. 199.

> Sergeant Anstin had forbidden him to leave the signal shop all morning . . . Wendell **sorted** colored wires with his hands and various tools of assassination with his mind.
>
> —Wright, *Meditations in Green*, p. 61.

SYNESTHESIA : *noun* a trope, figure of speech in which the subject and the image to which it is being compared come from different sensory domains: visual as sonic, tactile as olfactory, etc. See examples below:

Time as Vision

> The two **intervals of five days** each are seen by me as **twin dimples**, each brimming with a kind of smooth, grayish mist, and a faint suggestion of shed confetti. . . Synesthetia [sic] to which I am inordinately prone, proves to be of great help in this type of task. . . .
> —Nabokov, *Ada*, p. 549.

Sound as Vision

> His **laughter** cavorted forth in rollicking **yellow** bursts; it tumbled around inside the car like daffodils in a washing machine.
> —Nichols, John, *A Ghost in the Music*, p. 53.

Vision as Sound

> They collide in Gristede's: the baskets of these two maladroits lock together in a passionate embrace in front of the paper products. The collision causes a tremor which in turn causes a whole shelf of **toilet paper** to come down on their heads like a volley of Jewish **curses**.
> —Alexander, *Safe Houses*, p.63.

SYNESTHESIA : continued

Vision and Tactile as Sound

> . . . he felt the tropic sun embrace his shoulders, as his **eyes "heard"** the contrapuntal harmony of heat waves bowing saltato across glaring sand, and ocean blowing long, cool horn notes.
>
> —Koster, *The Dissertation*, p. 258.

Tactile as Vision

> And there is but one saliva and one flavor of ripe fruit, and I feel you **tremble** against me like a **moon on the water**.
>
> —Cortázar, *Hopscotch*, p. 33.

Emotion as Odor

> **Boredom** wafted from her like the **scent** of stale sweat so intense as to be the cause of boredom in others. . . .
>
> —Updike, *Roger's Version*, p. 35.

Odor as Sound

> A line of sweat droplets crossed his brow, a **stench** literally crashed from his damp armpits like a big bass **drum** of odor.
>
> —Nichols, *The Magic Journey*, p. 283.

SYNECDOCHE : *noun* a figure of speech, a trope, and a form of METONYMY in which a part is substituted for a whole or vice versa. Also see SYNECDOCHIC in main text.

. . . Southern ideals, of which the girls at Quinsy College, and like schools, were the most charming synecdoche. . . .
—Theroux, Alexander, *Darconville's Cat*, p. 38.

. . . a good part of Deborah's library consisted of books designed to **titillate the sweat glands**, books on mountain climbing, speed walking, water treading, muscle toning, gum massaging, and dumbell lifting.
—Exley, *A Fan's Notes*, p. 283.

I loved her, to be sure: but the love was fringed with restlessness. I grew jaded in my role of an Italian *cicisbèo*†: a carrier of fans, a flatterer of bosoms, a singer of duets, a sniffer of rose-water. . . I grew bored with being a slave to the **whims of the womb**.
—Prokosch, *The Missolonghi Manuscript*, p. 201.

. . . a **paunch** draped in candy-striped shirt and a greasey black mortician's suit pass[es] by. . . .
—Algren, *The Man with the Golden Arm*, p. 27.

SYNECDOCHE : continued

> The great secret of the ages is that man has evolved,
> is born, lives, and dies for one end and one end only:
> to commit a sexual assault on another human or to
> submit to such an assault. . . .
> Pascal told only half the story. He said man was a
> thinking reed. What man is, is a thinking reed and
> a **walking genital**.
>
> —Percy, *Lancelot*, pp. 222-223.

TALLAGE : *noun* feudal taxation of Crown lands and towns, a tax on dependents of a feudal lord. See AMERCED

THANATOID : *adj* from Greek deathlike. Compare LETHIFEROUS, THANATIZE in main text

> . . . genuine hopelssness, when faith has evaporated
> and the imagination is dead, when life seems to have
> come finally and irrevocably to a standstill.
> It might have been that—the stillness inside me, the
> thanatoid silence frightening me into a last-ditch
> effort to stay alive.
>
> —Conroy, *Stop-Time*, p. 178.

THRYSTAGEM : *noun.* See quotation

> Any ornament used to display or give display to a
> breast or breasts. (There are two kinds of thrys-
> tagems: Deceptive thrystagems are those that
> falsify the character, posture and/or existence of an
> unexposed breast. Embellishing thrystagems are
> those that adorn an exposed breast for the purpose of
> enhancing and intensifying its fascination.)
>
> —Burr, *BISBA*, p. 436.

TRICLINIUM : *noun* Latin from Greek for an eating-couch, where one accubates, reclines to eat

> . . . I would curl up like a caterpillar and fall asleep
> on top of the picture of a triclinium.
> —Cortázar, *Hopscotch*, p. 134.

TRIVESTA : *noun* Russian details of amorous doings

> How all these *trivesta* reached his comrades, is
> difficult to conjecture. . . .
> —Nabokov, *Bend Sinister*, p. 63.

TYCHISM : *noun* from Greek "chance, luck," the theory of chance as an objective reality; that evolutionary variation is purely fortuitous. Compare ALEATORY in main text

> There is only one reason for believing in this kind of
> unconditioned, universal, category-crossing tychism
> —since experience confounds it everywhere—and
> the reason is that language can be so arranged and
> manipulated.
> —Gass, "Representation and the War for Reality,"
> *Habitations of the Word*, p. 84.

ULLAGE : *verb* from French of a cask, filled up to replace leakage

> And to cap everything he had to call the gerent†
> over, or whatever the man was, to complain
> glowering about this champagne, was it ullaged or
> what? . . .
> —Spackman, *An Armful of Warm Girl*, p. 13.

UNIPYGIC : *adj* having only one buttock. See quotation. Compare ΠΕΜΠΥGIC, ΚΑΚΟΡΥGE in main text

> Of course the stewardess appeared on the instant, stretched to retrieve the case and in so doing showed an inch of sexless white slip between navy-blue jacket and skirt. As always with them, she was so girdled as seemingly to have but one buttock.
> —Berger, *Killing Time*, p. 194.

USTULATED : *adj* from Latin singed, scorched.

> Now I come, sir, to. . . the fire outside the cave. . . nothing has grown upon it since it was burnt . . . This ustulated patch is some nine paces across.
> —Fowles, *A Maggot*, pp. 276-277.

VERVENT : *adj.* See quotation

> Given to rapturous enthusiasms accompanied (momentarily, at least) by a show of great spirit and energy. (She jumps from one rapturous enthusiasm to another, more delighted with being enraptured than she is interested in accomplishment.)
> —Burr, *BISBA*, pp. 445-446.

VENEREAL NOUN : *noun* not AIDS, but a name for a collection of people, animals or things.

> Not long after our arrival in Ireland, we found ourselves in Kildare. We were quite without funds, cut off, and beleaguered by a gaggle or **bubble or squeak** of bog Irish of various species.
> —Nye, *Falstaff*, p. 219.

VENEREAL NOUN : continued

A boy leading a horse, an old woman who looked like Pestalozzi drinking a wine as black as ink, an **adagio** of nuns on a bridge.
—Davenport, "Lo Spledore della Luce a Bologna," *Eclogues*, p. 129.

VESPINE : *adj* from Latin for "wasp"

Not given to intruding on or interfering with others and in turn given to severe reproof and repulsion of any attempting to meddle or interfere in her life or affairs. (As the descriptive implies, she wasp-like minds her own business and stings you severely and deservingly if you don't do likewise.).
—Burr, *BISBA*, p. 446.

WHUFFO : *noun*. See quotation

In skydiving, there's a term "whuffo." Whuffos are people who hang around skydivers saying, "Whuffo you want to jump out of a perfectly good airplane?"
—Boyd, *The Redneck Way of Knowledge*, p. 25.

ZAHIR : *noun*. See quotation.

Zahir in Arabic means "notorious," "visible"; in this sense it is one of the ninety-nine names of God, and the people (in Muslim territories) use it to signify "beings or things which possess the terrible property of being unforgettable, and whose image finally drives one mad."
—Borges, "The Zahir," *Labyrinths*, p. 161; trans. by Dudley Fitts.

CORRECTION TO MAIN TEXT

INENUBILABLE : should read: literally "intensely uncloudy"; incapable of being made cloudy

APPENDIX SOURCES

Adams, Douglas. *Life, The Universe and Everything*. New York: Harmony Books, 1982.

—. *The Restaurant at the End of the Universe*. New York: Harmony Books, 1980.

—. *Dirk Gently's Holistic Detective Agency*. New York: Simon and Schuster, 1987.

Alexander, Lynne. *Safe Houses*. New York: Atheneum, 1985.

Algren, Nelson. *The Man with the Golden Arm*. Bath: Chivers, 1972.

Banville, John. *Kepler*. Boston: David R. Godine (reprint)1984. London: Martin Secker and Warburg, 1981.

Barthelme, Donald. *Guilty Pleasures*. New York: Farrar, Straus & Giroux; Dell, 1976.

Bellow, Saul. *Herzog*. New York: Viking Press, 1964.

Berger, Thomas. *Killing Time*. New York: The Dial Press , 1967.

—. *Nowhere*, New York: Dell, 1986.

—. *Who is Teddy Villanova*. New York: Delacorte Press, 1977.

Bishop, Michael. *No Enemy But Time*. New York: Timescape, 1982.

Borges, Jorge Luis. *Labyrinths*. New York: New Directions, 1964.

Bowler, Peter. *A Superior Person's Book of Words*. Boston: David R. Godine, 1985.

Boyd, Blanche McCrary. *The Redneck Way of Knowledge*. New York: Alfred A. Knopf, 1982; Penguin 1982.

Boyle, T. Coraghessan. *World's End*. Viking, 1987.

Brophy, Brigid. *The Adventures of God in Search for the Black Girl*. London: Macmillan London Ltd, 1973.

Burgess, Anthony. *Nothing like the Sun*. New York: W.W. Norton & Co., 1964.

—. *The Eve of Saint Venus*. New York: W.W. Norton & Co., 1970.

Burr, Timothy. *BISBA: The Burr Index of Systematic Breast Analysis*. Trenton, N.J.: Hercules Publishing Co., 1965.

Calisher, Hortense. *On Keeping Women*. New York: Arbor House, 1977.

Calvino, Italo. *The Path to the Nest of the Spiders*. New York: The Ecco Press, 1976. translated by Archibald Colquhoun.

Condon, Richard. *The Vertical Smile*. New York: Dial Press, 1971.

Conroy, Frank. *Stop-Time*. New York: The Viking Press, 1967.

Cortázar, Julio. *Hopscotch*. New York: Pantheon Books, 1966, translated by Gregory Rabassa.

Dali, Salvador. *Hidden Faces*. New York: William Morrow & Co., 1974.

Davenport, Guy. *Da Vinci's Bicycle*. Baltimore: Johns Hopkins University Press, 1979.

APPENDIX SOURCES

—. *Eclogues*. San Francisco: North Point Press, 1981.

—. *Apples and Pears*. San Francisco: North Point Press, 1984.

Davis, Terry. *Vision Quest*. New York: The Viking Press, 1979.

DeLillo, Don. *Ratner's Star*. New York: Alfred A. Knopf, 1976.

De Vries, Peter. *The Glory of the Hummingbird*. Boston: Little, Brown & Co., 1974.

—. Peckham's Marbles. New York: G.P. Putnam's Sons, 1986.

Deighton, Len. *Funeral in Berlin*. New York: G.P. Putnam's Sons, 1965.

Dillard, R.H.W. *The First Man on the Sun*. Baton Rouge: Louisiana State Univ. Press, 1983.

Durrell, Lawrence. *Monsieur*. New York: Viking Press, 1974.

Elkin, Stanley. *Boswell*. New York: Random House, 1964.

Exley, Frederick. *A Fan's Notes*. New York: Harper & Row, 1968 rp Vintage Books, 1985.

Faulkner, William. *The Mansion*. New York: Random House, 1959.

Fowles, John. *The Ebony Tower*. Boston: Little, Brown & Co., 1974.

—. *Daniel Martin*. Boston: Little, Brown & Co., 1977.

—. *The Magus*. Boston: Little Brown & Co., 1977.

—. *Mantissa*, New York: Plume Book, New American Library, 1983; Boston: Little, Brown & Co., 1982

—. *A Maggot*. Boston: Little, Brown and Co., 1985

Fraser, George MacDonald. *The Pyrates*. New York: Alfred A. Knopf, 1984.

Frayn, Michael. *Sweet Dreams*. London: Collins, 1973.

Friedman, Alan. *Hermaphrodeity*. New York: Alfred A. Knopf, 1972.

Garcia Márquez, Gabriel. *The Autumn of the Patriarch*. New York: Harper & Row, 1976; translated by Gregory Rabassa.

Gass, William. *Habitations of the Word*. New York: Simon and Schuster, 1985.

Gould, Stephen J. *The Flamingo's Smile*. New York: W. W. Norton, 1985.

Grubb, Davis. *Ancient Lights*. New York: The Viking Press, 1982.

Helprin, Mark. *Winter's Tale*. New York: Harcourt, Brace Jovanovich, 1983.

Irving, John. *Cider House Rules*. New York: William Morrow and Co., 1985.

Jarrell, Randall. *Pictures from an Institution*. New York: Alfred A. Knopf, 1954.

Jong, Erica. *Fear of Flying*. New York: Holt, Rinehart and Winston, Inc., 1975.

Kennedy, William. *Ironweed*. New York: Viking Press, 1983.

—. *The Ink Truck*. New York: Viking Penguin, Inc., 1984

Kimball, Michael. *Firewater Pond*. New York: G. P. Putnam's Sons, 1985.

Koster, R. M. *The Dissertation*. New York: Harper and Row, 1975.

—. *Mandragon*. New York: William Morrow & Co., 1979.

APPENDIX SOURCES

—. *The Prince.* New York: Morrow Quill Paperbacks, 1979.

Lafferty, R. A. *Space Chantey.* London: Dennis Dobson, 1976.

LeCarré, John. *A Small Town in Germany.* New York: Coward-McCann, 1968.

McCollough, Colleen. *An Indecent Obsession.* New York: Harper & Row, 1981.

McKenna, Richard. *The Sand Pebbles.* New York: Harper & Row, 1962.

Mano, D. Keith. *War is Heaven!.* Garden City: Doubleday & Co., 1970.

Morris, Wright. *Ceremony in Lone Tree.* New York: Atheneum, 1960.

Murray, John Middleton. "Metaphor." In: Shibles, Warren A. (Ed.). *Essays on Metaphor.* Wisconsin Language Press, 1972.

Nabokov, Vladimir. *Bend Sinister.* New York: Time Inc. , 1964.

—. *Lolita.* New York: G. P. Putnam & Sons, 1958.

—. *Ada.* New York: McGraw-Hill, 1969.

—. *Speak, Memory,* New York: G. P. Putnam's Sons, 1966.

Nichols, John. *The Sterile Cuckoo.* New York: David McKay Co., Inc., 1965.

—. *The Magic Journey.* New York : Holt, Rinehart & Winston, 1978.

—. *A Ghost in the Music.* New York: Holt, Rinehart & Winston, 1979.

Nye, Robert. *Tales I Told My Mother.* New York : Hill and Wang, 1969.

—. *Falstaff.* Boston: Little, Brown & Co., 1976.

Percy, Walker. *Lancelot.* New York: Farrar, Straus & Giroux, 1977.

—. *Lost in the Cosmos.* New York: Farrar, Straus & Giroux, 1983.

Prokosch, Frederic. *The Missolonghi Manuscript.* New York: Farrar, Straus & Giroux, 1968.

Raphael, Frederic. *California Time.* New York : Holt Rinehart & Winston, 1976.

Robbins, Tom. *Even Cowgirls Get the Blues.* Boston: Houghton Mifflin Co., 1976.

Robinson, Derek. *Piece of Cake.* New York: Alfred A. Knopf, 1984.

Salamanca, J. R. *Southern Light.* New York: Alfred A. Knopf, 1986.

Salter, James. *The Arm of Flesh.* New York: Harper & Brothers, 1961.

—. *A Sport and a Pastime.* Garden City: Doubleday & Co., 1967.

—. *Light Years.* New York: Random House, 1975.

—. *Solo Faces.* San Francisco: North Point Press, 1988.

Schneck, Stephen. *The Nightclerk.* New York: Grove Press, 1965.

Sinclair, Andrew. *Magog.* New York: Harper & Row, 1972.

Spackman, W. M. *An Armful of Warm Girl.* New York: Alfred A. Knopf, 1978.

Styron, William. *The Confessions of Nat Turner.* New York: Random House, 1967.

Theroux, Alexander. *Three Wogs.* Boston: David Godine, 1975.

—. *Darconville's Cat.* New York: Doubleday & Co., Inc., 1981.

—. *An Adultery.* New York: Simon and Schuster, 1987.

APPENDIX SOURCES

Theroux, Paul. *The Mosquito Coast*. Boston: Houghton Mifflin Co., 1982.

—. *The Old Patagonian Express*. Boston: Houghton Mifflin Co., 1979.

—. *Sunrise with Sea Monsters*. Boston: Houghton Mifflin, 1985.

Thompson, Earl. *Tattoo*. New York: G. P. Putnam's Sons , 1974.

Updike, John. *Roger's Version*. New York: Alfred A. Knopf, 1986.

Wiener, Norbert. *The Human Use of Human Beings*. Boston: Houghton Mifflin, 1950.

White, Patrick. *Voss*. New York: Viking Press. 1957.

Wolfe, Tom. *The Kandy Kolored Tangerine Flake Streamlined Baby*.

Wright, Stephen. *Meditations in Green*. New York: Charles Scribner's Sons, 1983.

—. *M 31*. New York: Harmony Books, 1988.

Zelazny, Roger. *This Immortal*. New York: Ace Books. 1966.